THE REAL ANCIENT
MARINER

THE REAL ANCIENT MARINER

pirates and poesy on the South Sea

Robert Fowke

Travelbrief Publications

travelbrief.org

TravelBrief Publications

23 High Street, Bishop's Castle, Shropshire, SY9 5BE

Published in Great Britain by
Travelbrief Publications 2010

ISBN 9780954835149

Set in Times New Roman

Printed in Great Britain by Lightning Source Uk Ltd. Milton Keynes

Cover: detail from *Ships Running Aground in a Storm* by Ludolf Bakhuizen, 1690s.

for Pinney

Praise the sea; on shore remain.
John Florio 1553 – 1625

Acknowledgements

Special thanks to my wife, Pinney. Without her help and encouragement I could never have written this book. Special thanks also to Clare Abbot of Oxford who was extraordinarily generous of her time and knowledge and who shared with me the adventure of the discovery of Hatley's identity, and to Robert Branton who also was endlessly generous with his time, advice and support. My thanks also to Andrew Mee, Philip Woolley and Emily Fowke who read the manuscript and made many useful comments.

The Authors' Foundation was kind enough to provide a grant which helped to finance research in South America. My thanks to them also.

CONTENTS

◆◆◆◆◆◆◆◆◆◆◆◆◆

List of illustrations

Significant voyages

1703-7 ◆ *St. George & Cinque Ports*

1708-11 ◆ *Duke & Duchess*

1719-22 ◆ *Speedwell & Success*

Significant works

1697 ◆ *A New Voyage Round the World* by William Dampier

1720 ◆ *Robinson Crusoe* by Daniel Defoe

1726 ◆ *Gulliver's Travels* by Jonathan Swift

1726 ◆ *A Voyage round the World by way of the Great South Sea* by George Shelvocke

1798 ◆ *The Rime of the Anyient Marinere* by Samuel Taylor Coleridge

Brief chronology

♦♦♦♦♦♦♦♦♦♦♦♦♦♦♦♦

1651 ♦ William Dampier born

1669 ♦ Sir John Narborough sails to the South Sea

1670 ♦ Henry Morgan sacks Panama

1680 ♦ First major buccaneer incursion into the South Sea

1680 ♦ Alexander Selkirk born

1684 ♦ *Buccaneers of America* published with Ringrose's supplement

1685 ♦ Simon Hatley born

1697 ♦ *New Voyage Round the World* published

1699-1701 ♦ Voyage of the *Roebuck* - Dampier sails to Australia

1701/2 ♦ Start of the War of Spanish Succession

1702 ♦ Anne crowned

1703 ♦ Start of the Voyage of *St George* and *Cinque Ports*

1704 ♦ Battle of Blenheim

1704 ♦ Alexander Selkirk marooned

1705 ♦ Start of Blenheim Palace

1707 ♦ Dampier returns without the *St. George*

1708 ♦ Start of the voyage of the *Duke* and *Duchess*

1709 ♦ Rescue of Alexander Selkirk

1709 ♦ Simon Hatley in prison in Lima

1711 ♦Return of the *Duke* and *Duchess*

1711 ♦ Edward Steele's article on Alexander Selkirk

1711 ♦ South Sea Company founded

1713/14 ♦ Treaties of Utrecht

1714 ♦ Anne dies, George I becomes king

1715 ♦ Louis XIV dies

1718 ♦ South Sea Company's assets in South America seized by Spain

1719 ♦ Start of War of the Quadruple Alliance

1719 ♦ Start of the voyage of the *Speedwell* and *Success*

1720 ♦ *Robinson Crusoe* published

1720 ♦ South Sea Bubble bursts

1721 ♦ Jonathan Swift starts writing *Gulliver's Travels*

1726 ♦ *Gulliver's Travels* published

1726 ♦ Shelvocke's *A Voyage round the World* published

1798 ♦ *Rime of the Ancient Mariner* published

Map

••••••••••••••••••

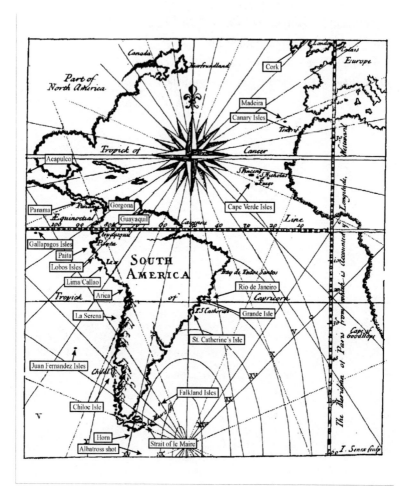

Preface

◆◆◆◆◆◆◆◆◆◆◆◆

They were building dens in the bushes, being aeroplanes on the tennis court, conducting a burial ceremony for a dead squirrel under a bush, somewhere a gang was forming and there might be trouble. It was a Saturday afternoon and the sun was frying the playing fields and I should have been out there with them, but instead I was indoors hunched over my desk.

I was memorising as much as possible of *The Rime of the Ancient Mariner* so that I could show off during the first lesson on Monday morning. We were meant to learn only a few verses but I intended to learn the lot. My friends had looked at me with a mixture of pity and admiration for about half a second when I told them of my plan, then gone out to play. Now, dead squirrel notwithstanding, I had to look like I was enjoying myself and it was not easy.

Monday morning. Our lesson was in the library, our desks crammed into the space between a billiard table and a bay window, open even at that early hour to receive the scent of poppy and dew-laden lawn. In contrast to the sunlit green outside, the library slumbered in gloom, its walls lined with cloth-bound books and its floor spread with dark linoleum. Mr Thurston straddled a chair on the other side of the table. He had a mane of lank, reddish hair and a voice that boomed. The class was quiet, unusually so. Word of my attempt had got round.

'Bradshaw,' he said (or words to that effect). 'You first.'

Bradshaw, two desks along to my right, stood up. He recited the first four verses without difficulty.

After Bradshaw came Pringle, then it would be my turn. I squirmed with anticipatory pleasure because I had managed to memorise quite a large chunk.

Pringle also recited the first four verses. Glances were sneaked out of the window, to where the gardener was pushing his wheelbarrow towards the compost heap, someone yawned, but I was all alert attention. I waited expectantly. My turn was next.

It was disconcerting that a look of irritation began to cloud Mr Thurston's beetroot face. He was thinking, I assume this in retrospect, that he should have allocated different verses to different children. Suddenly, his face softened and he straightened his back.

'Right, you little beasts. I'm going to let you off.'

No! How could this be? Thurston smiled, magnanimous. He dragged nicotine-stained fingers through his mane. We were to write down the first two verses only and he would let us off the rest. At this ostensibly glad news a chill of quiet tiptoed along the desks and all faces turned towards me and I felt a sudden pricking behind my eyes. I studied the bookshelves, stuffed with books by authors such as G.A. Henty and Rider Haggard. When you opened them, the smell of ink and paper rose in a beguiling, musty cloud and the words cradled you away to undiscovered lands. The further away the better. I tried to think about SHE of Rider Haggard but no image came, and meanwhile a tear was forming. Mr Thurston patrolled the desks.

'Just the first two verses.'

He came to my desk.

'Get on with it.'

How could I confess that I had spent the entire weekend learning the *Rime of the Ancient Mariner* when everyone else was out playing? My shoulders hunched.

'Please sir,' said someone, 'he's learnt all of it.'

Thurston was quick to understand. He stood in front my desk in an aroma-cloud of chalk dust and stale cigarettes. His voice was kind, if loud.

'Come on. Let's hear it.'

No, really, there was no point. It was too late. I'd forgotten it. I almost overdid the protestations, but he insisted. In the summer-drunk library, my eyes hot with gathering tears, I stood up and began to recite, and my classmates, I am pleased to say, were moderately attentive. I got quite a long way through.

It is an ancyent Marinere,
And he stoppeth one of three:
"By thy long grey beard and thy glittering eye
"Now wherefore stoppest me?

"The Bridegroom's doors are open'd wide
"And I am next of kin;
"The Guests are met, the Feast is set,
"May'st hear the merry din.

Nowadays, the words have almost all faded from memory but I still retain a handful of images: a man with a long white beard outside a church, a livid sea with things moving in it, a man naked to the waist, under a blazing sun, on a deck, grizzled and weather-beaten, his skin the colour of mahogany, shooting an albatross. Curiously, on re-reading the poem, I have found no references to anyone being naked to the waist. Coleridge is very clear about it. The Ancient Mariner shot the albatross when in the middle of a freezing fog and it would be more accurate to visualise him as being muffled to the ears at this point in the poem. This misapprehension seems to be widely shared. The pleasant statue of the Ancient Mariner, erected in 2003 in the little port of Watchet in north Devon where Coleridge started writing his poem, shows the Mariner bearded and naked to the waist exactly as I had always visualised him, although still holding his crossbow as if he has just shot the albatross.

The Ancient Mariner was cold because Coleridge based his central image on a real man who committed a particular deed in a particularly cold place. The image had arisen from a suggestion made by William Wordsworth while they were on a walk across the Quantocks in November 1797.

Wordsworth had been reading *A Voyage round the World by way of the Great South Sea* by Captain George Shelvock, published 1726. The *Speedwell* is rounding the Horn and has reached a latitude of about 61° south:

'... We all observed that we had not had the sight of one fish of any kind since we came into the southward of the streights of le Maire, nor one sea-bird, except a disconsolate black Albatross, who accompanied us for several days, hovering about us as if he had lost himself, till Hatley, my second Captain, observing in one of his melancholy fits, that this bird which was always hovering near us, imagined, from his colour, that it might be some ill omen .... he, after some fruitless attempts, at length shot the Albatross, not doubting (perhaps) that we should have a fair wind after it ...[1]'

To be exploited for someone else's imaginative purposes can sometimes be flattering but this is not the case with Hatley. Coleridge immortalised him (in a manner of speaking) because of the superstitious and unpleasant pointlessness of the incident with the albatross - although Hatley's life, for all we know, may otherwise have been quite saintly. Also, Coleridge neither wrote anything about him being a captain nor wanted his poetic Mariner to have a rank, aiming rather for something vague and universal. Throughout the poem the Ancient Mariner refers to the crew as 'we', whereas a captain would refer to them as 'my crew' or 'the crew' as would a senior officer.

The mariner behind the Mariner - a melancholic senior officer, possibly in gloves and a scarf and perhaps not a very good shot, a minor but unexpected footnote to the history of literature. In my mind's eye, I see a long, sad face and weak eyes.

This book is my attempt to track him down.

Shropshire 2009

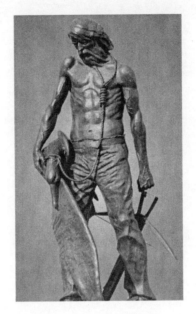

Statue of the Ancient Mariner, Watchet Harbour, by Alan Herriot

CHAPTER 1

Hatley

Hatley

Fortunately, there are a number of contemporary published books about the voyages in which Hatley participated as well as various journals and other documents. This is no coincidence. The voyages of British pirates and privateers into the south Pacific in the late seventeenth and early eighteenth centuries were among the longest and riskiest voyages undertaken at that time. The Pacific was a forbidden sea dominated by the Spanish, and it was dangerous to get to. Ships had to sail round the Horn, through the most dangerous waters in the world. In modern terms, these voyages were equivalent to voyages to the Moon. Landlubbers back home were fascinated by them.

There was a ready market for books by the tough, exotic sea-bandits and adventurers who made the journey. Some of these sea-bandits were aware of the potential interest in their ventures and a remarkable number scribbled away, describing their attacks and misadventures and also the plants and animals which they encountered. Crossing the Darien Isthmus in 1681, William Dampier was careful to keep his journal with him rolled up in a 'large Joint of Bamboo, which I stopped at both Ends, closing it with Wax so as to keep out any Water.'[2] Whenever opportunity presented, he and his companions would settle down to write up these precious journals. One is reminded less of pirates than of earnest students on holiday. There are *five* journals covering the buccaneering foray of Captains Bartholomew Sharp, John Watling and Richard Sawkins in 1680-81. When Captain Sharp split off from the main flotilla off the coast of South America in 1681, he took with him young William Dampier and two like-minded young colleagues, Basil Ringrose and Lionel Wafer, 'almost an accompanying press corps[3]'.

Simon Hatley sailed on two such voyages. The first of them was that of the *Duke* and *Duchess* which sailed from Bristol in 1708 during the War of the Spanish Succession. There are two published accounts of this voyage, by Captain Woodes Rogers, the commander of the expedition♣, and by Edward Cooke, Second Captain of the *Duchess*♠. Hatley, then a young man, was third mate of the *Duchess*, so a junior officer. This was the voyage when Alexander Selkirk, later in part the model for Daniel Defoe's *Robinson Crusoe*, was rescued from Juan Fernandez Island off the coast of Chile. Some time after Selkirk's rescue, Hatley was captured by the Spanish, taken under guard to Lima and slung into prison - into the hands of the Inquisition.

Somehow he managed to smuggle out a letter and a copy of it is now lodged in the National Archives at Kew[4]. It is addressed to the financial backers of the voyage and was possibly the first news they received about their venture. It is the only document that we have in Simon Hatley's own words and it is far from being the work of a rough, elemental, superstitious sailor of the type depicted by Coleridge. The voice is that of a competent and resourceful young man reporting back to the bosses, although in horrific circumstances. His tone is calm, except the last few lines when the tension breaks through:

... Some of our Countrymen here before we came they have made turn their Religion. We live a sorrowful life among them & always plagued by

---

♣ *A Cruising Voyage Round the World*, London 1712.
♠ Cooke, Edward *A Voyage to the South Sea and round the World*, London, 1712.

the Fathers putting us in Irons and in the Dungeon to make us turn. But we
are resolved to dye first. I and one more they have had to the Gallows
hanged until we were almost strangled before they cut us down ...

He survived of course, otherwise there would have been no episode
with the albatross. He returned to England in 1713/14 when the war ended,
and he next emerges in 1719 as Second Captain of the *Speedwell*. There are
two published accounts of this second voyage, which sailed from London
during the little-known War of the Quadruple Alliance, 1719-20. The first
is by George Shelvocke, *A Voyage round the world by way of the Great*
South Sea, published 1726, that read by Coleridge, and the second is by
William Betagh 'Captain of Marines', *A Voyage around the world, being*
an account of a remarkable enterprise begun in the year 1719, published in
1728. Unfortunately, both Shelvocke and Betagh could be shameless liars
on occasion and they loathed and contradicted each other. But, at least,
Simon Hatley was now a senior figure and through the fog of deceit and
authorial self-justification it is possible to piece together much of what he
did during the voyage.

If we are to believe Shelvocke, Hatley was drunk, depressed,
mutinous, a thief, a violent lout, a sexual predator and an incompetent
sailor. Betagh condemns less and is probably more reliable but he damns
with faint praise, portraying a skilled seaman but a heavy drinker, partly in
cahoots with the loathsome Shelvocke. One must tread with caution. One
thing is sure, the voyage was a nightmare for Hatley. Worse than a
nightmare - in 1719 he was captured again, wounded and flung into prison
in Lima for the second time.[5] One can only guess how he must have felt.
The Spanish authorities were unlikely to be merciful to a recidivist.

no. 6 High Street

That in outline is nearly all that was known about Simon Hatley until
now. Someone who figures in footnotes who first appears as a junior officer
and ends up as a Second Captain, who sailed on two extraordinary voyages,
shot an albatross, was twice imprisoned and finally came to the attention of
Samuel Taylor Coleridge. Through the mist of uncertainty which surrounds

him, he appears variously as a depressed brute, a pleasant young man, a lout, a skilled sailor or a pirate.

The Spanish Inquisition has little to be said in its favour but at least its bureaucracy was thorough. Casting around for a way to delve deeper into Hatley's life story, an obvious first step was to search for references to him in the Archives of the Inquisition in Madrid, which is the repository for many documents issued in South America in colonial times. I was fortunate. They have a little-known document, *Hereies Nacionales Espontaneos*[6], sixteen pages in neat, if slightly crabbed, clerkly hand. It is a report to the authorities in Spain on the 'spontaneous' ('voluntary') conversions to 'Our Holy Mother Church' of Protestant sailors held in prison in Lima during the War of the Spanish Succession. There are fifteen conversions in all, mainly English sailors but with a sprinkling of Dutch and Frenchmen. The reports follow a set pattern. Before the detailed account of each conversion there is a brief biography. At number twelve on the list comes a certain Simon Hatey[7] (*sic*). The report on the conversion of Simon Hatey tells us that he was born in 1685 in 'Jusdtoch' in the Kingdom of England, that his mother was a Catholic but his father was a Protestant and that he was brought up as a Protestant. It also tells us that Hatey trained as a pilot and took his 'vow' in Bristol. Spanish clerks were never too troubled about the spelling of English names. They wrote what they heard. 'Hatey' might be 'Hatley' and 'Jusdtoch' might well be a phonetic rendering of Woodstock given the Spanish habit of writing and pronouncing 'J' for 'W'.

I made my way to Oxfordshire. The local archives for Woodstock are kept in the Oxfordshire Record Office and in the local studies library in Oxford Central Library. In the parish register of St Mary Magdelene is recorded the birth of one Simon Hatley, 27 March 1685[8], son of Symon Hatley and Mary his wife, in Woodstock in the County of Oxon. I had my man - and I also had one of his secrets. When in prison in Lima, in 1709, Simon Hatley wrote in his letter to the owners that he would not become Catholic but would 'dye first'[9]. Two years after he wrote that letter, he had converted to Catholicism.

Woodstock is a little town which straddles the A44 about eight miles north of Oxford. The houses are built of soft, grey stone and it is still as

4

elegant as it would have been in Hatley's day. The neighbouring countryside is wide, the hills are low and the skies are big. Some days the clouds drift over like vast bales of cotton wool. The town is small enough that in spring the scent of may blossom and cow parsley penetrates from beyond the houses and competes, after a fashion, with the smell of traffic on the main road. In June, there are, or there used to be, poppies lining the wheat fields on the road down to Oxford and, not so long ago, you could hear larks sing in Woodstock Park nearby. But there's a price to pay for the wide landscape. In winter the wind blows almost all the way from Moscow without interruption. I've seen hoarfrost on the wild clematis along the A44 when the trees looked like sheeted ghosts.

Woodstock is pretty and it is also well situated, on the main tourist route from Oxford up to Stratford-on-Avon and the hometown of the Bard. Tourism is now the main source of income. Tourists frequently escape their coaches to wander the picturesque streets, a break on their journey to Shakespeare's birthplace further north. If they knew, Woodstock has literary associations of its own, and that is apart from 'Chaucer's House' on Park Street which was once rumoured to belong to Chaucer's son Thomas[10].

The town was once called 'New Woodstock' to differentiate it from 'Old Woodstock' on the other side of the little River Glyme. New Woodstock grew up to take advantage of trade along the entrance road to the royal park and manor of Woodstock, a favourite retreat of medieval English kings and queens. In the time of King Henry I, the manor was rebuilt into what was effectively a small palace. Henry also built a stone wall round the park and stocked it with a menagerie of exotic animals including lions and leopards.

Because of its proximity to the royal manor, Hatley's home-town was never as isolated as were most towns before the Industrial Revolution and the advent of trains and buses. Back then, the majority of inland English towns were rather isolated, self-contained worlds, but not Woodstock. It was near to Oxford and the great and the good frequently passed through it on their way to the manor. For two months in 1554, Princess Elizabeth, the future Elizabeth I herself, was imprisoned there[11] - but by then the manor itself was in such poor repair that she had to stay in the gatehouse. She scratched the following lines on a pane of glass with her diamond ring, one of the first verses to be associated with the town:

> *Much suspected by me,*
> *Nothing proved can be,*
> *Quoth Elizabeth, prisoner[12].*

To live in Woodstock was to be marginally connected to the fashionable world. In July 1680, five years before Hatley was born, the poet Hugh Wilmot, Earl of Rochester, libertine and one-time friend of Charles II, died in the Lodge nearby, a country retreat which came with his appointment as 'ranger and keeper of Woodstock Park[13]'. Wilmot once ran naked in the Park with a companion, 'upon a Sunday in the afternoon, expecting that several of the female sex would have been spectators but not one appear'd[14]'. The last lines of his poem *Love and Life* are typical of aristocratic *laissez-fair* attitudes in the period which immediately preceded Hatley's childhood:

> *Then talk not of Inconstancy*
> *False Hearts and broken Vows;*
> *If I by Miracle can be*
> *This live-long Minute true to thee,*
> *'Tis all that Heaven allows[15].*

At that time, when Carolingian rakes such as Wilmot passed through Woodstock, the royal manor was still standing. To a local child of the late seventeenth century such as Simon, it must have seemed as immortal as the surrounding woods and fields even though it was 'altogether ruinous',[16] an illusion brutally dismantled in 1723 when it was levelled by order of Sarah Duchess of Marlborough so as to improve the view from the Marlboroughs' new Palace of Blenheim on the hill opposite,[17] almost on the Hatley's doorstep. Blenheim Palace was begun in June 1705, a year after the Duke of Marlborough won his great victory at Blenheim, in Germany. Money for

6

construction was provided by Parliament while the park and the remains of the royal manor were donated by Queen Anne.

Back in the 1680s and during Simon Hatley's childhood, Woodstock consisted of just over a hundred houses.[18] It was dominated by a number of burgher families. Some were quite wealthy and the men considered themselves to be gentlemen. This local elite provided the six councillors or 'aldermen' and they shared the position of mayor among themselves, fighting off any competition as best they could.[19] Both Simon's father and grandfather were aldermen. His grandfather, Robert, was Mayor four times and his father, Symon, (I shall use the older spelling to distinguish him from his son, the Mariner) was Mayor twice.[20] They were part of the elite.

Simon Hatley's background was respectable. His parents, Symon and Mary, were married in 1684, a year before he was born[21] and the Hatleys can be traced back to the mid-seventeenth century in Woodstock, occupying roughly the same social position that they occupied in Simon's time, although it is just possible that Mary had a more elevated background. Her maiden name was Herbert. Given that, according to the Inquisition document, she was a Catholic, she may have been related, if only distantly, to the noble family of Herberts. One significant branch of the Herbert family was Catholic[22] and the Herbert Earls of Pembroke were stewards of the royal manor of Woodstock in the seventeenth century. The sowing of wild oats among the locals was not unusual for young aristocrats. The Earl of Rochester used to entice local girls to the Park Lodge, including one Nell Browne, 'who tho' she looked pretty well when clean, yet she was a very nasty, ordinary, silly creature, which people much admire'.[23] There is no reason to doubt Mary Herbert's respectability but who can speak for her mother? Mary could have been the illegitimate daughter of the disreputable Philip Herbert, Seventh Earl of Pembroke, convicted of manslaughter in 1678, who kept '52 Mastives, 30 Greyhounds, some Beares and a Lyon and 60 Fellows more bestial than they'.[24] He was just old enough, dying young in 1683. If Mary was the illegitimate daughter of the murderous Seventh Earl (or of the Fifth or Sixth Earl come to that), she was descended from the Second 'Incomparable' Earl who married the poet Sir Philip Sidney's sister in 1577. It is intriguing to speculate that the real Ancient Mariner may have been related to Sir Philip Sidney and a scion of the higher nobility. A promotion of sorts. Coleridge would have been amused, I think, if slightly disconcerted. However, Mary is more likely to have been the daughter of a certain William Herbert, one of the Woodstock elite and a prominent alderman and mayor, who died in 1715. This William, or his son, also called William, was witness to several Hatley family documents.[25] The murderous Seventh Earl is a less likely ancestor.

Remarkably, given Simon Hatley's obscurity, we can work out which house he was brought up in. Walk down Woodstock High Street towards the rather grand Town Hall. Just past Freeman's the Butcher, stop outside no 6 and look up. It is a handsome, three-storey, stone house with bow windows gazing out from either side of the front door. From beside the door on the left an old, lead drainpipe climbs upwards like an ivy branch. The rectangular head is clamped just below the parapet. On it is the letter 'H' with the letters 'S' and 'M' below and the date, 1710, all picked out in white. The 'H' stands for Hatley, the 'S' for Symon, the Mariner's father, and the 'M' for Mary, his mother.[26] Simon, eldest of their children, was born on this spot and spent his childhood here, as far as can be ascertained, along with his younger sister Mary and his younger brother William, although not in quite the same building.

Simon's father and his uncle Robert, 'haberdashers of hats',[27] bought numbers 6-8 High Street in 1682.[28] The brothers lived as neighbours for a while and Simon with his younger brother and sister grew up running in and out to visit their cousins, two boys and five girls,[29] next door. Simon grew up with Oxfordshire in his veins. Throughout his life he would have spoken with an accent similar to that of the poet Pam Ayres who comes from neighbouring Berkshire and speaks with one of the increasingly rare rural accents of the southern Midlands. By the 1680s his father was doing well. The hat business had been supplemented by malting and Symon began to describe himself as a 'maltster'.[30] In 1686, together with his wife Mary, Symon bought numbers 46-8 and 50 High Street as rental properties[31] and, in 1704, after Simon had left home, he knocked down the previous buildings at numbers 6-8 and began work on the building we now see there, a proper gentleman's residence. Suitably for the father of a son with piratical tendencies, it is said to have been built with stone filched from the then building site of Blenheim Palace.[32]

It was a small and secure world that Simon grew up in. The Inquisition document says that he was 'Latinate', which means that he could read and write Latin. He would have gone to the local grammar school, conveniently only about a hundred yards up the road, and run home down the cobbled street for lunch and supper. Founded in Tudor times, the school was then a single, long room built against the north side of the church. Nothing of it remains. It was pulled down in 1876 and the space where it once stood is now enclosed within the north aisle of the church[33].

The school, the house, the home. Everything points to a contented and comfortable childhood, the eldest son of a prominent citizen of a small, friendly town, borderline gentry, surrounded by a warm multitude of family and friends - and a thousand light years away from the man who shot an albatross in a fit of melancholy years later. But for Simon Hatley this secure world was evidently not enough.

one Spoon double gilt with Gold

The average age to start an apprenticeship in the late-seventeenth/early-eighteenth century was fourteen.[34] Some time around 1699, Simon Hatley made his way to Bristol. His tearful mother kissed him goodbye, the carter or whoever cracked his whip and off he went. It was difficult for his parents. One saying went:

Whosoever putteth his Child to get his living at Sea had better a great Deal bind him Prentice to a Hangman.[35]

It was Simon's own choice it seems. There was a family business to go into and he was the eldest son. There was no need for him to leave home at all. But many boys wanted to go to sea. Sailors were relatively well paid although from the accounts of contemporaries it appears that curiosity and a love of adventure were as much of a motivation.[36] Simon was educated and, like many other boys, he may well have read one or more of the books by the buccaneers which were just starting to roll off the presses. William Dampier's *A New Voyage Round the World*, the best-seller which set the trend for a flood of similar books, was published in 1697 when Simon was twelve.

Simon's father probably chose Bristol for the apprenticeship because of some business or family connection. The words of the Inquisition document are ever so slightly ambiguous. They say that he was 'apprenticed as a pilot' and that he took his 'vow' in Bristol, so the door is slightly ajar and he could have been apprenticed elsewhere to begin with. There was a Ralph Hatley living in London, part owner of the *New Nisbett*, a twenty-four-gun privateer,[37] who died in 1722 and who might have stood sponsor if related. This is unlikely however and the fact that the *Duke* and *Duchess* (named after the Duke and Duchess of Marlborough) later sailed from Bristol seems to clinch the matter.

Apprenticeship varied from three to seven years, with seven years being more common.[38] Simon finished his apprenticeship in 1706 at the latest, when he was twenty-one. Two years later, when he was twenty-three, he signed up as Third Mate of the *Duchess* (1708)[39] a junior position. Not that one should infer anything from this. Early progression up the ladder of promotion, in the merchant marine as well as in the Royal Navy, depended as much on contacts as ability. For an adventurous and ambitious young man without any very high-up contacts, signing up with the *Duchess* would have been a good move. The rewards and the opportunities for further promotion were potentially excellent - but it was a high-risk gamble.

Symon Hatley, his father, died late in 1712[40] while Simon was held in Lima. This was shortly after Symon completed his new house at 6-8 High Street, having marginally depleted Blenheim Palace's immense stock of stone. In Symon's will, he left Simon, his eldest son, the rental properties at the end of the High Street, numbers 46-8 and 50, and to Simon's younger brother, William, he left the new house at 6-8 and also his workshop and all the rest of his goods and chattels, all to be fully taken possession of after their mother's death. [41] William and Mary (the mother) were executors of the will - it was hardly practical to nominate Simon since he was in prison on the other side of the world.

Simon Hatley returned to England in 1713/14, aged twenty-nine, at the end of the War of the Spanish Succession. He had received some money from the voyage of the *Duke* and *Duchess* and he would have cut quite a glamorous figure - the voyage was already famous - if he made his way to Woodstock to see his family and his father's grave. He would have been less than human if he had not played up to this among family and friends in sleepy Oxfordshire. Perhaps he was tempted to find a star-struck local girl, settle down and take advantage of his new-won status. But no, he made no attempt to join the family business. It had become his younger brother's preserve.[42]

Simon Hatley sold his birthright. There is a parchment indenture, effectively a conveyance, dated 29 September 1718, in the local archives, part of a set of Hatley documents relating to numbers 46-8 and 50 High Street.[43] Simon's signature is on it alongside his mother's and the other parties'. He is described as 'Simon Hatley, Mariner, Gent.'[44] and beside his signature there is a seal, about the size of a five-pence coin, which is imprinted with a coat of arms.[45] In this contract, Simon and Mary agree to part with their interest in numbers 46-8 and 50 High Street to a certain Blagrove Gregory and his wife, also called Mary, in return for £110. This Mary Gregory was Simon's younger sister and Blagrove, her husband, was his brother-in-law.[46] They were keeping things in the family.

Mary Hatley, the mother, died that same year, leaving Simon 'one large Tankard, a Watch and One Spoon Double Gilt with Gold',[47] and, either shortly after or before, Simon signed on as Second Captain of the *Speedwell*. The following spring he turned his back on the land and set sail once more for the South Pacific. There followed his encounter with the albatross in October 1719. The melancholy fits described by Shelvocke may have been simple grief over the death of his mother, an event which causes many reassess their lives, although they are just as likely to have been caused by Shelvocke's unpleasant behaviour. Shelvocke returned to England in 1722 when he was briefly arrested for piracy, having circumnavigated the globe. There had been a piratical incident involving Simon Hatley.

Front page of *Hereies Nacionales Espontaneos*

Start of entry no.12 for 'Simon Hatey' in *Hereies Nacionales Esponaneos*

Woodstock Manor in 1711[48]

12

The Ancient Mariner's parents' house, Woodstock

The drainpipe of the house at Woodstock

Seal of Mary Hatley

13

Woodstock Grammar School before it was pulled down[49]

◆◆◆◆◆◆◆◆◆◆◆◆◆◆

CHAPTER 2

Language of the Sea

the South Sea

In September 1513, Nuñez de Balboa crossed the Isthmus of Darien and became the first European to reach the Pacific. Having tasted the water to see if it was salt, he put on his armour, drew his sword and waded into the waves, claiming the 'South Sea' and all the shores washed by it for God and the Spanish crown.[50] He called it the South Sea because the Isthmus runs from east to west at this point, so that to him it appeared to lie to the south of the Caribbean where he had started his journey. From the moment of its discovery by Europeans, the South Sea was a Spanish lake and others were kept firmly out.

The first Englishman to break the Spanish embargo was executed in Lima in 1580. This was Sir John Oxenham who crossed the Isthmus in 1577 and raided into the bay of Panama in a pinnace[*][51] manned by English sailors and a handful of escaped African slaves[52]. Following this there were

---

Pinnaces were of between ten and fifty tons, usually square-rigged and equipped with oars.

only fifteen English intrusions into the South Sea up to 1719 when the *Speedwell*, with Hatley as Second Captain, rounded the Horn and none at all in the seventy-seven years between 1593/4[53] and 1670 and the exploratory voyage of Sir John Narborough.

Right from the time of Sir Francis Drake, indeed from the time of Sir John Oxenham, there was keen public interest in British voyages into the Pacific precisely because of the rarity of such voyages, but in the late sixteenth and early seventeenth centuries this interest had been frustrated. *The World encompassed by Sir Francis Drake*, the account of Drake's voyage of 1577-8 by his chaplain Francis Fletcher, only appeared fully in print in 1628, fifty years after the event.[54] It had been withheld from the public by Elizabeth I for fear of offending the Spanish government and perhaps in order to keep English discoveries a secret. By the 1670s, other considerations prevailed and constraints on publishing had been reduced.

The voyage of Sir John Narborough was backed by Charles II. Indeed, all the few British intrusions into the South Sea up to this point had been backed, to greater or lesser extent, by the crown. But after 1670, a different type of British adventurer appeared on the scene. In 1671, while Narborough was on his way back to England, Henry Morgan and his buccaneer army marched over the Isthmus and sacked Panama in an unofficial act of war. Originally French masterless men from the island of Hispaniola, the buccaneers had grown into a ragtag international brotherhood of the sea. They included some of the original French buccaneers, French, English and Dutch renegade sailors, runaway servants, rogue captains, poets and scholars and various combinations of all these categories with the English by this time in the majority. They were anarchic and violent, motivated by hatred of Spain and a lust for adventure and gold. Only a minority were out and out pirates but they operated on the borderline between piracy and legitimate warfare.

Along with the appearance of the first buccaneers in the South Sea came a spate of publications about them. England was much richer than it had been a hundred years earlier and more literate. There was a much larger market for books and the accounts of these buccaneers were perfect for it. Travel books were second in popularity only to religious tracts, and the books of the buccaneers added an extra dimension of swash-buckle and adventure.[55] Enterprising London booksellers saw an opportunity and grabbed it.

a Pack of merry Boys

It was Gold was the bait that tempted a Pack of merry Boys of us, near Three Hundred in Number, being all Souldiers of Fortune, under Command (by our own Election) of Captain John Coxon, to list our selves in the Service of one of the Rich West Indian Monarchs, the Emperour of Darien or Durian[56]. Which Country has its Name from a River so called, running into the South Sea, almost across the Isthmus, which is between the two formerly Great Empires of Mexico and Peru ...[57]

Thus begins Basil Ringrose's introduction to his supplement to *Bucaneers of America*, the English edition with Ringrose's supplement being published in London in 1685, the year of Hatley the Mariner's birth. It reads like an adventure story. It is easy to see the appeal, especially for boys. A band of young men set out to march across the Isthmus of Darien to attack the Spanish on the Pacific coast. Like children out of school, they have elected their own commander and form themselves into companies. Each company has its individual, coloured flag. They plunge into the steamy jungle. Being a true account, no long-forgotten dinosaurs emerge from the trees nor do they come across Ancient Romans marooned there since the time of Christ, but everything else is so exotic and exciting that such wonders would hardly come as a surprise.

Bucaneers of America combined tales of cruelty with deeds of valour and adventure, mostly true, and its centre piece was Morgan's sacking of Panama. It was first published in English by two separate publishers[58] and both editions rapidly sold out, hence the second edition in 1685 containing Ringrose's supplement. It had been published first, without supplement, in Dutch in 1678, in Amsterdam, as *De Americanische Zee-Roovers*, the author being Alexander Exquemelin who 'of necessity was present at all these acts of plunder'.[59] He was probably a French Huguenot who had settled in Holland to escape persecution in Catholic France.[60] Mindful of potential criticism, Exquemelin went to great lengths to distance himself from his subject matter. He maintained a position of moral superiority but his readers could be forgiven for wondering how he managed to keep his hands clean when involved in quite so many pirate attacks. Fortunately for him, they were prepared to overlook this inherent flaw in his position and *Bucaneers of America* started a publishing fashion and ran through many editions in several languages besides English, spawning an industry of imitations and fictional spin-offs throughout the eighteenth century and beyond.

One of the key selling points of the books of the buccaneers was that they were all written by protagonists, men such as Exquemeling and Basil Ringrose, who had experienced the adventures they described at first hand. The period 1680-1720 was particularly fertile for British sailor-authors. There were only four British voyages round the Horn from 1700-1720 but they resulted in *six* books.* This compares to three French books in the same period derived from a far greater number of voyages.[61] British accounts became even more frenzied later in the century, to the extent that the British Admiralty began to confiscate all accounts of officially backed voyages to reduce them to just one official account per voyage. There are *eight* separate, published accounts of Commodore Anson's privateering circumnavigation of 1740. Put together, these accounts constitute a literary phenomenon, an anarchic mixture of adventure stories, objective descriptions, nautical travelogues, apologias and recriminations. There are tales of courage and accusations of abject cowardice. A bunch of madmen seem to have been let loose. The pirates/buccaneers/privateers, call them what you will, take on the Spanish with dare-devil brio, they hide or run away, they sit down and take notes, they quarrel, they attack Spanish ships five times their size and expect to win. It is small wonder that young men as late as Coleridge and Wordsworth enjoyed these books as much as they did.

On occasion the adventures take on an almost cartoon-like quality. In 1720 (Hatley was by then in prison for the second time), George Shelvocke was shipwrecked on the Juan Fernandez Islands. The *Speedwell* had sunk, he had lost all his guns except one cannon and his crew had almost voted

---

* Those by William Dampier (two), William Funnel, George Shelvocke, Woodes Rogers and Edward Cooke.

18

him out of office and decided to go 'on the account' (to turn pirate). But all was not lost. They voted him back into office. They built themselves a new ship using timber from the island and what stores they had been able to rescue. Forty of them crowded into this makeshift vessel and off they sailed. For food they had 2,300 smoked conger eels preserved in sea lion oil, the putrifying carcases of some seals, four live hogs and some beef - but only one frying pan. Frying had to be continuous. The smell and sound of the frying eels was almost unbearable according to Shelvocke. Eventually they saw a 'great ship' and tried to catch up with it even though it was much bigger than they were. Unfortunately, the wind got up and their prey easily outdistanced them. They had to row like demons when the wind fell, until by sheer persistence they managed to get close and attacked - and then ran out of bullets: 'which obliged us to fall astern to make some slugs', as Shelvocke casually explains.[62] That took all night. A gale blew up and their prey escaped. This is the stuff of Popeye.

In 1704, having just marooned Alexander Selkirk (Robinson Crusoe) on Juan Fernandez Island, Captain Thomas Stradling, then twenty-one years old, gave himself up to the Spanish, his ship having foundered. He was imprisoned in Lima, escaped and attempted to row the 1,400 miles north to Panama in an open canoe, planning to trek from there over the Darien Isthmus to the Atlantic. He was recaptured off the coast of Ecuador and was back in prison in Lima when Hatley arrived there in 1709.[63] Shortly after, Stradling escaped again, was captured by a French ship and shipped to France, France and Spain being allies in the War of the Spanish Succession[64]. He ended up in prison in Dinan in Britanny where he convinced the authorities that he had buried a huge, pirate treasure somewhere on an island in the South Sea. The Minister of Marine ordered prison regulations to be relaxed in the hopes of extracting further information. Sheets were allowed, whereupon Stradling and seventeen others escaped over the wall by tying their sheets together to make a rope, and thence via Jersey back to England.[65]

If some of these adventures had been described by professional writers, disbelief might well have prevailed. That being so, the authors are careful to emphasise their credentials as real sailors. They make a virtue of their direct seaman-like language and they punctuate their accounts with telling details and humorous episodes to add colour. William Dampier excels at this. In June 1686, William Dampier was a pilot or navigator on the *Cygnet*, Captain Charles Swan. They were in mid-Pacific, there were only three days' rations left and the men were plotting mutiny. They planned to kill Captain Swan and eat him once the rations were gone and then eat the others who backed him as the need arose. Swan uncovered the plot remarking: 'Ah, poor Dampier, you would have made them but a poor meal,' because, as Dampier writes, he was 'as lean as the Captain was lusty and fleshy'.[66] Woodes Rogers on the *Duke*, in 1709 after Hatley had been lost off the Galapagos Islands, uses a similar humorous tone to describe how he treated his Spanish prisoners:

We allowed Liberty of Conscience on board our floating Commonwealth to our Prisoners. For there being a priest in each Ship, they had the Great Cabin for their Mass, whilst we us'd the Church of England Service over them on the Quarter-Deck, so that the Papists were the Low Churchmen.[67]

Giants and Cannibals

As a teenager I would lie around in a fug of indolence while I ploughed through an endless supply of science-fiction paperbacks with spines that came easily apart. My eighteenth-century equivalents, right up to the time of Coleridge and beyond, would have done likewise, those who had the leisure. Their escapism involved leather-bound accounts of voyages where the text ambled between wide margins on thick-laid paper. In contrast to space ships and intergalactic wars, their imaginative universes were peopled with tall ships, exotic, undiscovered kingdoms, strange voyages, giants and cannibals. There was no need for intergalactic warfare when large tracts of the world were yet unmapped and unknown to Christendom. It was easy to believe in wonders when these wonders supposedly existed in the real world.

The boundaries between fiction and reality were easily blurred. El Dorado, the 'Golden', is a case in point. It was escapism but also, possibly, it was true. Jiménez de Quesada claimed to have discovered it in 1536 in the foothills of the Andes before he went on to found Bogota and the kingdom of New Grenada, now Colombia. Back in Spain once more, he was appointed governor of his *fictional* city by Philip II and returned to South America to find his city and take up his governorship, in 1568 aged sixty.[68] His account, now lost, was read by Cervantes, shortly after he was freed from slavery in Algiers, and Quesada and his exotic, futile quest became, in part and according to some scholars, the model for Cervantes's *Don Quixote* - and *Don Quixote* is, of course, a spoof on someone who believes what he reads*.

The Patagonians were another stock-in-trade. They added an exotic element to the accounts of the buccaneers, which were always in danger of degenerating into lists of storms, battles, loot and arguments. Patagonians were reputed to grow to over ten feet tall and people genuinely believed in them.

They were of a prodigious stature, fierce and barbarous, made a horrible roaring noise, more like bulls than human creatures; and yet with all that mighty bulk were so nimble and light of foot that none of the Spaniards or Portuguese could over take them.

What better way to tempt the public, especially in the early years? The Tudor writer Thomas Lodge* used them in the introduction to his experimental novel, *a Margarite of America*,[69] written on the second privateering voyage of Sir Thomas Cavendish in 1591. In his introduction Lodge explained to his lady readers: 'Touching the place where I wrote this, it was in those straits christened by Magelan; in which place to the southward many wondrous Isles, many monstrous Patagones withdrew my senses'.[70]

The sailor-authors of the late sixteenth and early seventeenth centuries were loath to give up on the Patagonians even though, by that time, doubts

---

* *Don Quixote* was a favourite book of Samuel Taylor Coleridge. Coleridge understood the limits of fiction better than Quesada: 'Reading made Don Quixote a gentleman, but *believing* what he read made him mad ...'.

* Antoniao Pigafetta, an Italian who sailed with Magellan in 1519, appears to have started the myth.

* Lodge is best known for his romance *Rosamunde Euphes Golden Legacies* which gave Shakespeare the plot for *As You Like It*.

had arisen. They got round it by discussing the earlier accounts in a superior manner. Woodes Rogers, Simon Hatley's commander in 1709, referred to giants 'whose Waste a middle-sized Man could scarce reach with his Head' but made it clear that he was unconvinced.[71] The Frenchman, Amadée Frezier, who visited South America on behalf of Louis XIV in 1711-14 and was in Lima while Hatley was captive there, gives details but with a scientific gloss to cover himself. The Patagonians' real name, he claimed, was the *Cacahues* and they were about nine or ten feet tall. They lived inland in the desert region of Chile[72]. Patagonians were still a temptation for George Shelvocke, Hatley's commander in 1719, who refers to Frezier in connection with them but then adds disparagingly 'I had sight of one or two ... who seemed to me to differ little or not at all from the other *Chilenians* as to their persons',[73] thus managing to knock the French, distance himself from such credulity and to mention Patagonians, all in one paragraph.

For amateurs, these turbulent sailor-authors were remarkably savvy about what would go down well with their readership. Apart from Patagonians, they made judicious comments on the charms of the local women, they inserted large tracts of 'useful' information, frequently copied wholesale from other authors, and they appealed to the reader's patriotism, or rather, jingoism. The French were lazy and had no stomach for a fight, the Spanish were confused and superstitious. The English or British were, by implication at least, resourceful and brave. John Bull was about to be invented (he derives from a satire written in 1712)[74] and the stereotypes were there to be exploited. Woodes Rogers writes disparagingly of the population of Peru as suffering under 'the burden of a numerous and luxurious Clergy that indulge all their Pride, Sloth, Effeminacy and Bigotry'.[75] Indeed, the Spaniards provided plenty of ammunition. They really were given to excessive religiosity and, more importantly, they were no longer great fighters. It was understandable. They wanted to enjoy the fruits of their conquests in peace and the last thing they needed or wanted was aggressive foreigners behaving as they themselves had done in the past. 'The easy Tranquillity they live in, makes them apprehensive of disturbing their Repose'.[76] Sometimes they fought back against the British marauders

22

but often they didn't. In 1680, when Captain Sharp took the town of La Serena in Chile, he did it with an advance guard of only thirty-seven men against several hundred, admittedly civilian, defenders. The defenders simply turned and fled. It made a good adventure story in England, but local histories of the town are hard put to it to forgive this craven behaviour even now.

Easy tranquillity: a Gentleman of Peru, 1711[77]

Sea Yahoos

Literary types back in London viewed the success of the amateur, nautical authors with both envy and disdain. They belittled the educational background and general culture of the writers. Jonathan Swift referred to sailors as 'Sea-Yahoos[78] and described travel literature in general as 'an abundance of trash[79]' (while reading it with relish), Daniel Defoe called Woodes Rogers and William Dampier 'illiterate sailors'.[80] This attitude arose from jealousy and a closed-shop mentality, and the accusations of illiteracy were wide of the mark. Even among common sailors as many as three quarters were literate to some degree.[81] The likes of Shelvocke,

23

Dampier and Rogers were all intelligent and well educated and came from middle-class backgrounds, in so far as a middle class existed in this period. If their language was less flowery than that of some professional authors', it was deliberately so and part of the appeal. Woodes Rogers at the start of his book explains, 'I rather chuse to keep the Language of the Sea, which is more genuine, and natural for a Mariner'.[82] Some of the buccaneers were scholars, albeit wayward scholars. Young Richard Gopson, who tramped across the Darien Isthmus with Dampier and Basil Ringrose in 1685, could translate from a Greek Testament extempore into English while bivouacking beneath the palm trees,[83] and Basil Ringrose is described as 'a good Scholar and full of Ingeniosity, had also very good skill in Languages'.[84] The rather superior Ambrosia Cowley, who sailed with Dampier from Virginia, was a Master of Arts from Cambridge University, and Major Stede Bonnet, a gentleman of Barbados who turned pirate in 1717, used to 'walk about the decks in his morning gown, and then to his Books of which he has a good Library on Board'.[85] One could go on indefinitely.*

Daniel Defoe may have belittled the sailor-authors but he knew a commercial opportunity when he saw one. His first novel, *The Life and Strange Surprising Adventures of Robinson Crusoe of York, Mariner*, was published on 25 April 1719 and purported to be a true account in the same vein. There is a map of Crusoe's travels at the beginning, and the preface claims it to be 'a just history of fact; neither is there any appearance of fiction in it'. Tongue-in-cheek to be sure, but to get that level of verisimilitude, Defoe was more than happy to plunder those he looked down on. Robinson Crusoe is based to a considerable degree, although specialists argue over the extent, on Woodes Rogers's description of the rescue of Alexander Selkirk from the Juan Fernandez Islands in 1709, the

---

* James Barrie made a play on this in a talk about Peter Pan that he gave to the boys of Eton College in 1927. Captain Hook was educated at Eton and Balliol, he explained. The books he borrowed from the library at his Oxford college included poetry, mostly of the Lakeland School. 'These volumes may still be occasionally picked up at second-hand bookstalls with the name "Jacobus Hook" inserted as the owner.' *cit.* Cordingly (2002) 31

same Alexander Selkirk who was marooned there by the adventurous Thomas Stradling in 1704.

Daniel Defoe was dandified, bumptious, prolific, a literary phenomenon, and it is impossible to dislike him, at least in retrospect. But his success, his general manner, his apparent lack of integrity and the fact that he was a dissenter and not a member of the Church of England made him unpopular with the likes of Jonathan Swift, Joseph Addison and other members of the literary establishment of early-eighteenth century London. They seem to have thought that Defoe was common in so far as they thought about him at all. An enemy described him:

One thing, Daniel, I want to know, whether you keep up your Beau habit, your long Wig, with Tassels at the End of it, your Iron-bound Hat, and your blew Cloak? As also whether you have left your old Wont, of holding out your little Finger to show your Diamond Ring?[86]

Defoe, always in and out of debt, was probably oblivious. He had a commercial success on his hands and he mined it to exhaustion, following up with: *Further Adventures of Robinson Crusoe* (also in 1719), *Serious Reflections during the Life and surprising Adventures of Robinson Crusoe* (1720) which was an attempt to draw high morals from the story, *The King of Pirates: Being an Account of the Famous Enterprises of Captain Avery* (1720), and *Memoirs of a Cavalier, the Life, Adventures and Piracies of the famous Captain Singleton* (also 1720). Singleton is a pirate whose accomplice William Walters is, of all things, a Quaker. Finally, several novels later, in 1724, came *A New Voyage round the World*, Defoe's last novel, the title was a direct crib from the sailor-author William Dampier's best-seller of 1697.

Jonathan Swift looked down on Daniel Defoe just as Defoe looked down on William Dampier and Woodes Rogers. Swift even pretended to be ignorant of Defoe's name (*'the Fellow that was pilloryed, I have forgot his Name'*),[87] having previously described him as a 'stupid, illiterate scribbler'.[88] But the success of *Robinson Crusoe* was irksome all the same. In 1720, then back in Dublin and Dean of St Patrick's, Swift began to write *Gulliver's Travels*. He too maintained the pretence of a real sailor-author, complete with phoney maps, but only as a spoof. The title begins *Travels*

25

into several remote nations of the World, in four parts ... and the author is
'Lemuel Gulliver, first a Surgeon then a Captain of several ships'. There's a
portrait of Gulliver on the frontispiece and the book starts with a letter from
Gulliver to his cousin Sympson asking him to hire some young university
gentlemen 'to correct the Style as my Cousin Dampier did by my Advice in
his Book called *A Voyage round the World*'.[89]

  The reference to William Dampier is deliberate. *Gulliver's Travels*
takes all the recent voyage literature as a target for its satire but Dampier's
books in particular. Dampier was an obvious target because he was the
most famous and the most talented of all the sailor-authors. His first book,
A New Voyage round the World, published in 1697, recounted his
extraordinary adventures as pirate, naturalist, buccaneer and explorer in the
years 1679-91 with a wealth of humorous and personal detail. On the
strength of it, he had been made a member of the Royal Society and was
commissioned to lead a voyage of exploration to New Holland (Australia)
'his qualifications to lead such a difficult expedition lying solely in his
literary talent'[90] and his portrait now hangs in the National Portrait Gallery.
Dampier's voice is woven into the language of *Gulliver*, which tends to
imitate his direct, descriptive style. There are also several parallels in the
narrative between fictional Gulliver and real-life Dampier. Gulliver sets off
in 1699, the year Dampier set off in the *Roebuck* to search for New
Holland. * It is commonly held that 'Captain Pocock of Bristol', in part four
of *Gulliver*, was directly modelled on Dampier: 'an honest man, and a good
sailor, but a little too positive in his opinions, which was the cause of his
destruction' (a reference to Dampier's court martial in 1702 after the
voyage of the *Roebuck*[91]). There is little doubt that Dampier's hostile
description of Australian aborigines was used by Swift for his Yahoos,
beastly humans ruled by horses. If Gulliver is anyone apart from Swift, he is
William Dampier, although not in a kind way.

  Jonathan Swift's parody of the sailor-authors seems shallow once one
has read about their extraordinary lives, but he had a point. For all their

---

* That same year Dampier spotted a ship called the *Antelope* off the Cape of Good
Hope. Gulliver's ship is called the *Antelope* - Swift is using Dampier as evidence
for Gulliver's reality - Williams (1997)

colourfulness, the buccaneers and privateers were sea-raiders of varying degrees of ruthlessness. They were at the front edge of European, colonial competition at a time when it was almost innocent in its high-handedness. In the last chapter of *Gulliver's Travels* there is the following passage:

A crew of pirates are driven by a storm they know not whither, at length a boy discovers land from the topmast, they go on shore to rob and plunder; they see a harmless people and are entertained by kindness, they give the country a new name, they take formal possession of it for the King, they set up a rotten plank or a stone for a memorial, they murder two or three dozen natives, bring away a couple more by force for a sample, return home, and get their pardon[92].

noble Savages

But if Swift had Dampier or another of the more sensitive of the sailor-authors in mind for his criticism, he was being unjust. Dampier was no angel and his attitude towards slavery, for instance, was no different to that of most of his contemporaries, but he was usually sympathetic towards native people, native Americans especially. This was not uncommon. Friendly relations between English buccaneers and South-American Indians were quite normal. Classically, in 1681, ship's surgeon Lionel Wafer, a friend of Dampier, along with Richard Gopson and three others, was left behind with the Cuna Indians of the Darien Isthmus while retreating to the Caribbean. A wound in his leg meant that he could not keep up with his shipmates. The five of them spent nearly three months with the Cuna, and Lacanta, the chief of the tribe, came to value Wafer so highly for his medical skills that he wanted him to settle permanently and even to marry one of his daughters.[93] Eventually, with the help of Indian friends, Wafer managed to reach the Caribbean and was reunited with his shipmates:

We went aboard the English Sloop, and our Indian Friends with us, and were received with a very hearty Welcome ... I sat for a while cringing upon my Hams among the Indians, after their Fashion, painted as they were, and all naked but only about the Waist, and with my Nose-piece hanging over my Mouth. I was willing to try if they would know me in this

Disguise; and 'twas the better part of an Hour before one of the Crew cry'd out, Here's our Doctor.[94]

Several of the sailor-authors made explicit use of the idea of the 'noble savage', of 'natives' who live happily and morally in a state of nature. It was a fashionable sentiment and therefore useful and it is no coincidence that the concept had its origins, indirectly at least, in South America. In 1555, the Frenchman Nicholas Durand de Villegaignon had sailed for Brazil[*] with around five hundred volunteer colonists and started a settlement on an island in the Bay where the modern city of Rio de Janeiro is now situated. His aim was to realise Plato's *Republic* in the New World and he was also influenced by Thomas More's *Utopia*.[95] Four years later, he gave up and the French returned home. Three years after that, in Rouen in 1562, the essayist Michel de Montaigne met a group of the Guarani Indians whom Villegaignon had brought back with him, and this encounter, together with Montaigne's reading of a book by one of the colonists,[96] led directly to Montaigne's famous essay *Of Cannibals*, in which the concept of the Noble Savage was first fully enunciated:

Each man calls barbarian what is not his own practice ... they are in such a state of purity that I am sometimes vexed that they were not known earlier.

George Shelvocke, writing in 1723, could almost be copying from Montaigne.[*] It is 1720 and the privateers have anchored off Puerto Seguro on the coast of California[97]. They have established friendly relations with the local native Americans:

By all that I could discern of their behaviour towards one another, and their deportment towards us, they are endued with all the humanity imaginable, and may make some nations (who would give these poor people the epithet of savages *and* barbarians*) blush to think that they deserve that appellation more than they: for all the time that we were there,*

---

[*] He had recently returned from accompanying the five-year-old Mary Queen of Scots to Scotland, Arciniegas (1969) 101.

[*] Daniel Defoe was influenced by Montaigne's noble savages and they were also central to the back-to-nature thinking of Jean Jacques Rousseau. In 1762, in *Émile ou traité de l'éducation*, Rousseau allowed Emile only one book before his twelfth birthday - and that book was *Robinson Crusoe*.

and constantly among so many hundreds of them, there was nothing to be perceived but the most agreeable harmony ... in a word they seem to pass their lives in the purest simplicity of the earliest ages of the world, before discord and contention were heard amongst men.[98]

Two Californian women

No, despite his humanitarian concern, what really irked Swift about Dampier, and by inference Shelvocke and some of the others, was not their attitude towards natives which was in the main quite liberal. It was Dampier's reputation as a scientific observer and that Dampier became a member of the Royal Society on the strength of *A New Voyage round the World.* Swift was suspicious of science. His book is in part a parody on how travel writers of the period loaded their books with endless, detailed facts. It was a sort of blindness on Swift's part, particularly with regard to Dampier and surprising in someone of Swift's literary sensibility. Dampier's descriptions are succinct and oddly pleasing to read:

The Cat-Fish is much like a Whiting, but the Head is flatter and bigger. It has a great wide Mouth, and certain small Strings pointing out from each side of it like a Cat's Whiskers, and for that Reason it is called a Cat-Fish.[99]

This entranced Coleridge. A description which is careful and without artifice. These qualities together with a degree of sensitivity distinguish the work of the best sailor-authors, such as Dampier (in particular) and Shelvocke (despite himself), from the rest. The worst, it must be said, such

29

as the rather repulsive William Funnel, first mate of the *St George* and no friend of Dampier, wrote accounts of their adventures without any sensitivity whatsoever. Funnel happily describes the sport of baiting sea lions to death in his *Voyage round the World* of 1707, going into graphic detail. The reader ends up feeling sorry for the sea lions.[100]

In complete contrast, when Shelvocke describes the albatross which Simon Hatley shot, he gives it a personality. It was 'disconsolate', 'hovering about us as if he had lost himself'. Good for Shelvocke as it turned out. If the albatross had had no personality there would have been no crime in Hatley shooting it, Coleridge and Wordsworth would not have picked up on the incident and there would have been no *Ancient Mariner* as we now know him.

William Dampier, 'Pirate and Hydrogapher'[101]

CHAPTER 3

the Hand of the most High

his Wonders in the Deep

At night, in their little bobbing ships, alone on the empty oceans, the adventurers got drunk, prayed, read books (some of them), missed their families, talked and argued. A ship at sea was a little bubble of Englishness or Frenchness or Spanishness or of some other nationality or mixture of nationalities. Apart from the particular, demanding interests of their profession, the sailors' preoccupations were broadly similar to the preoccupations of their countrymen back home. At the centre of such preoccupations were the eternally fraught areas of money, women, politics and religion. Sailors were less religious than most men[102] but it is still surprising the extent to which religion was practised even aboard buccaneer and privateer ships. In the seventeenth century and before, it was common practice for a crew to gather before nightfall 'all the seamen with the master to read a prayer and sing a psalm'.[103]

Free spirits such as William Dampier, Alexander Selkirk and Simon Hatley were hardly prone to religiosity - even if their fictional alter-egos, if one can call them that, showed signs - but they were not entirely immune. Even in Dampier's *A new Voyage round the World*, which is remarkable for its lack of religious feeling, religion has its place. In May 1688, having managed to escape from a crew of piratical shipmates, he and seven companions - two English, four Malayan and a 'mongrel' Portuguese - set out to sail from the Nicobar Islands to Achin in Sumatra in an over-laden, open canoe* with four paddles and a tiny square-rigged mast, a distance of about 150 miles. His companions being less experienced sailors were unaware of the risk they were taking, but Dampier was all too conscious of it. Three days out on the open sea, the weather turned foul. 'The Sea was already roaring in a white Foam about us. A dark Night was coming on, there was no Land in sight to shelter us, and our little Ark was in danger of being swallowed by every Wave[104]'. Dampier was certain that he was going to die:

... I had long before this repented of this roving Course of Life, but never with such Concern as now. I also called to Mind the many miraculous Acts of God's Providence towards me in the whole course of my Life, of which kind I believe that few Men have met with the like ...[105]

Nothing particularly unusual about that, and nothing specifically Christian. But the language is Protestant and this is of interest. Dampier was sharing a Protestant moment with his English readership, a readership that liked to think of the buccaneers as brave Protestant adventurers, common men making good. He was also enunciating his own belief. The passage calls to mind sentiments expressed in convoluted fashion in a book published in 1684, *Remarkable Providences* by Increase Mather, a prominent Puritan minister from Massachusetts. Mather set out to prove that God uses the weather to demonstrate his power and benevolence. The weather, indeed life itself, is all part of a long, hard lesson in why we should praise God and humble ourselves before him, a widely held opinion and especially pertinent to sailors. His first chapter was titled *Of Remarkable Sea Deliverances*:

---

* The larger canoes were long and thin and were called *piraguas* in Spanish. They could carry up to around twenty-five men and were either rowed or fitted with a single sail. Basil Ringrose's journal describes: 'our canoe, for it was nearly twenty-three feet in length and yet not quite one-and-a-half in breadth where it was the broadest'.

... they who go down to the Sea in Ships, that do Business in great waters, see the Works of the Lord and his Wonders in the Deep. And, in special, they see wonders of Divine goodness in respect of eminent Deliverances wrought by the Hand of the Most High, who stills the noise of the Seas, the noise of their Waves. It is meet that such Providences should be ever had in remembrance, as most of all by the Persons concerned in them, so by others, that the God of Salvation, who is the confidence of them that are afar off upon the Sea, may have eternal Praise...[106]

not because they are Spanish

Religion was often, as now, a poison that exacerbated national prejudices. The Spanish strongly identified themselves as Catholic and as defenders of their religion, but Spain, even at the height of her power, had quite a small population. From the very beginning, the Spanish were obliged to exercise a degree of ruthlessness in order to hang on to their conquests. If buccaneers were caught they were either killed on the spot, ransomed, executed as pirates or taken into slavery.[107] One Spanish edict stated that all trespassers in forbidden waters were to be hung as pirates with their commissions round their necks.[108]

Religion helped to justify such behaviour. God, the wise schoolmaster of Increase Mather's acquaintance, also manifested himself as God the intolerant tyrant. A Spanish note, left on the bodies of French Huguenot buccaneers massacred in the Caribbean, is said to have read: 'Not because they are French but because they are Lutherans'.[109] In answer to which the French left a note on some Spanish corpses which read: 'Not because they are Spanish but because they are Traitors and Murderers'.[110] And so it went on, Catholic *v.* Protestant.

Religious tensions were remarkably consistent from the sixteenth century right up to the early eighteenth century and beyond. There was no doubting Protestant attitudes. In the words of Francis Fletcher, chaplain to Sir Francis Drake back in the sixteenth century:

... in all parts of America, where the Spaniards have any government, the poisonous infection of Popery hath spread itself ...there is no City, as Lima, Panama, Mexico, &c. no Town or Village, yea no house almost in all

33

these provinces, wherein (amongst other the like Spanish virtues) not only whordome, but the filfithness of Sodom, not to be named among Christians, is not common without reproof: the Popes pardons being more rife in these parts than they be in any part of Europe, for these filthinesses whereout he sucketh no smal advantage.[111]

Contemporary reports to the Spanish Viceroy in Lima on Sir Francis Drake's depredations of the 1570s betray the mutual fear and disgust of the Spanish:

A red-haired, pock-marked boatswain led the fanatical English who profaned and sacked the church ...a tall hunch-backed Lutheran took down the bell of the church, and made off with it, wearing a chasuble he took from the church...they also carried off five pairs of altar-cloths, which they used either to wipe the sweat off their faces, or to drape over their shoulders, after they had hacked and cut the sacred pictures and images, greatly to the horror of the vicar and two laymen whom the English had made prisoners.[112]

Nearly two hundred years later, in 1740, Commodore Anson, having attacked and taken the small port of Paita in north-west Peru, entered the charming little church *la Merced* which stands on a little square near the harbour. He is said to have slashed at a statue of the Virgin Mary with his sword in an attempt to decapitate it. The statue is still there, the cut-marks still visible on the neck.

Relations between Catholic French and Protestant British buccaneers, while nothing like as bad as between the Spanish and British, were still uneasy. There was mutual scorn. Dampier sailed on a French freebooter in 1681 and described its crew:

The saddest creatures that ever I was among; for though we had bad weather that required many hands aloft, yet the biggest part of them never stirred off their hammocks but to eat or ease themselves[113]

In 1685, a French contingent separated themselves from the English because they were offended by the loutish Protestantism of the English buccaneers. The usual stuff: they complained of the English habit of taking pot shots at statues of saints in the Spanish churches, of hacking at crucifixes with their swords and, to complicate matters, of mocking and

34

jeering at the French sailors when the French sailors crossed themselves in horror at these profanities.[114]

Attempts to ignore or reduce the prejudices were fraught with difficulty. Charles II wanted a compromise between Britain and the Catholic powers. In the spirit of this, he intended the voyage of the twenty-nine-year old Sir John Narborough (1669-71) to be a peaceful, exploratory excursion into the South Sea. Narborough was to survey the Straight of Magellan and to make friendly contact with the Spanish.[115] He met hostility instead. The Spanish were unprepared for Charles's initiative. In his ship *HMS Sweepstakes*, together with a companion supply vessel, Narborough worked his way through the Strait braving ice and storms and emerged into the South Sea in November 1670 where he sailed up the Chilean coast to the port of Valdivia. At Valdivia after fruitless friendly overtures, four of his men were captured and imprisoned. Although completely innocent, they were taken to Lima and executed.[116] It is fortunate that his navigator, a Dutch/Spanish convert from Judaism by the name of Carlos Henriquez, was not among them or he would have suffered badly at the hands of the Inquisition. The Spanish reaction to Narborough bordered on hysterical. Rumour spread that a fleet of twelve British warships had come to mount a major attack on Panama and from his palace in Lima, the Viceroy ordered that regular shipments of silver to Panama be put on hold, causing financial embarrassment for the government in Spain. [117]

Meanwhile, to Charles II's huge embarrassment, Henry Morgan and his men came marching over the Darien Isthmus. Morgan's *ad hoc* buccaneer army included veterans of Cromwell's New Model Army. Some even wore faded, red, Model-Army uniforms taken from the government stores on the British colony of Jamaica.[118] These leathery, lapsed Puritans were reckoned 'among the most debauched' pirates in Kingston but they were still belligerent anti-Catholics. Their greed mixed with religious prejudice to form a potent brew. Morgan's men trudged and hacked through eighty miles of steep mountains and dense jungle, going without food for three days and eating leather bags,[119] fortified by dreams of the gold they would take from their cruel, Catholic enemies.

There was a particular animus between Spain and England. England, the largest Protestant country, had been a thorn in the side of Spain since the days of the Armada and before. Each country demonised the other. When Morgan took Panama, the inhabitants were surprised to discover that the Englishmen who burst out of the jungle in their motley uniforms looked much like themselves. Spanish propaganda had led them to believe that Englishmen looked like gorillas.[120]

Passions ran high. Panama was a beautiful city of white stone houses with rosy pan-tiled roofs, the churches and larger houses looming above the rest and showing their handsome profiles to the sea. Henry Morgan's men burned it to the ground in an orgy of destruction. Only the gutted tower of the cathedral was left standing. The sacking of Panama produced such fury back in Spain that attendants feared for the life of Queen Isabella who burst into uncontrollable paroxysms of weeping on hearing the news. It was fury fuelled by frustration. Morgan's attack was dramatic proof that Spain was unable to defend her colonies, even along the inaccessible shores of the South Sea. In reality, Isabella's tears came far too late. In 1661, ten years earlier, at the Court of St James, the French ambassador had demanded that his coach should precede the Spanish ambassador's coach and had tied up the reins of the Spanish ambassador's horses in order to delay him. The Spanish ambassador had thereupon attached his horses with iron chains. To no avail. Louis XIV had threatened war and Spain had backed down. From that time on, Spain gave precedence to France in all the courts of Europe.[121] The deed was done. Writer and administrator Melchor Rafael Macanaz expressed Spanish disillusionment with her decline in bitter words. Spain commits suicide, realising that she is about to die anyway:

Disillusioned as to what I am and in despair as to what I might have been (a torment which makes my ills more acute) and guessing from my weakness that my end is near, I beg all the powers of Europe to be present in person at my funeral, particularly England to whom I entrust my heart as a proof of my affection.[122]

Spain was weakening but France was growing stronger. From his immense, new, gilded palace at Versailles, Louis XIV ran his kingdom like the chief executive of some ambitious corporation, taking a personal interest in all important details of government. His goal was a Catholic Europe dominated by a Catholic France and he used war unapologetically to achieve his ends. As the seventeenth century moved into its final quarter, the Catholic threat to England was thus as real as it had been at the height of Spanish power, although the threat came from a different source. In fearful England, it was still easy to whip up anti-Catholic sentiment. In September 1678, Titus Oates, a defrocked Anglican priest, claimed that he had uncovered a Catholic plot to kill 'the Black Bastard',[123] which he said was the plotters' name for Charles II. According to Oates, the plotters planned to replace Charles with his Catholic brother James. Protestants would then be massacred in their thousands. In Oates's words: 'The General Design of the Pope ... is the Reduction of Great Britain and Ireland, and all His Majesties Dominions by the Sword'.[124]

This was just the sort of nightmare that honest Englishmen loved to believe in. Anti-Catholic hysteria gripped the country. Prisons were soon full of terrified, suspect Catholics. Paranoia ruled. Cannon were set up round the seat of government at Whitehall and the waves of fear or hatred spread outwards down the winding, muddy lanes of pre-industrial England. Even tranquil Woodstock was affected. Oates was given the freedom of the town.[125] One wonders what Symon Hatley, Hatley's father, thought of it, given that his wife was a Catholic. Before the hysteria had burned itself out, fifteen probably completely innocent men had been executed in London.

The tension was amplified in 1685, the year of Simon Hatley's birth, when Louis XIV revoked the Edict of Nantes, thus ending nearly a hundred years of freedom of worship for French Protestants. The Huguenots, already unpopular, were stripped of their rights overnight and Louis started a policy of vicious repression, enthusiastically supported by the majority of the French population. Huguenot refugees began to flood into Britain, many of them in a pitiful condition. In Britain the Revocation of the Edict of Nantes caused widespread revulsion:

To the eternal Infamy of Popery, and of the very Name and Memory of the late Lewis XIV it was disown'd, revok'd, and rescinded by the particular Order of that Prince in the Year 1685, and the Protestants thereupon treated with such Cruelty and Inhumanity, as can scarce be express'd by Words.[126]

In Woodstock a collection was made for the poor French refugees.[127]

Thus, at the height of productivity of the sailor-authors, escalation of the conflict between Catholic and Protestant was very much on the agenda. And refugees continued to move to England over the next two decades, with a wave after 1702, at the start of the Revolt of the Camisards, a doomed, last-minute stand by the remnants of Protestant France in the isolated, hilly Cevennes region of south-west France. Prominent among the Camisard refugees were the 'French Prophets'. The 'People of the Desert', as they called themselves, had adopted the most unbending millenarian beliefs. At their meetings they would whip each other into religious ecstasy, fall foaming at the mouth, trample on each other and speak in tongues. A female prophet stripped naked in the Sardinian (Roman Catholic) Chapel in Duke Street and ran to the altar 'where she appeared in several Strange and Indecent Postures'.[128] There was a sort of familiar novelty about the French Prophets for those who had experience of the early Quakers and Ranters. A number of low-church Anglicans and Dissenters were infected by their fervour and joined in.[129] Defoe was not among them but one of his publishers was a French prophet and he was probably referring to them in his description of a ship's crew rescued from fire in *the further Adventures of Robinson Crusoe*:

A Man that we saw this Minute dumb, and as it were stupid and confounded, should the next Minute be dancing and hallowing like an Antick; and the next Moment be tearing his Hair, or pulling his Clothes to Pieces, and stamping them under his Feet, like a mad Man; a few Moments after that, we should have him all in Tears, then sick, then swooning[130]

traitorous Clubs

Religious anxieties were especially complicated in England. In England, moderate Protestant opinion was hemmed in on both sides. It was

38

possible for the average citizen to be anxious about Catholics and their High-Church, crypto-Catholic sympathisers on the one hand and at the same time to be anxious about Dissenters, who felt themselves unable to join the Church of England because, broadly speaking, it was too papist for them. Dissenters included Presbyterians and Quakers among others. There were representatives of all religious tendencies among the nautical fraternity. Alexander Selkirk was a Presbyterian if not a very good one. George Shelvocke was probably a high-church Tory. William Betagh, the Captain of Marines on the *Speedwell*, was born a Catholic.[131] Simon Hatley, as we have seen, had a Catholic mother but was otherwise most likely an Anglican.

The fear of Dissent is harder to understand than the fear of Catholicism, given that by far the greatest threat to Protestant England came from Catholic France. However, in England, the Civil War and Cromwell's Commonwealth were fairly recent memories. Those joyless years were resented. Dissenters were suspected of wanting to plunge the country back into a gloom-cloud of Puritan piety. The Dissenter, Daniel Defoe, while no extremist, had something of the killjoy about him. He objected to cosmetics, maypoles and masturbation.[132] English Sundays were certainly unbearably dreary thirty or forty years on from the restoration of Charles II. In London no pubs were allowed to open on Sundays, no hackney cabs or river taxies were allowed to ply for trade and in many houses music was forbidden all day.[133] In the words of one foreign observer: 'This is I suppose, the only point in which the English profess to be Christians, certainly from the rest of their conduct one would not suspect it of many of them'.[134]

Allowing for this understandable reluctance to be made gloomy, the sheer hatred and loathing directed at Dissenters is still staggering. Malicious rumour claimed that they met in 'traitorous clubs' once a year to toast the execution of Charles I. They sang subversive songs and ate a symbolic menu of calves' heads (for Charles's followers), a cod's head (Charles himself), a boar's head (Charles's greed) and a pike (for tyranny).[135] There were several bursts of vicious persecution: in 1662-64, 1670 and 1681-85.[136] As many as 60,000 Dissenters are said to have

39

suffered for their opinions during this period, perhaps 15,000 families were ruined financially and as many as 5,000 may have died in prison.

Partly it was to do with class. In the minds of many high-Church Tories, all Dissenters were Levellers, crypto-republicans bent on starting social revolution - radical sentiments which were echoed by many a mutineer. Indeed, it would be interesting to ascertain the proportion of men from dissenting backgrounds who went on to become mutineers and pirates, the old division between church and chapel, but on the high sea.

Most dissenting sailors were never mutineers of course, although Selkirk came close to it when he argued with Stradling on the Juan Fernandez Islands. There is no reason to suppose that Simon Hatley and William Dampier were anything other than Protestant, Church-of-England men who kept their noses clean, and they were officers too and thought of themselves as gentlemen.

With regard to their literary alter egos: Robinson Crusoe reflected the views of his creator. He follows Defoe's Puritan path of error and repentance and sees evidence of God's providence in the wonders of the world. The Ancient Mariner, informed by Coleridge's Unitarianism, moves from error to reconciliation with an abstract, universal God through the discovery of love for all creatures.

Gulliver is harder to pin down. He is definitely Church of England but as he ends up preferring to live with his horses rather than his wife, can one be completely sure? Jonathan Swift, who had secured the position of Dean of St. Patrick's Dublin by the time he wrote it, could be elusive:

> The place he got by wit and rhyme
> And many ways most odd;
> And might a bishop be in a time
> Did he believe in God.[137]

tђe Voyage of tђe *Cinque Ports*

Commanders of the whole South Seas

On 23 April 1680, sixty-eight British buccaneers in a flotilla of open canoes arrived off Panama City, recently rebuilt five miles to the south west of the city burned by Morgan seven years earlier. The new city was girdled by a strong wall, with neat, white-washed houses and new, stone churches peering over. The buccaneers had paddled and sailed across fifty miles of open sea from the Gulf of San Miguel. Their leader was Captain John Coxon, who had fought under Morgan and who once captured a Spanish governor and a bishop but was too drunk to demand a ransom.[138] Among his men was William Dampier, then aged twenty-nine. The canoes had been provided by 'Prince Golden Caps' in the interior of the isthmus, so called from his brass helmet, eldest son of the 'Emperor of Darien', 'one of the richest of the West Indian monarchs'.[139] On arrival, the buccaneers were confronted with a fleet of five Spanish 'great ships' and three 'pretty big barques' with combined crews of several hundreds of men. The Spanish could hardly believe their eyes. The buccaneers formed their canoes in a line and charged.

Images of football hooligans creep unwelcome to mind. One of the Spanish barques got off a broadside then the helmsman of the Spanish

41

admiral's barque was shot and, during a brief moment of confusion, the buccaneers were up and over the side. In the ensuing battle, during which three of the 'great ships' never came close, the buccaneers captured two enemy ships for eighteen killed and a few captured. The slaughter on the Spanish ships was appalling.

In subsequent negotiations, the governor threatened to execute his prisoners. The buccaneers replied that they would do likewise:

We will bring our Ships near your Walls that you may have the pleasure of seeing them hanged at our Yard Arm. We will make you know that we are the Commanders of the whole South Seas, so consider what to choose, for we wait your Sentence of Life or Death with impatience; if Death, you shall certainly have the Heads by Monday Morning ...

From the commanders of the whole South Seas[140]

In the event, nothing so bloody took place on either side. Foiled of a ransom the Commanders of the whole South Seas proceeded south down the Pacific coast of South America in search of further targets. This 1680 incursion, with the spate of books which followed it, ushered in the high tide of buccaneer activity in the South Sea. There was a sort of feeding frenzy. Footloose sailors and other masterless men flocked to join strong captains who they believed might lead them to riches. They dreamed of some significant prize, a wealthy town perhaps or a treasure ship. One such success and, in theory, a sailor could retire for life.

The inhabitants of the scattered towns along the Pacific coast of South America suffered severely from this surge in buccaneer activity, some of them being raided repeatedly, and the period is remembered in South America much as the Viking period is remembered in Europe. The Spanish felt themselves besieged by brave, cruel, warlike thugs. Not entirely without reason. They took belated steps to defend themselves. In Chile, all male inhabitants were trained to carry arms, and a new governor instituted a system of regular patrols by coastguards.[141] Letters captured on a Spanish ship during this period from the Governor of Costa Rica advised that it was a religious duty for the Spanish to annihilate these 'new Turks'.[142]

In 1685, the year of Simon Hatley's birth, things moved towards a *crescendo*. That year, around a thousand buccaneers of various nationalities gathered in the Bay of Panama in a fleet of ten ships and with a flotilla of canoes. Their intention was to seize the annual silver ship which sailed north up the coast from Arica* to Panama where the silver would be transhipped across the Darien Isthmus to the annual treasure fleet for Spain. On 28 May, the buccaneers, spread out in a line over the blue water, saw, instead of a silver ship, fourteen Spanish vessels plus canoes sailing towards them. Six of the Spanish ships were substantial warships and the buccaneers had only two of comparable size. For once the Spanish had got their act together. They put out false lights once darkness fell. In the grey dawn, the buccaneers discovered that they had been outmanoeuvred during the night and the Spanish had got the weather-gage of them.* In Dampier's words, 'we ran for it'.[143]

This episode in 1685 marked the high tide of buccaneering activity in the South Sea. Three years later, in the 'Glorious Revolution' of 1688, Catholic James II fled to France and was replaced on the throne of Britain by Dutch, Protestant William III. A year later, in 1689, William, whose life was dominated by his struggle with France, formed a brief alliance with Catholic Spain and it became impossible for the buccaneers to claim any legality for their depredations. The heady, anarchic days of the South-Sea buccaneers, the first chapter in the saga of the sailor-authors, were over.

relative to annoying the King's Enemies

William died on 8 March 1702, of pneumonia, a complication caught after breaking his collar bone following a fall from his horse after it tripped on a molehill in Richmond Park. William had never been popular. Woodstock had greeted the news of his accession with 'sullen silence'. Now, in many quarters, there was celebration.

---

* Arica was at that time part of Peru. Since 1880 it has been the northernmost city of Chile.
* To have the weather-gage was to be upwind of one's opponent.

43

The new ruler of Britain was William's sister-in-law Anne,* a moderate, mainstream, Church-of-England sort of woman, respectably anti-Catholic and not foreign. It was reasonable to expect a respite from William's bitter feud with France. The last thing that homely, peace-loving Anne wanted was a war. Unfortunately, almost her entire reign was taken up by the first major war of the eighteenth century, 'the War of the Spanish Succession', also known as 'Queen Anne's War'. It began in 1702 and continued until 1713/14, dominating the lives of the next generation of South-Sea men, men such as Simon Hatley and Alexander Selkirk.

The War of the Spanish Succession was fought over who should succeed Charles II of Spain, 'the Bewitched'.* Before the start, there were two candidates, each supported by one of the two major, mainland European powers. Austria backed eight-year-old Prince Joseph Ferdinand of Bavaria, and France backed Philip duc d'Anjou, a grandson of Louis XIV. When Charles the Bewitched died in 1700, Louis XIV installed his grandson on the Spanish throne as Philip V, welding Spain and France into what was effectively a single super-power. Hostilities broke out soon after (September 1701) and Europe took sides. Protestant Britain and Holland joined the war on the side of Austria, while Bavaria, Spain, Portugal and the Italian kingdom of Savoy sided with France.[144]

In late 1702, William Dampier, now aged fifty-one and a respected and well-known figure following the publication of *A New Voyage Round the World*, was commissioned by Thomas Estcourt, a wealthy, young Bristol merchant, to command a voyage to the South Sea.[145] Dampier came originally from the village of East Coker* in Somerset and had many West-Country connections and it was probably because of this that Estcourt contacted him. Estcourt's partners in the venture were Thomas Goldney, a

---

* Anne did not like William either. She was in the habit of making hostile reference to him as 'Caliban' in private letters to her friend, Sarah Churchill. On William's death, Sarah complained that she had not got as much pleasure from it as she expected.
* Charles II was of reduced intelligence. He could not sit up until he was six and had an abnormally large tongue. He was incapable of producing an heir so a crisis over the succession had been long foreseen.
* Whence T.S.Eliot's ancestors first sailed to America in the nineteenth century, *vis The Four Quartets - East Coker*.

Bristol Quaker and three London businessmen: a lawyer, a scrivener and a vintner.[146] At a cost of around £4,000 they fitted out the 200-ton, 26-gun frigate *St. George*, previously the *Nazareth*, the name changed for patriotic reasons.[147]

The *St. George* was a privateer. During the War of the Spanish Succession, and in most previous European wars, none of the belligerent countries could afford to maintain the size of fleets they needed, not even Britain backed by the Bank of England.* To make up their strength they authorised large numbers of privateers such as the *St. George*. Essentially, governments outsourced much of their naval warfare. Privateers were warships on the cheap and their authority to make war, the crucial document that distinguished them from pirates, was a letter of 'marque and reprisal' issued by their government. It was a very ancient system. In England, the earliest known letters of marque date from the thirteenth century when Henry III, in February 1243, gave letters to George Pyper, master of the barque *Le Heyte* and another to Adam Robenolt and William le Sauvage:

Relative to annoying the King's enemies. The King to all etc., Greeting. Know ye that we have granted and given licence ... to annoy our enemies at sea or by land wheresoever they are able ...[148]

Differences between the French and British methods of setting up their privateers reflected their respective cultures. British privateers were privately financed and, after 1708, kept all the profits to be divided between owners and crew. The French were more centralised. In France the ships were financed and equipped by the government which then leased them fully armed to entrepreneurs who provided the crew and provisions. The French formula was very efficient. Between 1695 and 1713, French privateers captured nearly 10,000 ships, almost three quarters of them British.[149]

There was always some level of official concern about privateers. The opportunities for abuse were legion and the dividing line between piracy and privateering was easily blurred - as was evident in the activities of the

---

* Established 1694 and often considered to be one of the main reasons for British success in the war.

buccaneers. The buccaneers had regularly carried letters of marque but these letters were often corruptly purchased from the governor of one or other of the Caribbean colonies. When issuing the Letter of Marque for Dampier and the *St. George*, the Lord High Admiral asked for a security for £2,000 'for the civil and honest behaviour of officers and men'.[150] Dampier had recently been censured by a Court Martial following the voyage of the *Roebuck*[151] to Australia. His buccaneering past gave cause for concern.

Following Dampier's appointment by Thomas Estcourt and his partners, the senior officers were recruited, including a tough, experienced sailor by the name of John Clipperton (as Mate), and Edward Morgan, an old buccaneering friend of Dampier, as Purser. The authorities were right to be wary. Morgan first had to be released from prison where he was being held on a charge of theft.[152] A young man by the name of William Funnel was taken on as Second Mate. Funnell's account, *A Voyage Round the World*, published 1707, is our main source of information for the voyage. This is the Funnell mentioned earlier whose description of sea-lion baiting is so repulsive.

By early 1703, the *St. George* was almost ready to sail. Apart from basic victuals for her crew of 120 men, she bristled with guns, cannon, cutlasses and thirty barrels of powder and she had spare sails for the long journey ahead. She moved to an anchorage in the Downs, out from the fat, wide shore of Kent, and final preparations were put in hand. She set sail on 30 April 1703. She was without her intended consort, the *Fame*, due to a disagreement between the owners of the two ships and she arrived alone at the port of Kinsale in southern Ireland on 18 May. At Kinsale she waited a further nearly three months until she was joined by the galley *Cinque Ports*, 90 tons and 16 guns, Captain Charles Pickering.[153]

A 'galley' at this date meant a manoeuvrable, single-decked vessel, which could be either sailed or rowed. After Pickering, the most senior of the officers of the *Cinque Ports*, holding a position perhaps equivalent to First Lieutenant or First Mate, was twenty-one-year-old Thomas Stradling, a gentleman mariner. Prominent among the crew was a rough, twenty-three-year-old foremastman, a Scotsman by the name of Alexander Selkirk.[154] Selkirk was originally from Largo on the windswept coast of Fife in east

Scotland. In 1695, aged fifteen, he had been disciplined by the elders
local Kirk for unspecified 'Undecent Behaviour' and had left for t
shortly after, rising to become a skilled mariner.

On 11 September 1703, the two ships weighed anchor from Kinsale
for the start of the long journey south. It was an easy voyage with easy
weather but from the first Dampier had trouble with his officers. He left his
first Lieutenant, Samuel Hoxford, at the Cape Verde Isles following a duel
between Hoxford and Edward Morgan, where Hoxford 'three months
afterwards miserably ended his days, partly with Hunger'.[155] In November
1703, having crossed the Atlantic, Dampier quarrelled with his Second
Lieutenant, James Barnaby, they 'being both drunk together in the Cabbin'.
Next day Barnaby left along with eight others 'About ten at Night, he and
eight more of our Men put their Chests and Cloaths in the Pinnace ...
Captain Dampier being in his Cabbin quite drunk'.[156] They were at Grande
Island, about a hundred miles south-west from Rio and sometimes called
Placentia, to wood and water.

The quarrels with Hoxford and Barnaby were part of a pattern
repeated throughout the voyage. Dampier's senior officers trickled away.
Charles Pickering, Captain of the *Cinque Ports* 'another main pillar of our
voyage' died shortly after Barnaby's departure, having fallen ill of a fever.
He was buried 'at the watering place' on Grande to a salute of guns. Young
Thomas Stradling took over command.

The two ships, having replenished their water and made necessary
repairs, left Grande Island on 8 December 1703 and sailed south past the
coast of what is now Argentina, passing the 'Cibald de Ward Islands[157] on
29 December 1703, great clouds of seabirds clustering like foam around the
masts. By 9 January 1704 they were past Cape Horn and heading north into
the calmer waters of the Pacific.

The remote Juan Fernandez Islands, about three hundred miles out
from the coast of Chile on the latitude of Valparaiso and Santiago, loom
lonely as asteroids above the emptiness of the Pacific and, on most days,
clouds can be seen hanging suspended over their peaks which rise abruptly
as high as three thousand feet. The larger of the islands, *Mas a Tierra*, now
called 'Robinson Crusoe Island', is wrapped in forest and laced with silvery

47

waterfalls. It was a favourite haunt of buccaneers from when they first began raiding into the Spanish Pacific in the seventeenth century, a remote and temperate retreat with 'Trees and Grass verdant all the Year … there being only a small Frost and a little Hail, but sometimes great Rain'.[158] It was too far from the coast for the Spanish to maintain a permanent colony, yet very well situated for ships to recuperate, to wood and water, after the long and demanding passage of the Horn.

The *St George* and the *Cinque Ports* arrived in the great bay of Mas a Tierra in early February 1704. Now it was Stradling's turn to have problems. Twenty of the *Cinque Ports'* men had been lost since leaving England, some by desertion but most dying of cold and exposure during the long, gruelling voyage round the Horn. The remainder were at the end of their collective tether. Probably led by Selkirk, they now deserted and set up tents along the shore leaving only Stradling and the ship's monkey on board.[159] The men seem to have objected to Stradling's style of command, and perhaps his age and his background were against him. Selkirk in his later deposition to the court[160] claimed that Stradling failed to consult properly. For two days the *Cinque Ports* 'lay as it were without men'[161] until Dampier intervened and coaxed them back on board.

Work resumed. The ships were careened, heeled over on one side then the other and their hulls scraped clean of barnacles and other detritus of the sea. Water casks were replenished. For meat and fuel the men killed seals and sea lions. There were goats as well, which lived there in vast numbers having been introduced by the Spanish over a century before. The men dined on roasted goat and boiled 'cabbage' from the cabbage palms, short, straight trees, 'void of leaves except at the top', the 'cabbage' nestling at the base of the leaves of the crown and tasting remarkably like the real thing.

At noon on 22 April 1704, the sail of a ship was spotted approaching the bay. The men were summoned aboard and the two privateers hastily slipped their moorings and sailed after her. Dampier was fearful that the strange ship would report their presence and raise the alarm along the coast of the mainland. In the rush to get under way all of the *Cinque Ports'* spare sails were left behind as well as much of her stores and five of her crew who were on the west side of the island.

So great was the rush to get under way that, as the wind took their sails on the open sea, the *St. George's* pinnace was 'towed under the water' and the tow rope of the *Cinque Ports'* boat broke. The boat was left bobbing on the empty ocean, in her a lone sailor and a dog. Dogs were common aboard ships. It would be good to know more about this one. Did it relish its experience, forepaws on a thwart, barking madly, the wind in its ears? Robinson Crusoe had a dog: 'he jump'd out of the Ship of himself and swam on the Shore to me the Day after I went on Shore with my first Cargo ...'.[162]

The long, slow-motion ballet which was naval warfare in the age of sail got under way. The slow manoeuvring for position and the tortoise-slow closing of the gap between ships. By eleven that night *St. George* and *Cinque Ports* were close up with the stranger and the following morning they came along side. She was a French frigate, the *St. Joseph* from St. Malo, 400 tons and 30 guns, well manned.

This was no surprise to Dampier and Stradling. The French were taking full advantage of their position as defenders and wartime allies of the Spanish. French smugglers had managed to break the very strict Spanish colonial trading system. Spanish policy was that only Spanish ships could trade between Europe and Spanish colonies in America. All European and colonial goods destined for South America had to be carried from Spain in a Spanish fleet which was unloaded at Portobello on the Caribbean. The economic consequences of this policy were disastrous.[163] Before the ships had even anchored, the Spanish merchants got together and fixed their prices to ensure a profit of as high as three hundred percent, and things only got worse thereafter. From Portabello the goods were transported overland to Panama and from there by ship or overland to Lima and other places, usually on mule carts or *carretas*, clumsy, two-wheeled vehicles, the wheels up to ten feet in diameter to stop them getting stuck in the mud. With every mile and with every change of ownership, the price increased. Goods destined for Potosi and the Atlantic coasts of what are now Uruguay and Argentina had to travel overland up to two thousand miles. By the time it arrived in Buenos Aires, a simple piece of tableware might cost eight times what it did in Lima and perhaps fifteen to twenty times what it cost in Europe.[164]

It was an absurd system. French smugglers were welcome to break it - if they were careful. (Smuggling remained a hanging offence for both sides of the transaction.) Trading commonly took place at night on some desolate beach or near a small, remote port. The French merchant captain would fire a cannon to warn of his presence and, in the darkness, canoes and other small vessels would put off and slip across the silver surf. Out at sea they would tie up alongside the smugglers and trading could begin.

The French were formidable operators. Their economy was bigger than Britain's and their ships tended to be better built. Because of the war, Spain had asked for French help to crack down on the smugglers as well as on British privateers. French efforts with regard to British privateers were robust, those towards their own smugglers were, for obvious reasons, lukewarm and there was really nothing to stop French merchants from making a financial killing. Which is precisely what they did. French ships came flooding into the South Sea. Lace, perfumes, mirrors, ribbons, all the fine things of France, were suddenly available to the inhabitants of South America at a fraction of their former cost. Glass window panes became widely available for the first time[165]. When the British took notice, they were horrified and extremely jealous. In the preface to *A Cruising Voyage round the World*, Woodes Rogers calculated that the total return trade from South America to Europe on French ships amounted to £25,000,000 in the first years of the war, a vast sum in those days.[166]

Fortunately, the French made themselves unpopular. They tended to give themselves 'extravagant airs ashore by frisking and drinking'.[167] And not all Spanish colonials were happy with the new trading conditions. Colonial merchants were resentful of French inroads into their markets. There were tensions and fights. In Callao, the port of Lima, the French were forced to go around in gangs for their own safety. A French sailor was killed by a shot from a window and the French threatened to bombard the town[168] if the killer was not punished. For the English, it was a small wedge to drive between enemy allies but it was better than nothing.

The *Cinque Ports* came level with the *St. Joseph* first. She fired a broadside then retired. After that, the *St. Joseph* and the *St. George* slogged it out 'broad-side and broad-side' for seven hours until the Frenchman broke off and sailed away. The French lost a great many killed and of their wounded thirty two had 'either lost a Leg or an Arm or and Eye'[169] but they had escaped to raise the alarm. The privateers returned to Mas a Tierra disappointed. There they found two further French ships at anchor in the bay. Bruised and battered from the fight and not wishing for further unprofitable action the *St. George* and *Cinque Ports* stood for the north leaving *Cinque Ports's* spare sails and her five sailors uncollected.

During their approach to the island, one is glad to learn, one of the French ships had picked up 'a Boat at Sea, in which there was an Englishman and a Dog'.[170]

the reason of his being left there

Dampier's first intended target was the little town of Santa Maria on the Gulf of Panama. He knew from the buccaneer attacks of the 1680s that this was the collecting point for gold from the nearby mines before transhipment by mule train across the Isthmus of Darien. He had once harboured 'golden dreams' that these mines could be held and exploited by a band of determined Englishmen.[171]

On 25 April 1704, having taken various prizes along the way, the *St George* and *Cinque Ports* arrived at the Gulf of San Miguel about a hundred miles south-east of Panama. Leaving the *St George* and *Cinque Ports* at Point Garachina on the southern side, Dampier and Stradling with 102 men paddled and sailed deeper into the gulf in a small prize 'barque' and various boats and canoes. Steamy with insects and lined with dark mangrove forests, this was a remote region where small vessels could easily avoid discovery. That night they anchored hidden among some islands which lay scattered near the shore. It was dark and rainy weather, the tossing, angry woods lit by lightning and with thunder echoing between the hills.

Next morning, five Indians came by in a canoe and shouted across the water. Dampier, unusually for him but fearing that they would give the alarm, ordered his men to shoot. The Indians got away. The expedition then proceeded to the mouth of the Santa Maria river at the end of the gulf and an advance force entered it, paddling between towering green and silent banks towards the village of the Indians which was about nine miles inland and taking three other Indians captive along the way. Night fell, hiding the village in darkness, but the privateers were alerted to its presence by the barking of dogs. They moored at the bank and took it, two of their captives escaping overboard during the attack. The inhabitants had fled.[172]

On the afternoon of 30 April 1704, with a reduced force of eighty-seven men in three launches, leaving John Clipperton, mate of the *St George*, and fourteen others to guard the barque, Dampier and Stradling made their way further up river towards the town of Santa Maria itself. Things went badly wrong. The Indians had warned the town of the privateers' arrival and Dampier and his men returned to the barque at midnight, empty-handed, having suffered three ambushes with one man killed and several wounded. Tired and dispirited, the following morning the entire force made its way back down river and across the gulf to the relative safety of the *St. George* and the *Cinque Ports*. The whole exercise had been a hopeless disappointment and the men's faith in Dampier's knowledge of the South Sea was badly dented. They were short of provisions, most having been consumed during the long voyage up the coast of South America, down to a diet of five boiled green plantains per day between every six men.

Miraculously, at this low point, fortune unexpectedly smiled. Around midnight on 6 May 1704, the very night of their return on board, a large ship came innocently to anchor nearby. She was Spanish, 550 tons, and her captain had no idea of the danger he was in. The privateers drew quietly alongside and took her 'without any resistance'. She was carrying barrels of wine, brandy, sugar and flour, bales of linen and woollen cloth and thirty tons of quince marmalade.♣[173]

♣ It is surprising how much marmalade (originally from the Portuguese *marmalada*, a quince) was captured by buccaneers and privateers during this period. It was a way of preserving fruit. Shelvocke took 'bales and Boxes of marmalade' from the *Concepción de Recova* in 1721 and, in 1709, Woodes Rogers took 'Fails of Quinces' as well as 'Marmalet' from a barque in the Gulf of Guayaquil, and Simon

William Funnell and Alexander Selkirk were transferred to the new prize as 'chiefs' along with a skeleton crew, Funnell to represent the *Cinque Ports* and Selkirk to represent the *St. George*. Neither captain was taking any chances.

The little flotilla crossed the Gulf of Panama in unpleasant, squally weather to the uninhabited island of Tabago, about twenty miles from the city of Panama to 'rummage' their prize. Tabago was a high, bejungled island rich with fresh water. It was perfect cover. Here the two captains agreed to part, a decision partly fuelled by copious quantities of prize brandy. Funnell says that they quarrelled although Dampier in his brief *Vindication* denies this.[174] They divided up the proceeds of the voyage, the *Cinque Ports* receiving £1,100 to be shared among officers and crew. Goods were transferred from the prize to the two warships and the sailors of both ships were allowed to choose on which ship they wished to continue the voyage. Five from each ship changed places but Selkirk chose to remain with the *Cinque Ports*.

Stradling sailed south with a crew of just forty men, in his small, leaking ship and with the coast alarmed and Spanish men of war patrolling for the British 'pirates'. He made for the Juan Fernandez Islands again to regain his lost sails and provisions and to pick up the five men left behind. It was September 1704 when he arrived at Mas a Tierra. Of the five[175] men left behind only two remained. The others had been either captured or killed by the French. The spare sails and stores were gone as well.

Cinque Ports was heeled over and work begun on careening her hull which was eaten 'to a honycomb'[176] by the worm. Selkirk advised that she was unfit to sail. There was a row. Stradling ignored him. Stores were taken on board, seals and seal lions killed and their meat preserved and stowed, the water casks replenished.

By early October 1704, they were ready to sail but Selkirk was still adamant. The *Cinque Ports* was a death-trap he said. They were putting their lives in danger. He refused to sail and asked others to join him

---

Hatley took 'three or four boxes of marmalade' off a Portuguese ship off Cape Frio in 1719. The most famous advocate of South American marmalade is, of course, Paddington Bear, who arrived at Paddington Station in 1958 having sailed from 'Darkest Peru', surviving on a diet of marmalade, his favourite food.

although none did. Stradling left him alone on the shore with 'clothes and Bedding; with a Firelock, some Powder, and Tobacco, a Hatchet, a Knife, a Kettle, a Bible, some practical pieces, and his Mathematical Instruments and Books'.[177]

Selkirk changed his mind at the last moment, suddenly fearful of the immense loneliness which was about to engulf him. He begged to be allowed to rejoin the ship. Stradling ignored him and sailed away:

The reason of his being left here was a Difference betwixt him and his Captain; which, together with the Ships being leaky, made him willing rather to stay here, than go along with him at first; and when he was at last willing, the Captain would not receive him...[178]

Stradling sailed north in his hopeless craft, hoping to make contact with the *St. George* once more. But *Cinque Ports* was beyond repair. Off Malpelo Island, a grim speck of land far out from the coast of what is now Colombia, the thirty two remaining men transferred to two makeshift rafts and struggled ashore to survive as best they could, abandoning *Cinque Ports* to the depths. Of these, eighteen including Stradling lived long enough to give themselves up when a Spanish ship chanced by. They were taken in chains to prison in the colonial capital of Lima.

Clipperton's Betrayal

Having left Stradling and the *Cinque Ports*, Dampier cruised between the gulfs of Guayaquil and Panama. On 22 July 1704, he came up against a Spanish man-of-war close in to land, one of two which had been fitted out to hunt him down. The wind was blowing fresh across the waves and Dampier reckoned he could out-sail her - but his crew thought otherwise. They raised the 'bloody flag',[179] a sign that no quarter would be given or taken. Dividing themselves into two watches (Dampier seems to have lost control at this point), they fired continuously, one watch resting while the other fired - 560 shots to the Spanish 110-115. The battle raged from midday until half six in the evening when, dusk descending, both ships stopped their fire. Not a single Englishman had been killed or wounded and in the morning the Spanish ship had gone.

54

It was Dampier's intention to capture the Manila Ship. All the trade across the Pacific between the Spanish Philippines and Spanish America was carried in one or two officially-sanctioned ships per year, known as 'Manila ships'. Carrying, as they did, the entire annual trade between Asia and America in their holds, they were fabulously rich targets, usually built very large in order to accommodate sufficient bulk. Some were giants of 2,000 tons although most were between 600 and 1,000 tons. It was while they were on the Asia-America leg of their great circular journey that they were of most interest to buccaneers and privateers, their holds crammed with nutmeg, pepper, silks, lacquer-work and porcelain, the near-countless treasures of the Spice Islands and China.

The Manila ships departed from the Philippines in late summer. Their route took them on one of the longest, regular, almost-uninterrupted voyages in the world, an astonishing ordeal which took well over six months[180]. First they sailed to Guam and then to Hawaii or the Aleutian Islands far out in mid-ocean and from there they sailed north without sight of land for a vast distance in order to avoid the easterly trade winds which blow in the tropics. On such an immensely long journey, water was a major problem. The ships were festooned with jars and other receptacles which hung from the rigging like fruit. Special mats were placed to direct rain water into the jars.[181] Usually, it was winter by the time they came up with the coast of North America, somewhere in the region of the modern boundary between Oregon and California. From there they followed the coast south for a further two thousand miles to their destination, the Mexican port of Acapulco. By the time the ships were within striking distance of Acapulco, their crews and passengers were vulnerable and exhausted like birds at the end of a long migration.

The *St. George* sailed north along with a small captured barque, which they named the *Dragon*, anchoring for a few days on the Esmeraldas coast of what is now Ecuador for provisions. These were wild lands, unsuitable for a long stay. The Indians of the Esmeraldas had never submitted to the Spanish. 'With their Arrows they easily annoy anyone that shall land there'.[182] Those with the temerity to do so could expect 'to be exposed all the way to the Arrows of those who would lie purposely in Ambush in the

Woods for them'.[183] They would, if given the chance, 'rob and kill any white Men, thinking all white Men to be Spaniards'.

The *St. George* and *Dragon* arrived at the Gulf of Nicoya on the coast of what is now Costa Rica on 16 August 1704 and moored in a deep, sheltered bay at the island of St. Lucas, one of the Middle Islands, deep in the gulf. It was rich with lush forests where streams of fresh water tinkled, the woods brilliant with macaws, the shores teeming with fish. With five guns mounted on promontories on each side of the bay the two ships were safe and snug as could be. The privateers proceeded to move as much as possible that was heavy and removable from the *St. George* to the *Dragon*, including several other guns and all their remaining powder and shot. The *St. George* was then heeled right over in the shallow water so as to 'bream' her hull, to burn off the detritus of the sea, a thorough cleansing. The planks were almost eaten through with worm, 'like a Honey-Comb'[184] again, in some places eaten to a few millimetres thick, so crumbled that 'we could thrust our Thumbs quite through with ease'.[185]

In that secluded bay, the macaws screaming between the tree tops and the sailors working on the battered hull, the *St. George* upended like a sick whale, Dampier and John Clipperton, fell out. Like Stradling and Selkirk far to the south, they argued about the state of the hull. Clipperton then seized the *Dragon* with all their goods on board and sailed away with twenty-one of the crew, taking also Dampier's commission, the proof that he was no pirate. Clipperton relented to the extent that he left most of the powder and shot in an Indian house nearby where Dampier's men were able to retrieve it.

The time of the arrival of the Manila ship was fast approaching. Dampier sailed north-west up the coast of Mexico in his honey-comb craft, pilfering two further prizes along the way. On the morning of 6 December 1704, three hundred miles north of Acapulco, the *St. George* was just out from the Bay of Navidad, near where the grey volcanic bulk of Mount Colima towers above its green foothills. His men sighted a great ship breasting the waves towards them. She was the Manila ship and she was huge but the Englishmen attacked anyway.

The contest was hopelessly uneven. The Spaniards advanced one tire of their eighteen or twenty-four pounders and began to fire. Each accurate shot was enough to drive in up to four foot of the St. George's planking and there were many, and one shot 'between Wind and Water in our Powder Room'.[186] In return, the *St. George's* five-pounders made almost no impression on the Spaniard's massive hull. The *St. George* stood away and the Manila ship continued majestically south, scarcely interrupted in her journey. This was the end of all their hopes of sudden riches. Dampier's authority ebbed away. On 6 January 1705, more than half of his crew mutinied and sailed for home in a captured barque, leaving him and twenty-seven men alone on the ocean in the rotting and battered *St. George*. The ship's carpenter, fortunately, stayed with Dampier. He 'stopped the shot Holes with Tallow and Charcoal, not daring, as he said, to drive in a Nail for fear of making it worse'.[187] The adventure was almost over. They sailed south once more, capturing the small town of Puna and then yet another Spanish ship to which they transferred leaving the *St. George* abandoned. In their new ship they crossed the Pacific to Dutch Batavia (Jakarta) where Dampier was taken for a pirate and imprisoned because Clipperton had stolen his commission. He returned to England, penniless, in late 1707.

CHAPTER 5

◆◆◆◆◆◆◆◆◆◆◆◆◆◆

the Voyage of the *Duke* and *Duchess*

all are in a Hurry

There were two roads into Bristol from the east. The high road led through the villages of Bitton and Kingswood, now part of the city-sprawl. In the 1700s, this road was usually packed with carts, in particular the dirty black carts of colliers bringing coal for the city's innumerable fires. Most people preferred to enter by the turnpike road through Keynsham and Brislington.[188] From the top of Brislington Hill, notoriously treacherous in wet weather, the city suddenly came into view below, a dense mass of spires, roofs and chimneys with a river of masts winding through the middle. Alexander Pope described it in a letter to his friend Mrs. Martha Blount: 'a key along the old wall, with houses on both sides, and, in the middle of the street, as far as you can see, hundreds of ships, their masts as thick as they can stand by one another, which is the oddest and most surprising sight imaginable. This street is fuller of them than the Thames from London Bridge to Deptford'. [189] The city clustered in a wide valley beneath the rolling heights of Clifton and with the green fields of Somerset to the south. There was a sense of excitement about the place even at a distance, of pent-up energy. This was one of Britain's greatest cities, an ant heap of activity, already industrialising even at that early date. On windless days the view was often obscured by smoke from the tall cones of around twenty glass kilns that hung like a cloud over the clustered buildings, sometimes so low that it seemed to consume the spires of the churches. On some such day, fourteen-year-old Hatley, fresh from Woodstock, first looked down on the city where he would spend much of his youth.

Hatley's apprenticeship was based in a city given over to money and trade. Bristol had only recently been overtaken by Liverpool as the second port in the kingdom. It was still immensely wealthy. At the city's centre stood the ruins of Berkley Castle, demolished by Oliver Cromwell, where Edward II had met his grisly end, and the port itself, consisting of the muddy, tidal waters of the River Avon and its tributary the Frome. As early as the thirteenth century the Frome had been diverted to create an anchorage for ocean-going ships, but even so, the tides were extreme and at low tide the ships flopped over on their sides like beached whales. They had to be strongly constructed - 'shipshape and Bristol fashion' - to withstand this treatment and to withstand the force of the tides in the narrow confines of the Avon Gorge leading from the city to the open sea.

Bristol looked west, an improbable port perched at the end of a narrow channel near the edge of what was once the known world. It had risen to prominence in the fifteenth century when the focus of Europe shifted away from the Mediterranean and outwards to more distant lands. It was from Bristol that the young Italian Giovanni Cabotto, John Cabot, set sail in 1497 and 'discovered' North America while in search of a northern route to China. He had been in Spain in 1493 and had seen Columbus return from his momentous voyage and he had tried for backing in several cities before approaching the Bristol merchants. There he found that he was pushing at an open door. Bristol sailors were already travelling regularly to the fisheries off Iceland and possibly to Greenland and they may well have heard of Vinland, yet further to the west, where the Vikings established a brief colony. Not so long before, in 1480, a Bristol ship had sailed in search of the 'island of Brasile', reputed to lie far out in the Atlantic beyond Ireland. Its navigator, John Jay, set his brass memorial in the church of St.

Mary Redcliffe on the Somerset side of the Avon before departing, just in case. Belief in Brazil, the 'Isle of Seven Cities', fabulous cities of gold, was common among merchants and sailors before the discovery of America.[190] According to Irish legend, it was the 'Promised Land of the Saints' where 'the sadness of life could be escaped', searched for by the Irish monk St Brendan in the sixth century. The only problem was that it was always hidden by mist or it only emerged from the ocean every seven years.

The air of Bristol was rich with tales such as this, in striking contrast to rural Woodstock. In 1577 Martin Frobisher, a Tudor thug but a brilliant sailor, captured four Inuit off Greenland, one of them brought down with a rugby tackle that 'made his side ake against the grounde for a moneth after'[191], and exhibited two of them, a man called Callico and a woman called Ignorth, with their canoes on the Avon although they died soon after.[192] From Bristol, John Guy, a local merchant, set sail in 1610 with the backing of the Newfoundland Company and established 'Cupid's Colony' on the Avalon Peninsular, the first English settlement in Newfoundland, although it didn't last. From here too, Captain Thomas James, previously a barrister, set out in search of a North-West Passage in 1631, returning to write his bestseller *The Strange and Dangerous Voyage* ..., one of Coleridge's favourite books, disarmingly and ambiguously introduced:

Gentle Reader, expect not heere florishing Phrases or Eloquent tearmes; for this child of mine, begot in the North-West's cold Clime (where they breed no Schollers), is not able to digest the sweet milke of Rhethorick, that's food for them.

The voyage was strange because he refused to include any sailors in his crew who had sailed that way previously and dangerous because, among other things, he deliberately sank his ship over winter in Hudson's Bay.

Hatley would have walked through streets bustling with people and animals, past rich merchants in wigs, leathery seamen in their bell bottoms, men from the ship-building trades, genteel ladies, fishwives and loose women from the taverns of the port. 'All are in a hurry, running up and down with cloudy looks and busy faces, loading, carrying and unloading goods'.[193] The streets were 'narrow and something darkish, because the rooms on the upper storeys are more jutting out, soe contracts the streete

60

and light'.[194] Among the jostling crowds there would have been quite a number of black servants, a novelty to a child from the country. The slave trade was in full swing.

The Bristol pilots were a well organised fraternity with a long tradition. The very first pilots are said to have been two barge-masters, James Ray and James Shepherd, who were employed by Sebastian Cabot in 1497, their usual business being to supply the forts at Avonmouth. The pilots' base was at Crewkerne Pill, a couple of miles up the River Avon towards the Bristol Channel on the Somerset side, a tough little village nestling below steep, wooded escarpments and entirely given over to the water. There was so much for a young boy to learn. Pilots were kings of the river. They had to know every twist and turn between the city and the river mouth, where it was shallow, where it was deep, where best to moor up and sit out the flood of the tide. In addition to an expert knowledge of the river, a pilot needed to understand the art of sailing in order to take command of the ships as he sailed them to and from the harbour. He had to master the intricate, arcane language of the sea, a specialist, technical language common to all sailors. Every sail, every rope, every knot had its name, as did every type of wind and weather: 'fresh gales', 'foul winds', 'cats' paws', 'variable breezes'.[195] Commands must be clear and unambiguous for sailors to follow them. Without this knowledge, Hatley would not have been a sailor, let alone an officer. He would never have ventured so far from home.

Not all apprentices were treated equally. In all likelihood, given his prosperous background, Hatley would have been treated more equally than most. A child of prosperous parents could expect to receive more respectful treatment and better education in the ways of his trade than a child of poor parents because his parents could afford to pay a premium to the master.

At some stage, perhaps towards the end of a seven-year apprenticeship, Simon made the transition to deep-sea sailor and learned the art of navigation. There were good reasons why he might choose that route. The ships he helped guide into harbour came from the four corners of the world. Those from remote parts might come back loaded with exotica, carrying the world with them in the stories of their sailors, in their parrots and monkeys, their exotic cargoes and strange beasts. It was not unusual to see leopards or other strange beasts in cages on the decks, and foreigners crowding the gunwales, pigtailed Chinamen and dark-skinned Indians. Sheer curiosity was sufficient reason to want to go to sea, powerful enough to cancel out the fear of danger and discomfort. The danger could be an incentive:

I know not by what Deity incited,
To see the Ocean-seas I was delighted,
Or for to take Delight in such a Way
Where many Men and Ships have lost their Way,
In such a dangerous watery Element,
Where many times both Ships and Men are sent
Unto the Bottom of those gulfey Waves ...[196]

And if neither danger nor curiosity were sufficient incentive, there was always money. The War of the Spanish Succession had brought plentiful new opportunities for making it. Bristol continued to trade but privateering, although risky, promised quicker returns and many traders were turning to it.

The turning point of the war came quite early on. In May 1704, while Hatley was still an apprentice and at about the time that Dampier and Stradling were trying to take the town of Santa Maria, John Churchill, Britain's commander on the continent, led a combined Anglo-Dutch army on a secret march of over 250 miles from near Maastricht in modern Belgium, through appalling weather by the end of which his army was marching through rivers of mud. In five weeks he arrived at the Danube in Bavaria and the French and Bavarian armies were caught almost completely unprepared.

The Battle of Blenheim took place on 13 August 1704 near the small Bavarian village of Blindheim near the Danube and was an overwhelming Austrian, British and Dutch triumph. It was as significant for the War of the Spanish Succession as Dunkirk or D-Day were for the Second World War. France never regained the upper hand. The significance of Churchill's victory was reflected in his lavish reward. He had been elevated to the Dukedom of Marlborough a short while previously and now he was voted the finances to build Blenheim Palace outside Woodstock by a grateful nation, Queen Anne providing the land. Shortly after, Hatley's parents began the construction of their fine house at numbers 6-8 High Street with stone filched from the building site.

The victory at Blenheim was followed, in May 1706, by another stunning victory at Ramillies and, in September 1706, by the Battle of Turin when Prince Eugene forced the French from Italy. When, in late 1707, William Dampier, penniless once more and recently returned from the voyage of the *St. George*, spoke up for a major new privateering voyage to a group of Bristol merchants, his advocacy met sympathetic ears.[197] There was a sense of urgency about it. That winter, conditions in the French countryside were appalling. There was a real danger that the French would sue for peace.

Merchants were the elite of Bristol. Business was conducted along the Merchants' Tolzey, a walk by the side of All Saint's Church right in the centre of the city. The merchants in their wigs and embroidered waistcoats haggled in the open air around the 'nails', flat-topped brass pillars, the first installed during the reign of Elizabeth I. When agreement was reached the buyer would slam his money down 'on the nail'.[198] The merchants whom Dampier approached were all members of the prestigious Society of Merchant Venturers, incorporated by Letters Patent in 1552, during the reign of Edward VI.[199] Among them were Sir John Hawkins who had been Mayor in 1701, John Hollidge who would be Mayor in 1708 and Christopher Shutter who would be Mayor in 1711.[200]

Dampier suggested a voyage to the South Sea with the aim of capturing the Manilla Galleon, the great Spanish ship which crossed the Pacific from the Far East to South America once a year, and which he had failed to take with the St. George. Two ships were needed he said. The *St. George* had been too weak to be successful on her own, with only the *Cinque Ports* galley as consort. Such an undertaking, he was still certain, would return astronomical profits if properly executed.

His proposal fell on willing ears. Shares were issued. On 20 January 1708, an agreement was signed between Dampier and the 'owners' by which Dampier would receive a sixteenth of the net profits in return for his expertise but, evidently, the merchants were wary of giving Dampier another command. A twenty-eight-year-old Bristol captain and freeman of the city by the name of Woodes Rogers, was chosen to be commander, perhaps on Dampier's recommendation - Dampier was probably a friend of Rogers's father. In his book of 1697, he refered to a friend, Captain Rogers, 'a very ingenious person and well experienced'. The younger Woodes Rogers was well-placed for such a command. He was a prominent local citizen, a member of the Society of Merchant Venturers and a freeman of the city. He lived in a substantial house on Queen's Square, named for Queen Anne and the most prestigious address in town.* The younger Rogers had suffered at the hand of a French privateer at the beginning of the war and had become a privateer himself to seek compensation. He had undertaken two such voyages in nearby waters in 1707.[201]

The merchants Dampier approached were decisive, hard-headed businessmen. They were prepared to lay out large sums to achieve their ends. They immediately purchased two hulls from a Bristol ship builder. The *Duke* cost £1,310 and was commissioned for the voyage. The smaller *Duchess* cost £850 and was second-hand. Both were moored at the riverside.[202] A Mr J Welch was sent to London that February to purchase guns, either new or second hand.

The senior officers were appointed. Mr Stephen Courtney, 'a man of birth, fortune and very amiable qualities',[203] was to be captain of the *Duchess* serving under the overall command of Rogers. The Second Captain of the *Duchess* was to be Edward Cooke, a friend of Alderman Batchelor, whose account, *A Voyage to the South Sea and around the World* published 1712, is one of our main sources for the voyage. Like Woodes Rogers, and in fact the majority of officers who signed on to the *Duke* and *Duchess*, Cooke had suffered at the hands of the French. He had

---

* No.127 was completed in 1704/5 by the elder Woodes Rogers, also a mariner. Unfortunately, it was bombed in the 1939-45 war and has been replaced by an office block. It is marked by a blue sign.

been attacked off Beachy Head and had been taken wounded to Le Havre, where the French had treated him with 'extraordinary civility'.[204] Next time, he had tried his luck with a twenty-gun galley and had come up against a fifty-gun, French man-of-war and had to surrender for a second time. He too was in need of compensation.

Both the *Duchess* and the *Duke* were three-masted frigates, which at that time implied a long ship of medium size, the length being good for broadsides, with slightly raised poop and forecastle. Soon workmen were swarming over them and the general officers were recruited. Deliberately, the owners took on twice the normal compliment of officers for such a voyage. This was to reduce the risk of mutiny, always a problem for privateers, especially on long voyages when the arm of the law and of the owners were stretched to breaking point. Not all of the officers were sailors. George Underhill and John Parker were 'two young Lawyers design'd to act as Midshipmen, and there was a John Finch 'late wholesale oilman of London[205]' who was to be a ship's steward.

By April 1708, Hatley, now just turned twenty-three, had been taken on as Third Mate of the *Duchess*. If reward is the best indication of status then this was nearly as low as it got for an officer. Remuneration was based on nominal shares in the voyage. A third mate received four shares [206] (although Simon received five), as opposed to eight for a third lieutenant, sixteen for a first lieutenant and twenty-four for a captain. It may have been a junior position but it was not atypical for a man of his age and it had prospects. The drawback was that he was not a lieutenant. In 1677, Samuel Pepys, then Secretary of the Navy, had instituted the lieutenants' exams in order to create a professional, elite officer core, a deliberate attempt on Pepys's part to attract more sons of gentlemen to the sea. To become a lieutenant a young man had to be proficient in seamanship and navigation and he could make use of those skills and of his status outside the Royal Navy on a privateer. Those who became skilled mariners by mere apprenticeship and experience, such as Hatley, were at a disadvantage compared to qualified lieutenants. That having been said, attitudes were less rigid than they were to become later in the century and many men such as Hatley could still end up as senior officers or captains.

Bristol, view towards St. Mary Redcliffe with glass kilns just visible
behind the ships

go with what Speed you can to Holy Head

Privateers of this period often combined trading with private warfare, turning their hands to whichever was most advantageous. This was not the intention for the *Duke* and *Duchess*. They were warships pure and simple. By the time the loading was complete, they were stocked with guns, powder and armed men and the provisions to keep the men alive, with little space left over except for the booty which they hoped to capture. Considering the immense voyage which they were about to undertake, these ships were quite small. The *Duchess* was 260 tons and carried twenty-six not particularly large guns, the *Duke* was 320 tons and carried thirty guns.[207]

Gradually, masts rose skywards, guns were hoisted aboard and provisions stored away. Supplies were lifted from the quayside using an array of slings, derricks and other equipment. The heavy stuff was winched aboard using a windlass or, for the heaviest items, the capstan.[208] The captains and senior officers would have paid close attention. It was vital that the heaviest goods were stored low down and near to the keel to give the ship a good balance. For a ship to sail well, a basic necessity for privateers which had to be able to outrun their prey, she had to be just right.

Too 'crank' (light) and she might roll excessively, too 'stiff' (heavy) and she would be slow and ponderous.[209]

That spring of 1708 the danger of an early peace was passed and war clouds loomed closer once more. While *Duke* and *Duchess* were being prepared for the sea, Anne's chief minister (and Daniel Defoe's protector), Robert Harley, resigned, exacerbating tensions in Anne's Tory government, and James the Pretender attempted to land in Scotland bringing with him the threat of Catholic invasion.

Sailors were sworn in. We know quite a lot about sailors of this period. The men who signed up for the *Duke* and *Duchess* would have been dressed in wide breeches, tarred against the cold and wet and reaching down to just above the ankle in the English style. Weather-beaten and well tattooed, they often wore a checked linen shirt with buttons made of hardened cheese or carved from sharks' vertebrae.[210] On average, they were in their late twenties, although there were older men also.[211] The ship's cook was typically such an older man, too frail to work the rigging any longer.

Merchant and privateer sailors were better paid than men in the regular navy, an average of fifty-five shillings per month as opposed to twenty-three shillings[212], so merchant captains and also privateer captains had an advantage over Royal Naval recruiters. Men had to be forced into the Navy as if 'dragged to execution[213]'. But all captains, whether naval or privateer, had recourse to 'crimps'. These were portside agents who specialised in providing crew. Frequently unscrupulous, they would get men drunk then cart them off or even raid local taverns and kidnap their quarry. In addition, and in order to level the playing field with the merchantmen and privateers, the government had the press gang. All agreed that the press gang was evil, it was just that it was a necessary evil. To get round it, Daniel Defoe, from the best of motives, proposed a scheme around this time which would not go amiss in a modern totalitarian state. He suggested that all British sailors should be enrolled in the Royal Navy without exception on a fixed scale of wages. Once in the Navy they could be assigned either to merchant ships or to warships. Thankfully, his scheme was disapproved of 'upon some Scruples about Liberty and Compulsion'.[214]

If it had been, the life of Hatley and many others would have been very different.

Press gangs roamed the pubs and boarding houses of ports looking for victims. As the demands of war had exacerbated the existing shortage of manpower, sailors on shore had begun to live like fugitives. It was unsafe for them to walk around in the open. One tactic used by the press gangs was especially resented. Naval press boats would waylay ships returning to harbour before they could enter port. They would then take off the best men. At the end of a long voyage this could be heartbreaking. Sailors would find themselves faced with another long period at sea without having been able to touch land or see their loved ones. Often there were pitched battles and the sailors would fight off the press boats. Guns might be fired, fingers slashed off with cutlasses, bones broken. Sailors also had more passive forms of resistance. They might give themselves self-inflicted injuries, feign lunacy or idiocy or an infectious disease.[215] Press gangs had little luck in Bristol however:

> *Here is our chief encouragement, our ship belongs to Bristol*
> *Poor Londoners when coming home they surely will be pressed all;*
> *We've no such fear when home we steer, with prizes under convoy,*
> *We'll frolic round all Bristol town, sweet liberty we enjoy.[216]*

A long privateering voyage such as that proposed for the *Duke* and *Duchess* was relatively attractive for sailors. It was an effective way to avoid the pressgang for those based other than in Bristol; privateer discipline was slack; if a crewman sailed on the basis of 'no purchase no pay' he could share in the plunder. But despite these advantages, by 1708, six years into the war, the owners of the *Duke* and *Duchess* still had difficulty finding sufficient crew, in particular for the *Duchess*. A recruitment flysheet was printed describing the distribution of potential prize money.[217] The owners met, on 23 June, and decided that Captain Courtney should proceed to Portsmouth to search for men and Hatley with an assistant should proceed to Ireland. John Hollidge and Woodes Rogers undertook 'their particular directions for their management of the men they

68

shall procure'.[218] Simon was to proceed from Dublin to Cork along the Irish coast, collecting men along the way, there to await the *Duke* and *Duchess*. It is interesting that Simon Hatley, only twenty-three and a third mate, was sent on a similar mission to that of his captain.

Time was passing and the shortage of crew threatened to undermine the entire endeavour. A letter to Hatley, dated July 8, 1708, conveys something of the pressure they were all under. Probably from John Hollidge, it is written in such haste that the latter part is indecipherable:

You are requested by the owners of the Duke *and* Duchess *to go with what speed you can to Holy Head and to take passage from there to Dublin. At your arrival your are to deliver the enclosed letter to Mr Humphry French on which he will assist you in procuring what men are to be had ...*[219]

Mr French was to provide money for the purchase of the men and to find the master of a ship who would assist Hatley and if necessary accompany him to Cork. An entry in an account book records that Hatley took with him £2 15s 10d toward expences.[220]

the Sound of the Sea

It was high summer. The two ships were towed down the Avon, passing through the Avon Gorge where now the Clifton Suspension Bridge defies the sky. There were poppies and corn flowers in the wheat fields and cows fattened contentedly, knee-deep in the lush Somerset meadows. The ships moved between banks lined with silvery-grey mud, fading towards green at the top where sparse blades of grass pierced through like pigs' stubble. The art of the pilots was to catch the retreating tide so that the rowers in the long boats who did the pulling were assisted by the flow, until the water fell too low and the ships were temporarily grounded. The deep water channel was narrow and the ships flopped over on their sides inert as logs until the tide came back again and slowly lifted them so that they were able to continue their cautious journey to the sea.

For a while they moored at Hong Road, along the north bank of the river just before it emerges into the sea, and from there on 15 June they were towed down to King Road, to complete fitting out and because it was more difficult for the men to abscond at that distance from the city, desertion was a major concern for owners and captains.[221] King Road is out in the Bristol Channel off Portishead, a stretch of deep, relatively sheltered water where ships commonly anchored before proceeding from or to the River Avon. On quiet days, the water lies flat and mud-brown all the way to the Welsh coast and you can pick out scattered buildings on the further side and the steel-grey Welsh hills rising behind. On the English side, hillocks tousled with pine trees provide a thin shelter from the wind. The narrow, tidal flats are speckled with thrift. Here the two ships lay anchored for another six weeks while they fitted out their rigging and while, over on the Continent, on 11 July, the Duke of Marlborough won another crushing victory, this time at Oudenard in modern Belgium.

At last, at 1.00 in the morning on Monday 1 August 1708, *Duchess* unmoored and at 2.00 weighed anchor and set sail with *Duke* close behind her. They were in company with eight other ships and two small sloops. There was safety in numbers for merchant ships. The little fleet set off down the Channel but one is reminded yet again of the unpredictable nature of travel in the eighteenth century. The wind faded and their sails hung limp. At 10.00 in the evening *Duchess* and *Duke* anchored in Bridgwater Bay, about five miles to the south of Steep Holme Island. Above them and only a couple of miles or so away hung the Quantock Hills, fading blue-grey in the dusk. Someone walking over them to Watchet that evening, on looking down, would have been able to see the two ships quite distinctly and, while the light lasted, even the men on deck or in the rigging as they clambered to make last-minute preparations for the open sea. Coleridge and Wordsworth, ninety years later, saw many such ships and sometimes heard the sounds drifting up from below, more easily so in winter than summer according to Dorothy Wordsworth, who wrote in her journal for 23 January 1798:

The sound of the sea was distinctly heard on the tops of the hills, which we could never hear in summer. We attribute this partly to the bareness of the trees, but chiefly to the absence of the singing of birds, the hum of insects, the noiseless noise which lives in the summer air.[222]

At one in the morning, *Duke* and *Duchess* weighed anchor again and set sail before an easterly breeze. The next evening, drawing close to Lundy Island, they saw a sail straight ahead and *Duchess* gave chase. A thrilling moment, the first chase of the voyage, cramming on sail, the ship straining forward among the waves. The target was a large ship by the look of it but it got away when night fell, although they kept their hammocks up* all night and the decks cleared for action. There was information that the *Jersey*, a forty-six-gun French man-of-war, was cruising in the Irish Sea and it may have been the *Jersey* that they challenged. On they bucketed, heading for Cork. Despite the careful preparations, they were slow and ungainly, their masts and rigging 'all unfit for the sea'.[223] It was Thursday 4 August 1708 when *Duchess* finally let go her anchor in the peaceful water of Cork Harbour, to be joined later by *Duke* which over-shot the entrance to Cork Cove.

The City of Cork, nestling on the many-fingered estuary of the River Lee, thrived on providing provisions to English merchants and navy vessels. It was part of Britain, but not quite. Since the time of Oliver Cromwell it had been firmly if uneasily under Protestant control, fortified by further Protestant settlers from England and, since 1685, by Huguenot refugees from France. In the outer suburbs the Old (Catholic) English and the native Irish were still in the majority and most of them would have backed the Catholic French and Spanish enemy given the chance. The native Irish were known at that time as 'the domestic enemy'.[224]

Here Hatley met up with his shipmates.[225] Forty men defected soon after the two ships let go their anchors but the new men procured by him and by a Mr Noblett Roger, the owners' agent in the city, made good the shortfall. Many of the fresh intake were landsmen. This was in line with government policy, although perhaps not deliberately so. An Order in Council of 1695 ruled that at least one half of the company of any privateer were to be landmen.[226] Conditions on privateers were so much preferable to conditions on regular naval ships that the authorities were afraid there would be insufficient experienced sailors for the Royal Navy if privateers

---

* When action was imminent, the sailors' hammocks were rolled up and jammed into racks along the gunwales as a protection against enemy fire.

could take their pick. The new men on the *Duke* and *Duchess* included haymakers, fiddlers, foreigners and a black man, only twenty of them being professional sailors. They appear to have been delightfully innocent. They were 'continually marrying while we staid at Cork'[227] according to Woodes Rogers. A Dane married an Irishwoman although neither could speak each other's language and they were obliged to use an interpreter in order to communicate with each other. They were among the most upset when finally the ships set sail and they had to part.

Captain Woodes Rogers when he was governor of the Bahamas[228]

Letter to Simon Hatley, instructing him to proceed to Holyhead, July 1708:
'Mr Simon Hatley You are requested by the owners of the *Duke* and *Duchess* ...'

King Road, Bristol Channel

the length of our Voyage

At 10.00 in the morning of Wednesday 1 September 1708, *Duke* and *Duchess* set sail from Cork. The ships were cleaned and tallowed and in good shape for the voyage ahead. They had waited a week for the wind and they set off in company with the *Hastings*, a powerful British man-of-war along with twenty merchant ships bound for the West Indies and other distant parts. Both privateers were deep-laden with provisions. There was livestock penned on the decks along with chicken coops. Their hulls were stocked with bread and water casks between the decks.

Six days later, well out into the Atlantic the convoy split up. *Duke* and *Duchess* left letters home onboard the *Hastings* and set their course for Madereira with only one merchant ship still accompanying them. They needed more alcohol, in particular wine and brandy:

We began to consider the length of our Voyage ... and the excessive Cold which we cannot avoid, going about Cape Horne; at the same time we had but slender Store of Liquor, and our Men but meanly clad, yet good Liquor to Sailors is preferable to Clothing ...[229]

73

At six the next morning, they spied a sail and both ships gave chase. They caught up with her at three in the afternoon only to discover that she was a Swedish ship bound for Cadiz. As Sweden and Britain were not directly at war, they could not legally plunder her. Finding no evidence that she was carrying contraband they were obliged to let her go.

Only ten days out, but the release of the Swede sparked their first mutiny. Some of the *Duke's* men, led by the boatswain,* felt that they had been cheated of their rightful plunder. All that night, Rogers and his officers were holed up in the after-part of the ship and it was not until the next day that they eventually reasserted control. The boatswain was flogged and ten others were put in irons. Hatley would have been aware of the danger because it was equally tense on the *Duchess* and mutiny was only averted because the potential mutineers were intimidated by what happened on the *Duke*. Punishment and a period in irons followed by an apology was the usual method for dealing with mutinous outbreaks at that time. Five days later, the offenders were released after apologising, and those who were minor officers were restored to their positions. All except Giles Cash, the mutinous boatswain, who was transferred to the accompanying merchant ship disgraced.

On they sailed, borne by moderate gales. There was as yet no effective method of establishing longitude and they discovered that they had passed too far to the east of Madeira without being aware of it. They decided to give it a miss after all. The merchant ship changed course and left them, taking the recalcitrant boatswain with him.

Woodes Rogers was an effective commander. William Dampier, the old buccaneer who had been denied the overall command in spite of proposing the expedition, must have felt out of place beside him. This neat voyage was very different from the dissension and mutiny on the *St George*. A mutiny quelled, order established, the most disciplined of privateering voyages, so orderly that at times it seemed positively respectable. The senior officers clamped down on swearing, an almost insufferable imposition on the crew although not uncommonly attempted by naval captains[230] because swearing was part of the language of the sea. Sailors

---

* The boatswain acted as foreman and was responsible for the rigging.

were said to go about their work 'with volleys of oaths', 'the very shambles of a language'. There was even an expression: 'with seamanlike profanity'.[231] But Rogers and Courtney were determined and they had a point. With the swearing went a lack of deference. Any privateer captain who showed signs of weakness could expect to negotiate a minefield of egos, insolence and argument and might even be deprived of his office and perhaps *voted* or *allowed* back into position, with considerably less authority, as happened to George Shelvocke in 1720. As for pirates, almost by definition the least deferential of sailors, they swore worst of all. A certain Philip Ashton fell into the hands of pirates in 1722:

I soon found that any death was preferable to being linked with such a vile crew of miscreants ... where prodigious drinking, monstrous cursing and swearing, hideous blasphemies, and open defiance of Heaven, and contempt of hell itself, was the constant. Employment ...[232]

Rogers ordered *ferulas*[*] to be made, to punish offenders.

The late seventeenth and early eighteenth centuries enjoy a reputation for gin-swilling moral laxness, but a case can be made that it was in this period that the seeds of Victorian primness first took root, so Rogers and Courtney were following a trend. The Society for the Reformation of Manners was founded in 1695 with Daniel Defoe a member of Society No. 2.[233] Its purpose was to discourage 'public vice'. This included swearing and drunkenness, drunkenness being defined as 'unable to stand on his legs'.[234]

On Thursday 16 September 1708, the two ships came up with the Canaries and on 18 September they saw the black volcanic finger of the Peak of Tenerife, longed-for landmark of sailors since ancient times. It was said to be visible from a distance of 180 miles, the site of the fabulous rain tree, 'always covered by a little cloud which hangs over it, which wets the leaves as with a perpetual Dew, so that fine, clear Water constantly trickles down from it into little Pails set below to catch it as it falls'.[235] Further out into the Atlantic, so legend had it, lay the Isle of St. Brendon where no sailor could ever land.

---

[*] Flat rulers with a widened end used for punishing boys - OED.

Here they took their first prize, a small Spanish barque of twenty-five tons, which they spotted between the islands of Fuerteventura and Grand Canaria. They chased her for five hours until *Duchess*, which was a little ahead, fired a gun and forced her to stop. As it turned out, the passengers were thoroughly relieved to have been captured by an English ship and not by Turkish pirates which would have meant almost certain slavery. One of them was the padre of Fuerteventura whom 'we made heartily merry, drinking King Charles the Third's Health'.[236] The rest, including several other priests, were the 'wrong sort' whatever that might be.

The *Duke's* boat put in to land carrying the master of the Spanish barque and the padre in order to negotiate a ransom for the prize. With them, against the advice of Woodes Rogers, went the Owners' agent on the *Duke*, an obnoxious young man by the name of Carlton Vanbrugh. Carlton was a cousin of the famous architect who designed Blenheim Palace and, although young, he was a senior figure. His job as owner's agent was in some respects similar to that of financial director in a modern enterprise. On landing, he was promptly arrested by the Spanish authorities, thus converting himself into a bargaining chip in their favour. Angry letters were exchanged and mutual threats. There was a small colony of British merchants on the Canaries who were very anxious not to alienate their Spanish hosts and these merchants attempted first to get the privateers to give up their prize and then to mediate a deal. Eventually a ransom was produced in the form of wine, grapes, pigs and other items and the barque and prisoners were released, the priests being allowed to keep all their Catholic impedimenta including crucifixes. The padre got a cheese as well.

They sailed on. Saturday 25 September they crossed the Tropic of Cancer and the greenhorn sailors were baptised in the traditional way. This involved hoisting them halfway up to the main yard and then dropping them into the water while attached to a rope to stop them drowning. 'This proved of great use to our fresh-water Sailors, to recover the Colour of their Skin which were grown very black and nasty'.[237] A mood of optimism prevailed. Next day they auctioned the loose plunder from the Spanish barque - small personal items belonging to the passengers and crew. Hatley purchased a pair of silk hose. The accounts books give no date, just the fact that he bought them. Compared to some of his shipmates he was thrifty.

With every mile it grew hotter but the fair winds continued. On Wednesday 29 September 1708, they at last saw the Cape Verde Islands, owned by the Portuguese, their next port of call. The Cape Verde Islands, a scattered and lonely archipelago far out from the coast of Senegal, were a useful stopping off point but they were not much liked by sailors. They were originally colonised by the Portuguese back in 1456, but the Portuguese persecuted their black slaves so viciously that a great many escaped, a state of affairs already under way when Sir Francis Drake touched on the Cape Verde Islands in 1577.

The Portugals ... used that extream and unreasonable cruelty over their slaves, that (their bondage being intolerable) they were forced to seek some means to help themselves, and to lighten that so heavy burden; and thereupon chose to flie into the most mountainy parts of the Island: and at last, by continual escapes, increasing to a great number and growing to a set strength, do now live ...[238]

The descendants of escaped slaves formed the majority of the population but they were desperately poor and addicted to theft. 'They will take your Hat off your Head at Noonday, although you be in the Midst of Company'.[239] The privateers let go their anchors off St Vincent's, one of the larger islands, now completely treeless but then still wooded in places, the woods being infested by huge spiders the size of walnuts, their webs as strong as thread.[240] Some of the men began to sell their clothes in return for small items from the inhabitants. They had no understanding of the severity of the conditions which they would encounter when they rounded the Horn.

While at anchor in the sickle bay of St. Vincent, the arid hills behind and the beautiful view of Santo Antão Island across the water, there was a meeting on the *Duke*. The owners (at the instigation of Woodes Rogers) had set up a managing committee before they left Bristol in order to avoid contention between the senior officers and because Woodes Rogers wanted to be sure of consensus before he took any controversial decision. If decisions were fully discussed and minuted he was less likely to end up in court on his return, the fate of so many privateer commanders. The president of the committee was Dr Thomas Dover,* an irascible but wealthy Bristol doctor and the largest investor in the voyage, who seems to have come along for the adventure as well as to protect his investment. On this occasion Rogers wanted to change the articles of agreement regarding plunder. The mutiny off the Canary Islands had given everyone a scare. New articles were drawn up which gave a greater share to the ordinary seamen.

After two weeks at the Cape Verde Islands, the ships had taken on all the fresh water and provisions that were needed or were available. On the evening of Thursday 8 October 1708, *Duchess* weighed anchor and sailed out of St. Vincent Bay into the open sea and there waited with a light out to mark the way for the *Duke*. At eight o'clock, with night falling, both ships turned their bows to the south west, towards Brazil and the Atlantic crossing.

In the seventeenth and eighteenth centuries, the crossing southward from the Cape Verde Islands could take three months or longer. For sailors going about their regular tasks, it was a slow, timeless, experience. No human contact of any kind apart from the narrow circle of one's shipmates. No living creatures but the creatures of the deep:

Nothing but sea beneath us and aire above us was to be seen, as our eyes did behold the wonderful works of God in his creatures, which he made innumerable both small and great beasts in the great and wide seas ...[241]

The two ships were alone and the old world was behind them. The immensity of what they were undertaking must have struck home as they settled down to the routine of the sea, one watch on, one watch off, four hours each watch, day after day. Ships were little island universes. Divided island universes. The officers and men worked, drank, sang and argued in their separate quarters, two little worlds per ship, the officers in the steerage and cabins aft, and the men in the forecastle.[242] The senior officers relieved the monotony by dining on each others' ships. It is remarkable how they

---

* The inventor of Dover's Powders, a popular medicine right into the Victorian era. He was also known as Dr Quicksilver because of his preference for prescribing mercury for many ailments.

would ply backwards and forwards in mid ocean in the small ships' boats without a second's thought to the wind and waves.

It was a slow and timeless world but also a hothouse with no safety-valve available. Inevitably, such long passages on the open sea were punctuated by outbreaks of dissension. A fortnight out and there was trouble with William Page, Fifth Mate on the *Duchess* to Hatley's Third Mate:

October 22. Close cloudy Weather all night, with Squalls of Rain. At ten this morning it clear'd up: Capt. Courtney came aboard of us, and sent back his Boat for Capt. Cook, with Orders to bring Mr. Page, Second Mate [actually Fifth Mate], with him, to be in the room of Mr. Ballett, that we exchang'd out of our Ship. Page disobeying Command, occasion'd Capt. Cook, being the superior Officer aboard, to strike him; whereupon Page struck him again. And several Blows last: but at last Page was forc'd into the Boat, and brought on board of us. And Capt. Cook and others telling us what Mutiny had pass'd, we order'd Page on the Fore-Castle into the bilboes.* He begg'd to go into the Head* to ease himself; under that pretence the Corporal and the rest left him for a while: upon which he leapt over board, thinking to swim back to the Dutchess, it being near calm, and the Captains out of the Ship. However, the Boat being along side, we soon overtook him, and brought him on board again. For which and his abusive Language he was lash'd to the Main-Geers and drub'd; and for inciting the Men to Mutiny, was afterward confin'd in Irons board the Duke.[243]

All this in mid-ocean. Page was let out of irons a week later after an apology. Hatley, his fellow mate, appears to have been made of more sensible stuff.

a remarkable high Land

South America makes itself felt long before it comes into view. First there are seabirds. They wheel in the blue, their shrill cries punctuating the

---

* Bilboes were irons which held a miscreant's ankles.

* A wooden construction over the sea at the bows, made up of two or three boxes with holes in them.

slap of water against the bows. There is a change to the rhythm of the waves. Strange scents invade the air. Far out from the rivers Amazon and Orinoco and in some other places, the water changes colour to a muddy yellow - sometimes, more dramatically, to blood red, as it did for Ambrosia Cowley in 1683: 'the sea as red as blood which was occasioned by the great shoals of shrimps which lay upon the water in great patches for many leagues together.'[244] Finally there is the land itself. On Saturday 13 November, *Duchess* struck ground at thirty fathom water.

Nowadays the coast of Brazil is necklaced by cities. Sail close in to the major centres of population and the skyline is distorted by gap-toothed apartment blocks. In the eighteenth century, the cities were little more than pinpricks in the vast wilderness. It was still much as Amerigo Vespucci had known it in 1499 when he sailed down almost the complete Atlantic coastline of South America and saw, or thought he saw, nothing but forests and only here and there the tiny settlements of native Indians.

Islands were the best places for privateers to wood and water after the crossing because they afforded the least likelihood of meeting an enemy. *Duke* and *Duchess* headed for Grande, where William Dampier had anchored in the *St. George* in 1703 in company with the *Cinque Ports*, where Captain Pickering died and was buried 'at the Watering place[245]' and where young Thomas Stradling had taken over as captain with Alexander Selkirk as a difficult member of his crew. It was also a favourite port of call for the French.

On the afternoon of 19 November 1709, they let go their anchors about twelve miles out and Dampier went ahead in a pinnace to check that they had indeed arrived and that there were no French warships at anchor. As evening drew on, they first sailed then rowed and towed into the channel between the island and the mainland. A magical moment, the ships with furled sails slipping silently past the dark, forested shore, the tropical air pierced by the night-hoots of alien birds and animals. It was 'A remarkable high Land ... has plenty of good Timber, Fire-wood, and excellent Water. It is hot like an Oven'.[246] At midnight they dropped anchor again. For Hatley it was his first experience of South America.

It was pouring with rain.

Grande is now a nature reserve and wonderfully unspoiled. Luxuriant forests tumble down steep hills to the sea and, at sunset, the black, broken backbone of the hills cuts off the sky like torn cardboard. It can feel as wild as it did back then. 'It is not inhabited by any other than Jackals, Lyons, Tygers etc which in the Night make a most hideous Noise, enough to terrify any man[247]'. A few days after the arrival of the *Duke* and *Duchess*, two Irishmen deserted, only to return the next morning having been scared out of their wits by the howls of the 'lions', in reality by monkeys. 'They ran into the water, hollowing to the Ship till they were fetch'd aboard again.'[248]

The men got to work, still in pouring rain. Empty water casks were rowed ashore to be scraped clean and refilled, the carpenter set off in search of timber to replace various items of rigging which had broken during the crossing. The ships were heeled and scraped clean, and a week later, the weather having improved although still 'violent hot', Woodes Rogers, Stephen Courtney and most of the officers of both ships set off for the village of Angra dos Reis or 'Grande town'[249] about nine miles down the coast on the mainland, 'sixty low Houses built of mud'[250], which supplied fruit and other commodities to Sao Paulo inland. Rogers was anxious to keep in with the locals so that they would return any deserters who sought haven in the village. The English officers were invited by the 'governor' to join in a local festival to the Virgin Mary. Edward Cooke writes primly of a dinner with music and sweetmeats[251] but in Woodes Rogers's description his rough English sailors thoroughly enjoyed the occasion. Not all Catholics were demons:

He ask'd us if we would see the Convent and Procession: we told him our Religion differ'd very much from his. He answer'd we were welcome to see it, without partaking in the Ceremony. We waited on him in a Body, being ten of us, with two Trumpets and a Hautboy, which he desir'd might play us to Church. Our Musick play'd, Hey Boys up go we! and all manner of noisy paltry Tunes: and after Service our Musicians, who were by that time more than half drunk, march'd at the head of the Company, next to them an old Father and two Friars carrying Lamps of Incense with the Host, next came the Virgin Mary...[252]

There followed a convivial dinner in the convent.

Interdenominational fraternising continued the next day when the Portuguese were asked on board the *Duke* for a return visit:

We treated 'em the best we could. They were very merry, and in their Cups proposed the Pope's Health to us; but we were quits with 'em, by toasting that of the Archbishop of Canterbury: to keep up the Humour, we also propos'd William Pen's to them; and they' lik'd the Liquor so well; that they refus'd neither.[253]

The interlude on Grande was almost idyllic but marred by the killing of an innocent Indian. Early on the morning before the festival, a canoe came paddling across the channel close by the *Duke*. It was steered by a Portuguese friar with two Indian slaves at the paddles and it ignored calls to stop. Carlton Vanbrugh took command of the *Duke's* boat without permission and went off in pursuit. He ordered the boatmen to fire, first at a distance and then at closer range. An Indian was shot and died soon after. As a result of this, the committee agreed that the troublesome Vanbrugh should be swapped with William Bath, agent of the *Duchess*.

By Tuesday 30 November, after eleven days at Grande, both ships were stocked with food and water and their rigging and hulls all made good. They were ready for the next stage of their journey, the long, dangerous voyage round the Horn into the Pacific. They would not touch land again until around four thousand miles later at the Juan Fernandez Islands off the coast of Chile. They weighed anchor and prepared to leave the jungle-fringed channel.

A false start. On reading the accounts, one is constantly struck by how differently people experienced time in those days, particularly on journeys by sea. Days could be lost with as little regret as hours or minutes are today. As a result of adverse winds *Duke* and *Duchess* were forced to come to anchor again close by the island. And the wind continued to be unhelpful. It was not until the afternoon of Friday 3 December that they were able to get under way properly. At last a brisk gale filled their sails and they were able to set their course for the south. The jagged outline of the island gradually blended with the hills of the mainland until both were reduced to a green-grey smudge on the horizon.

It was raining again. It would be ten years before Hatley was back.

Their course took them down the east coast of what is now Argentina. By mid-December, they were on the latitude of Port Desire (*Puerto Deseado*) so named by Thomas Cavendish in 1586. There they saw their first albatross 'a large Bird called an Alcatros who spread their Wings from eight to ten Foot wide, and are much like a Gannet[254]', probably Hatley's first sight of the bird that he is associated with. By Tuesday 21 December they were level with *Puerto St. Julián* where Francis Drake executed Thomas Doughty for witchcraft and treason in 1578 and where Ferdinand Magellan marooned John Cartagena, cousin of the Bishop of Burgos, for mutiny in 1520 after the executing of Gaspar de Quesada and Luis de Mendonza for the same reason. Shortly after, they saw the Falkland Islands to the east and ran along the green, rolling coast, looking 'like some Part of England'.[255]

It was Christmas Eve 1708, but they were far from their loved ones and this was no festive occasion. *Duchess* spotted a sail and gave chase, losing the strange ship in the night but sighting her again on Christmas morning. Both ships crammed on all possible sail and set off in pursuit but then the wind fell and they had to put out their ships' boats and row and tow. On they went right through Boxing Day, rowing then sailing, sailing then rowing. The wind was infuriatingly patchy. *Duchess* drew so far ahead that eventually Captain Courtney felt he had to wait for the *Duke* or they might be separated. The chase escaped.

On they sailed, into a colder and bleaker climate. By New Year's Eve they were at Latitude 58°, to the south of the latitude of Cape Horn. Woodes Rogers ordered a large tub of hot punch to be made ready on the quarter-deck of the *Duke* and allowed a pint for every man on board. They drank 'our Owners and Friends Healths in Great Britain, to a happy new Year, a good Voyage and a safe Return',[256] then drew close to the *Duchess* and the two crews cheered each other across the freezing waves. Meanwhile the wind grew stronger and the waves more mountainous. They ran through great banks of freezing fog.

The cold began to bite. Men went about their tasks in grim misery, their clothes permanently damp, fingers numb, eyes streaming, lips chapped and sore. Spare blankets and clothes were dished out to them. Officers gave away what they could spare to be altered for the men's use. The weather became ferocious. In the southern hemisphere, the prevailing winds spin round the earth from northwest to east so that, in the far south, storms blow up in the Pacific and are driven clockwise (seen from above) into the southern ocean. Those travelling from the Atlantic must sail into them. Cold winds are more powerful than warm winds because cold air is denser so cold wind packs more punch.[257] Immense waves battered into the wooden hulls and blasts of wind tore through the rigging, screaming like demons in anguish. Not for nothing are these regions referred to as the 'Furious 50°s' and the 'Screaming 60°s'. By Wednesday 5 January 1709, they were in a peak of very bad Weather. *Duchess* reefed both courses of sails and lay by until five in the afternoon, wallowing and heavy between the waves. The waist of the ship was almost continuously full of freezing water and they were constantly battered by the huge seas. They expected to drown at any moment. Courtney ordered out the sprit sails* and wore the ship round, hoping thus to lessen the impact of the waves. *Duke*, following, fired a gun ordering *Duchess* to bring to. Woods Rogers was worried that they might run into ice floes in the extreme cold, but *Duchess* kept on. Finally, at nine in the evening, *Duchess* shipped a huge sea at the poop just as the officers were going into the main cabin to eat. It broke through the cabin window like a fist, filling it with water and the first lieutenant was thrown 'halfway between decks'.[258] Luckily, this monster wave also smashed right through the bulkhead which separated the cabin from the rest of the deck, thus allowing the water to drain forward, if not the officers 'must inevitably have been drowned',[259] like rats in a bucket, Hatley among them. As it was, miraculously, no one was badly hurt.

Next morning the storm abated and *Duke* drew close again. *Duchess* had got six of her guns down into the hold for better balance and all her rigging was festooned with clothes put out to dry, so that she looked like a giant clothes horse. She was still afloat and her crew were all intact, although some of the men had fallen very sick and they were all very wet

---

* Sprit sail: a fore-and-aft sail spread from the mizzen mast of a barque-rigged ship.

84

and freezing cold. Commodore Anson, passing that way in 1770, described the sort of conditions they were experiencing:

The ship, by labouring in this lofty sea, was now grown so loose in her upper words, that she let in water at every seam, so that every part within board was constantly exposed to sea-water, and scarcely any of the officers lay in dry beds ...[260]

They were now, by Cooke's estimation, at latitude 61°20 south, not far from the northernmost tip of the continent of Antarctica, probably the furthest south that any European, or perhaps anyone, had sailed until that date. There were no maps to tell them what to expect. All they knew was that the ocean grew more hostile and more enraged the further south one sailed. As the saying went: 'below 40° there is no law; below 50° there is no God' - but what of below 62°? What then?

Just over a week of 'raw cold Weather' later, amid squalls of rain and hail, they at last corrected their course northward. It was Friday 14 January 1709 and the worst was over. That day, one of the *Duchess's* men died of scurvy, the first such death of the voyage. The following Wednesday they crossed the fiftieth parallel. The passage round the Horn is commonly said to be from 50° south in the Atlantic to 50° south in the Pacific, so at this point they could be said to have rounded the Horn.

el Mar Pacifico

When Magellan emerged from the straits which bear his name, on 28 November 1520, he wept tears of joy on seeing the calm ocean which lay before him and named it *el Mar Pacifico* out of gratitude for his safe arrival, and indeed the calmer waters of the Pacific were always welcome after the rigours of the Horn - although the accounts of both Cooke and Rogers are imbued with a sense of weariness at this point in their voyage. They had now been almost two months at sea and many of the men, especially on the *Duchess*, were sick and incapable of working. They limped their way up the coast of Chile, aiming for the Juan Fernandez Islands which lie about three hundred and sixty miles out to sea on the latitude of Santiago. Three more died as they worked their way north.

At last, on Monday 31 January 1709, at eight in the morning, they saw 'high ragged Land'[261] a little to port. The Juan Fernadez Islands at last. They had made it. A fire was flickering on the shore and so, tantalisingly, they held off landing fearing that a Spanish or French ship was there before them.

To the voyagers' relief, it transpired that the fire had been lit by Alexander Selkirk. He had been living alone on the island ever since George Stradling marooned him there in 1704, a total of four years and four months to the moment when *Duke* and *Duchess* rounded the bay. Selkirk had dined on cabbages from the cabbage trees and on the flesh of goats, descendants of the goats left there by Spanish sailors many years before, which he ran down bare-footed once his ammunition was expended. He had domesticated feral cats to keep the rats at bay and, when his clothes wore out, he had dressed in goats' skins, looking 'wilder than the first Owners of them'.[262]

This was the figure which greeted Dr Thomas Dover and seven others who went ahead in a ship's boat to check out the fire, while *Duke* and *Duchess* were manoeuvring to enter the bay. Relieved to find that there were no Spaniards or Frenchmen on the island and only this solitary, ragged figure, they carried Selkirk back across the choppy water to the *Duke* together with 'an abundant catch of craw fish'. On first coming aboard, Selkirk was barely able to speak, his tongue had been unused to speech for so long. His words came out 'by halves'. He refused liquor when it was offered to him, a thing rarely seen in a sailor, let alone a Scottish sailor. He said 'he was a better Christian in this Solitude than ever he was before, or than, he was afraid, he should ever be again'. Woodes Rogers's description of the ordeal and rescue of Alexander Selkirk which holds within it the bones of Defoe's *Robinson Crusoe*, was a major selling point for Roger's book when they got home. There was small respite for Selkirk however. No sooner was he on board than William Dampier (showing more generosity than accounts of the voyage of the *St. George* and the *Cinque Ports* might suggest) recommended him and Woodes Rogers promptly made him second mate on the *Duke*.[263]

Duke and *Duchess* came to anchor in Cumberland Bay. The sick were transferred to land and put up in sail-cloth tents specially erected for the purpose. They recovered rapidly on a diet of goat meat, caught in the main by Selkirk, and greens from the island, including 'cabbages'. It was summer in the southern hemisphere and in the warm nights, the senior officers lay in spacious tents with views over the sea. They relaxed and watched the stars in the clear night air, clean-scented from the pimento trees.

The island was almost a Garden of Eden, teeming with all manner of wild birds and animals. By day, the bay rang with the shouts of the sailors as they hewed wood and fetched water and prepared provisions for the next stage of their journey, the boats busy ferrying water and supplies to the ships. But at night, the perpetual bleating of the seals and sea lions took over. They lined the shore in vast numbers and during the mating season, Selkirk reported, they lay so thick and were so aggressive that it was impossible to force a way through them. The seals and sea lions were easy prey for the sailors who killed and rendered enough of them to produce eighty gallons of sea lion oil for use in the ships' lamps and for frying.

Juan Fernandez Island[264]

By 13 February 1709, all was in order. The provisions were stowed, the water casks made fast and the sick all recovered apart from two more from the *Duchess* who died while on the island. The two ships weighed anchor and rowed and towed out of the bay on a calm flat sea. Then the wind rose and they set sail north-east towards the mainland, *Mas a Tierra* fading from dark green to misty turquoise behind them until it was little more than a jagged mark on the horizon. Selkirk, looking back, must have wondered at his ordeal.

It was time to start work, and work meant plunder. About eighteen miles off the mainland they turned northwards. At that distance they would be unidentifiable from the enemy shore but in a perfect position to scoop up coastal shipping. In order to avoid dissension and any suspicion of unfairness between the crews of the two ships, it was agreed at a meeting of the Committee, held on board the *Duke*, that each ship should appoint agents, two for the officers and two for the men. One of each would stay behind on his own ship and one of each would transfer to the other ship. Orders for the agents from the *Duke* applied also to the agents from the *Duchess*:

... search all Persons that return from such Prize or Prizes that may be taken by either Ship: as also all Persons that the Captains of either Ship shall give leave ... and immediately inform of any Persons belonging to either Ship, that shall be perceived to use clandestine Methods to hide Plunder, or endeavour to avoid the searching of them ...observing that you be not overaw'd, nor deceived of what is your Due ...[265]

Hatley was appointed agent for the officers of the *Duchess* on board the *Duke*.

Thus it was that on 17 February 1709, at latitude 28°50 and within sight of the Chilean shore, Hatley, together with one Simon Fleming, agent for the *Duchess's* men, was rowed across to his new quarters 'to prevent any Wrong being done to the Company of the said *Duchess*'. A responsible task and one which would only have been given to someone considered reliable and reasonably popular, as well as someone able to stand up for himself.

So there we have it. From 17 February 1709 for a period of several weeks, Simon Hatley, Plunder Manager for the *Duchess*, Alexander Selkirk, recently-rescued castaway and now second mate on the *Duke* and William Dampier, former pirate and author and now navigator, were all on board the *Duke* and sailing northwards. The Ancient Mariner, Robinson Crusoe and Captain Pocock/Lemuel Gulliver were shipmates together. It leads nowhere, but it is a unique occurrence. Literary models do not usually cluster like this, not when recruited from different books by different authors. As if the originals for Shakespeare's Hamlet and Marlow's Dr Faustus once bumped into each other in a pub in London and one of Webster's characters joined them, or Barry's Peter Pan attended the same church as Carroll's Alice in Wonderland and Christopher Robin happened to be another member of the congregation. I doubt that anyone would have been more surprised at this strange coincidence than the prototypes themselves if they had been able to fly into the future and look back on themselves. Their lives, already rather too large for life, touch unreality at this point in their journey.

the Coast of Chile

Hatley continued his journey in the *Duke* in 'fine, pleasant Weather', the sea 'as smooth as in the River Thames but hazy and no Sight of the Sun'.[266] On Thursday 24 February 1709, they crossed the Tropic of Capricorn. Temperatures were less hot and unpleasant than anticipated, the nights almost cool. Edward Cooke remarks on the Megallanic Clouds. Invisible from Europe, they hung among the stars, two puffs of smoke beyond the Milky Way. Far to the east, the snowy peaks of the Andes shimmered against the blue, rising like ghosts, detached from the land which lay hidden below them. To the west, nothing but ocean. The days merged into each other, the familiar routine of the sea. On Sunday 27 February, they crossed the Bay of Arica, the port for the silver mines of Potosi near the border between modern Chile and Peru and Woodes Rogers reduced water rations to three pints per day per man, determined that they should keep to sea for as long as possible so as to avoid premature discovery. Once their presence was known, all coastal shipping would be

89

confined to harbour immediately and Spanish defensive plans put into action. By early March they were level with Lima. They slowed down and began to cruise 'under easy sail', side by side but well spread out in hopes of catching vessels on their way to Lima's port of Callao.

At last, on Monday 14 March 1709, they took their first prize in the Pacific Ocean, a small sixteen-ton vessel on its way from the port of Paita some five hundred miles to the north. The Spanish captain surrendered without a struggle. Further actions would have to wait however. It was now over a month since they had left the Juan Fernandez Islands and it was time to repair and recuperate yet again. They made for the twin islands of *Lobos del Mar*, the 'Sea Wolves', to the south of Paita. It was near these islands that William Dampier had been forced to abandon the honey-comb hulk of the *St George* in 1704.

An English privateer about to take a prize
Samuel Scott *c.*1701

The islands of *Lobos del Mar* are two small low-lying ragged smudges of land which lie about fifty miles out from the coastal town of Chiclayo, then a mere satellite of the neighbouring town of Lambayeque, now a city of almost a million people carved from the coastal desert. These islands were another convenient stopping off point for buccaneers and privateers, lying between Paita and Callao, right beside a busy shipping lane. They were called *Lobos del Mar* to distinguish them from the *Lobos de la Tierra* which are situated nearer to the coast. They were not the most welcoming of islands however. Their soil was 'hungry white' and sandy and there were no trees and they were home to vast numbers of pelicans and other birds which are alternatively described in the accounts as 'carrion-buzzards' or 'carrion crows' but which were probably vultures. The flesh of the pelicans was black and fishy-tasting and the vultures stank. The three ships anchored in the middle of this teeming if foetid zoo in the sheltered water between the two islands, where the 'ugly noisom' smell of huge numbers of seals blew across from the land and gave some of the men headaches.[267]

Seals, vultures and pelicans notwithstanding, the sick men - and by now there were quite a few yet again - were made comfortable in tents on land and the narrow channel was made noisy with the shouts of the men as they took on water and began to fit out the new prize as an attack privateer. Rogers gave her a new main mast and guns and a crew of thirty-two men and renamed her the *Beginning*, placing Edward Cooke, second captain of the *Duchess*, in her as captain. *Duke* had to be careened. Hatley had little to occupy him with no plunder to take care of as yet. True to form, Carlton Vanbrugh went off to shoot vultures and also threatened to shoot a sailor for refusing to carry them.

Duke lay anchored between the islands of *Lobos del Mar* for a fortnight while *Duchess* and *Beginning* cruised between the islands and the mainland. The two ships captured a fifty-ton barque which was brought back to base and renamed the *Increase* and Selkirk was made master of her. At last at ten in the evening of 30 March, *Duke* weighed anchor and left the channel between the two islands for the open sea, ready to resume her leadership of what was becoming a small fleet. Prisoners taken on the *Increase* had information that the widow of the last viceroy of Peru was expected to sail south from Acapulco to Paita shortly, with her family and all her riches. Hopes ran high. On 1 April the sea turned red as blood for miles in every direction 'from the spawn of fish'[268] and the following

91

morning they sighted a sail to the west and *Duke's* pinnace set off after it, a tiny vessel compared to the 'chase' which was a grand, old, high-galleried Spanish galleon, heavy with cargo, beating southward. She surrendered without a fight. There were fifty or sixty black slaves on board as well as a number of Spanish passengers but no wealthy widow. Next day they took a thirty-five ton barque loaded with timber with a crew of eleven white men and a black man. They discovered that they had just missed a rich bishop due to sail that way shortly in a great ship.

Rogers now commanded a fleet of seven vessels. He worked his way yet further to the north. By Monday 7 April 1709, they were level with Paita and shortly after, at a meeting of the Committee on board the *Duke*, it was agreed that they would attack the port of Guayaquil, in what is now Ecuador. 'We resolve to attempt it'.[269] The resolution was signed by all the senior officers of the expedition.

Guayaquil

Guayaquil was the third most important port on the Pacific coast of South America after Callao (the port for Lima) and Valparaiso (the port for Santiago). It is now a sprawling, urban mass of around two million people but even then it was a significant place. As the main ship-building and repair centre for the continent, it was often, if not usually, the first port of call for ships making their way south from Panama and Mexico. Founded in 1538, it was governed by a president with five or six *oidores* (judges) and it answered only to the Viceroy in Lima on military matters. It had been the subject of a brutal attack by buccaneers in 1687, when among other things four prisoners had been decapitated,[270] but, by the time *Duke* and *Duchess* and their fleet were in the area, it had recovered and was probably larger than the two thousand population estimated by Woodes Rogers. Certainly it could call on more than the few hundred men he had at his disposal. This tempting but formidable target lay about twenty miles inland up the grey-brown waters of the River Guayas.

The privateers planned their attack while still well out on the open ocean. It was agreed that Dr Dover, Woodes Rogers and Stephen Courtney were to command three equal parties of seventy-eight men each, with another twenty-one-man party under William Dampier to take care of the guns. Together with officers, the attack party would comprise 238 men in total. Two small barques were to lead the attack fleet, together with the two ships' pinnaces and a launch. These small vessels were to take the attack party up the river to the waterfront of the town. The big ships, *Duke* and *Duchess* and the rest of the prizes, would stay back in the Gulf of Guayaquil with Edward Cooke as temporary captain of the *Duchess* and Edward Fry, First Lieutenant, as temporary captain of the *Duke*. The rearguard would amount to eighty-four men including officers and they would be heavily outnumbered by their 266 prisoners.

Two days later the fleet rounded Capo Blanco into the Gulf of Guayaquil, staying well out to sea to avoid detection. The attack boats were prepared with arms and ammunition and all was nearly ready when, at break of day on Friday 15 April 1709, in a virtual calm, they spotted the slack sails of a large ship between themselves and the land. There was almost no wind, the two ships' pinnaces were rapidly lowered into the water and began to row across the glassy surface towards the strangers. So great was their haste that neither of the pinnaces was properly prepared and neither had their full compliment of men. Hatley was in the *Duchess's* pinnace[271] which was commanded by Edward Cooke. The *Duke's* pinnace was commanded by Robert Frye and had on board John Rogers, younger brother of Woodes Rogers, who stepped in at the last moment against his brother's wishes.

The men in the pinnaces expected a quick surrender but they were in for a nasty surprise. The Spanish ship, French-built and then called the *Havre de Grace*, was about the size of the *Duke* and it had six guns mounted. Instead of striking its flag in surrender, it raised the Spanish flag and the men on board moved one of their guns to the stern to be able to fire down on their attackers. *Duke's* pinnace was quickest across the water but, having got almost within range of the target which was edging towards land and safety, moving slowly in the almost still air, Robert Frye held back and waited for his colleague to catch up. Cooke and Fry held a hurried conference just out of range. They decided to bluff it out and pretend to be

Spanish while they edged closer and to keep out of the field of fire of the 'stern chase', the gun now positioned at the stern of the enemy ship.

The air was electric-tense, the two boats and the ship warily watching each other across the water with the green-fringed shore beyond. Unfortunately, *Duke's* men panicked, fearing that they were about to receive a murderous volley. They blasted off with their muskets then fell to their oars, rowing as fast as they could to get alongside the tall hull of the enemy. The plan had been for *Duke's* pinnace to board by the stern and *Duchess's* to board from the bows. All hell broke lose. The men in the small, bobbing pinnaces fired off their muskets and pistols and the Spanish answered from their high decks, peppering the water with partridge shot from their guns. The still water of the Gulf echoed with the sound of gunfire. White smoke drifted in the warm air. Twice the pinnaces were forced to fall back. *Duke's* lost one man killed and one wounded. *Duchess's* had two wounded. They forced their way forward yet again, into the hail of bullets and this time young John Rogers was shot in the head 'to my unspeakable sorrow' as Woodes Rogers described it.[272]

Duke's pinnace had taken too much punishment. She fell back, transferring some of her men to the *Duchess's* and taking off the *Duchess's* wounded. *Duchess's* pinnace then began to work her way round to the other side of the *Havre de Grace* in order to cut her off from the land but still with the intention of boarding. The Spanish captain guessed what they were up to and now edged out to sea. The pinnace altered course and followed her like a terrier after a bull. Meanwhile, while this bloody fight was going on, *Duke* and *Duchess* had inched closer, cramming on as much sail as possible in order to benefit from what wind there was. *Duchess* was first within range and suddenly ,magically, it was all over. Two shots from her guns was all it took. The Spanish captain struck his flag and surrendered. Hatley had survived. He had been in the thick of the fight from early in the morning until around two in the afternoon. He had proved himself and would soon be rewarded.

The estuary of the River Guayas enters the Gulf of Guayaquil at its north-east corner. At the mouth of the estuary lies the island of Puna which is about the size of the Isle of White, a fertile place, still quiet farming

94

country, then mainly used by the Spanish as pasture for cattle. At its northern point, towards the river, there was a village of around twenty-five thatched houses built on stilts along the waterfront and entered by ladders. The plan was for the main fleet to hang back in the Gulf for forty-eight hours out of sight of land and then to move forward and anchor off Point Arena at the southern tip of the island, there to await the return of the attack party. The attack party would capture Puna village and then make their way up river to Guayaquil on the flood tide.

On Monday 18 April 1709, at one in the morning, the attack party cast loose from the main reserve fleet and set off across the silent moonlit water towards Puna village. The attack boats prickled like hedgehogs, crammed to the gunwales with men and guns. They took with them the captains of the various prize vessels to keep an eye on them. Hatley would have watched them go. He was one of the rearguard, detailed to mind the reserve ships and guard the prisoners. Possibly he needed a rest following the attack on the *Havre de Grace*.

Rest might be too fine a word for it. The *Havre de Grace* had provided another fifty Spanish prisoners and a further mixed hundred of blacks, Indians and mulattoes. There was now a total of 416 prisoners, half black and half either Indian, mulatto or Spanish, and there were only eighty-four men to guard them. Next day, to make matters worse, they took yet another small barque and added yet more prisoners. They sunk the barque shortly after, it was of no use to them. Hatley, as one of the small number of officers left behind, must have been worked off his feet managing this dangerously exposed situation.

As arranged, after forty-eight hours, what might be called the 'prison fleet' moved to Point Arena and cast anchor. The prisoners were allowed to walk the decks in the daytime but were shut up below at night. Although on the *Havre de Grace* where the discrepancy in numbers between jailers and jailed was most extreme, they were put in irons. All communication between prisoners on the various ships was strictly forbidden for fear of a conspiracy and the English sailors 'had their Arms always ready and kept the after-parts of the Ships for themselves'.[273]

95

Six days of this guard duty was hard going and things became very difficult. Two of the wounded from the attack on the *Havre de Grace* died and there was a desperate shortage of water. It had not been planned that they would need water for so many. The prisoners were rationed to a pint per man per day. On Wednesday 27 April 1709, Hatley and Henry Duck, Second Mate of the *Duchess*, were sent to Puna village to collect water and with instructions to sail up the River Guayas for news of the attack party. Duck commanded the *Beginning* and Simon commanded a slightly larger barque of fifty tons which they had found swinging at anchor and abandoned by her owners off Point Arena when they first arrived there.[274] It was presumably his first command.

Hatley and Duck made their way up the coast of Puna Island. There was no word from the attack party and they cannot have known what to expect when they reached the village, but the following morning, to their great relief, they met Woodes Rogers on his way downstream from Guayaquil ahead of the rest. Rogers brought excellent news. The attack had been a success, although not quite as profitable as it might have been.

Woodes Rogers, Dr Dover and the others, together with their men, had begun with the capture of Puna village in the early morning of 20 April 1709, as planned. Having taken the local 'captain' prisoner, they had set off up the River Guayas on the flood tide. When the tide changed the following evening, they hid in the mangrove trees which lined the banks, making themselves as comfortable as they could in the bathroom heat and among clouds of mosquitoes. They set off again, when it was dark and the tide was once more in their favour, and got their first sight of the waterfront of Guayaquil around midnight on 22 April 1709. Although it was midnight, the town was far from asleep. Across the water, they could see that a bonfire was burning and there were lights shining and they could hear scattered gunshots among the buildings. Unknown to them, they had arrived during the festival of the 'Eve of the Invention of the Holy Cross', one of the many Catholic festivals which enliven life in South America that the Protestant English were almost completely ignorant of. One of their Indian guides advised them that what they saw and heard was the town in a state of alarm and preparing for their arrival, so the little flotilla fell back down

96

river to consider their options. They took refuge under the mangrove trees once more and the senior officers crammed into a small boat and moved a short distance off from their men in order to discuss things in private. Rogers was all for immediate attack, fearing that delay would lose them the element of surprise and would allow the Spanish to remove their most valuable possessions from the town. Courtney and Dampier were more cautious. Stalemate. Tempers frayed. Voices were raised in the darkness. Unfortunately they were overheard by a passing Indian. He hurried to the town and found the *Corregidor* of Guayaquil, a young, army officer, a native of Tenerife by the name of Don Iéronimo Bosa,[275] at around three in the morning. There were perhaps a thousand English pirates on the river, he said.

This was the reason that the men back at Point Arena guarding the prisoners had had to wait so long. By hanging back, the attack party had missed their opportunity for a quick, surprise victory. There followed two days of fruitless haggling while the English tried to extract a ransom for not attacking the town, with a separate ransom for the ships in the docks. Don Iéronimo was put under intense pressure. In his later *Apologia*, he said that he could count on only seventy men to defend the town against four hundred hardened privateers so he had to do all he could to avoid a conflict. He went twice to meet the privateers to negotiate in person. He sent them presents of food and wine to keep them sweet. He prevaricated; they threatened. At last, their patience exhausted, the English attacked. They landed on 24 April 1709, on the waterfront, probably where the clock tower now stands, at the end of the short road leading up to the Cathedral. Nowadays, the river is edged with concrete and overseen by a walkway where joggers parade and couples saunter, but then it was just a muddy, tidal river bank. The sailors rammed their boats into the mud and leapt forwards. 'We landed, and fired every Man on his Knee at the Brink of the Bank'.[276] Don Iéronimo had posted a troop of Spanish horsemen across the end of the street who fired a volley and then retreated. The English charged forward and captured the guns outside the Cathedral. Within half an hour, the town was in British hands. Captain Courtney took his party of men to the northern end of the town to secure it and Rogers took possession of the cathedral as his base.

In Woodes Rogers's account of the four-day British occupation of Guayaquil, the British are well disciplined and under strict orders not to overindulge in the local wine. Spanish sources tell a different story. A later witness, at the unfortunate Iéronimo Bosa's trial in Lima, asserted that on the night after the attack the English were so drunk that a counter attack would have routed them.[277]

There followed four days of negotiations and the gathering in of booty while the townsfolk nursed their anger at a distance and ever larger parties of Spanish horsemen patrolled menacingly through the woods on the outskirts of the town. Selkirk and another officer led a party further up the river to search for valuables in the riverside villas of wealthy locals. In one such villa they came across about a dozen well-brought-up girls from Guayaquil who had taken refuge there. The girls had hidden their valuables on their persons. The women of Latin America of the period eschewed the stiff stays and corsets of their European cousins preferring to show a hint of their figures through soft materials, a fact commented on appreciatively by many foreign observers. Selkirk's men, by 'pressing', felt the gold chains and other treasures 'which were wound about their Middles Legs and Thighs etc.'[278] and asked the girls to remove them. It was done with decorum, according to Woodes Rogers, and the girls were so impressed by the courteous behaviour of the English sailors that they prepared food and drink for them.

Woodes Rogers knew how to spin a good tale for the readership back home, but he left out quite a bit. In particular he made no mention of the fraternisation which took place between the senior British officers and some of the Spaniards. At one point during the occupation, Don Iéronimo invited Rogers and others to dine at his house, which presumably was outside the town since otherwise it would have been in possession of the British. Dinner was served by his wife. Don Iéronimo's later accusers suggested that he tried to cultivate the friendship of the British in order to protect his own property.[279] Neither Don Iéronimo nor Woodes Rogers had any interest in publicising this event. Don Iéronimo's fraternisation was clearly suspicious from a Spanish point of view but, from a British point of view, the behaviour of the British officers would hardly have looked any better. Friendly dinners with the Catholic enemy were not what was expected of tough, Protestant, privateer captains.

All these negotiations and contacts had their result. The British agreed to spare the town from burning in return for a ransom of 30,000 pieces of eight, to be paid within six days at Puna in return for four hostages. Although this was a less than perfect result from their point of view, the British, having loaded up all they could carry, left with flags flying and drums drumming. Rogers came away last with a group of picked men 'and pick'd up Pistols, Cutlasses and Pole-axes, which shew'd our Men were grown very careless, weak and weary of being Soldiers'. [280] The Spanish were able to return to their homes.

Having met up with Hatley and Henry Duck, Rogers went to Point Arenas to see Edward Cook and check on the reserve fleet and the prisoners. He was then followed by the rest of the attack party. Having been reunited, the privateers then spent a further nine days off Puna Island because the Spanish had difficulty raising the ransom, or so they claimed. The four hostages became very anxious, fearing that they would end up being taken back to Britain, a fate 'worse than death'.[281] The delay in payment caused further tensions between Woodes Rogers and the other senior officers. Rogers calculated that they could afford to wait a few more days in the Gulf of Guayaquil to gather more ransom before the Spanish were able to send ships against them from Lima; Courtney, Dover and Dampier wanted to be gone as soon as possible. Meanwhile they released most of their prisoners except a few important hostages and sold the *Beginning* which went to one of the Guayaquil hostages. To the Spanish captains of the various ships, who had suffered as a result of losing their ships, they donated slaves and some clothes. Eventually the Spanish handed over 26,810 pieces of eight (Spanish silver dollars), not quite the full total, but enough.

Thus ended one of the most audacious privateering actions of the eighteenth century and Hatley, although not in the thick of it, had more than played his part, as had both Alexander Selkirk and William Dampier.

Fig. 5.9. VISTA DE GUAYAQUIL, desde el río, sector Ciudad Nueva, c1790. (Expedición Malaspina)

View of Guayaquil, 1790

Where the men of the Duke and Duchess landed, modern Guayaquil

the Enchanted Isles

On Sunday 8 May 1709, the little fleet emerged once more into the Pacific, heading for the Galapagos Islands to wood and water. Simon was still in command of his barque. He had a crew of four English sailors with five or six captives to see to, three of them black according to one account, six according to another.[282] The privateers had done well. Only three dead in the attack on Guayaquil and four wounded in return for a sizeable sum of money and much other booty. The Spanish had lost fifteen killed or wounded.

A sense of tiredness, of anticlimax almost, pervades the accounts at this point. The air was hot. There was only a small breeze. There was 'an abundance of dead birds on the Water'.[283] The privateers were still far from able to relax. They had advertised their presence in the South Sea in the most blatant manner imaginable and the small size of their force was now known. They knew that the Viceroy in Lima would be swinging into action. He quickly embarked a special force of three powerful Spanish ships and two French ships to hunt them down, and all along the coast the local governors were ordered to prepare against attack. Coastal shipping was confined to port. The Viceroy also equipped six companies of cavalry. In a rather pathetic postscript, some of the Guayaquil councillors went to the Viceregal palace in Lima to protest about what they saw as Don Iéronimo's spineless behaviour and Don Iéronimo was arrested and thrown into prison. Judgment was long in coming. He was a native of Tenerife and had been *corregidor* for just two years but it was not until 1730, twenty-one years later, that he was brought to trial, then in his forties, and eventually released.[284]

The little fleet crawled slowly westward. It became apparent that some of the men had picked up an infection in Guayaquil. While occupying the town, the men had been bivouacked in various churches. It was customary for the citizens to bury their dead beneath the floors of their churches and Guayaquil had recently suffered a severe contagion. The British sailors had been sleeping directly above the semi-decayed bodies of the victims of a 'plague'. So many of the people of Guayaquil had died from this plague that the authorities had been forced to create an additional, communal grave next to the Cathedral. To make matters worse, some of the sailors had rifled the infected graves looking for plunder. This virulent illness now began to spread through the ships. By 11 May, twenty men were ill on the *Duke* and fifty on the *Duchess*. Captain Courtney himself went down. Soon more than 120 men were sick and on 14 May the first one died. Dr Dover blamed Woodes Rogers for the lack of medicines. Rogers suggested punch, finding it 'did preserve my own health'. They were also very short of water. They were tired and many were ill and they seemed to be lost. Where were the Galapagos Islands?

William Dampier had last been on the Galapagos in 1684 but they were not where he expected them to be. These islands, the abode of strange birds and beasts and of giant turtles which eventually gave their own name, *Galapagos*, had always been slightly mysterious, indeed their original name, given at their discovery in 1535, was *Islas Encantadas*. They were further out in the ocean than Dampier had calculated and *Duchess*, now in desperate straits with most of her crew sick, put on sail and moved ahead of the rest of the fleet. At last, on 14 May 1709, in hazy weather, her sailors saw land ahead and slowed to allow the rest of the fleet to catch up. The following day they were among the islands and *Duke* sent her boat ashore to look for water.

In vain. At first inspection, the islands appeared to be dry. They would have to hunt for water. A meeting place was agreed at a 'remarkable rock'[285] and *Duchess* and the *Havre de Grace* turned towards an island to windward, with *Duke* heading in a different direction. Hatley in his barque (which they intended to convert into a fireship once at the Galapagos)[286] followed *Duchess*. Two days later, having plied between the islands but still without finding water, the fleet met up again by the remarkable rock.

All except Hatley's barque and the old fashioned galleon captured at the beginning of April.

It was all too easy to lose company at sea, even for very skilled navigators. Fearing for the safety of the two missing ships, the little fleet placed lights at their mast heads and fired guns throughout the night but in the morning there was still no sign and *Duke* set off to search for them, standing 'on the Wind to eastward'. Rogers was fearful: 'Here are very strange Currents among these Islands.' By three in the afternoon he had met up with the galleon but still no sign of Hatley or his barque. The following afternoon all the ships were once more gathered near the 'remarkable rock'.

All except Hatley and still no water.

We all bewailed Mr Hatley and were afraid he was lost: We fir'd our Guns all Night, and kept Lights out, in hopes he might see or hear us, and resolved to leave these unfortunate Islands, after we had view'd two or three more to Leeward. We pity'd our 5 men in the Barque that is missing, who if in having a melancholy Life without water, having no more but for 2 Days, when they parted from us. Some are afraid they are run on the Rocks, and were lost in the Night, others that the 2 Prisoners and 3 Negroes had murder'd 'em when asleep; but if otherwise, we had no water, and our Men being still sick, we could stay little longer for them'.[287]

After three more days of fruitless searching, the fleet set sail, still without water and with no sign of the lost ship. They set their course north-west, heading for the tropical island of Gorgona which lies off the coast of what is now Ecuador.

CHAPTER 6

good Dogs were Tories

a Wall of soft Stone

Duke and *Duchess* dropped anchor at the tropical island of Gorgona on 14 June 1709. They were there for more than two months while they 'rummaged' their booty, stowing the most valuable items and selling the more bulky materials back to the Spanish hostages and captains, who managed to raise cash ashore. The privateers were slimming down. Seventy prisoners were freed and most of the captured ships were sold, the *Havre de Grace* was refitted as a warship and renamed the *Marquis*. Briefly back at the Galapagos Islands, it appeared possible that Hatley and his crew might have survived a shipwreck. Some men sent ashore to look for water came across the rudder of a small barque, abandoned on a lonely stretch of coastline. Closer examination however showed that it had been there too long and 'nothing to give us further Hope of poor Mr Hatley':

I order'd a Gun to be fired at a venture, to see if it were possible Mr. Hattley could be there alive, and then seeing or hearing us, might make a Smoake a-shore, as a signal, but we had no such good luck; so that our hopes for him are all vanished, and we finally conclude, that we can do no more for him than we have done already'.[288]

It was time to try for the Manila ship, the original aim of the expedition when it was proposed to the Bristol owners by Dampier. *Duke*, *Duchess* and the *Marquis* sailed north, picking up one or two small prizes along the way. They headed for the remote and desolate bay of Puerto Seguro near the southern tip of the long arm of Baja California, then thought to be an island. Their intention was to loiter off the coast of southern California ready to intercept their prey but there was no time for loitering. At nine o'clock in the morning on 21 December 1709, while they were still manoeuvring to enter the bay by Puerto Seguro, a lookout at the masthead of the *Duke* sighted a sail well out to sea and both the ships' pinnaces went to investigate. She was a large frigate-built Manila ship, *Nuestra Señora de Begoña*, heading for home. The smell of success in their nostrils, the privateers sailed and rowed all through the night over the near-calm water. They had run out of alcohol but even that did not deter their enthusiasm. By the following morning Woodes Rogers was ordering a kettle of hot chocolate on deck to warm the men before they attacked. The crew had just begun to say prayers when the Spanish guns roared out. The captain of the Manila ship, a Frenchman by the name of M. Pincherty, was in no mood to surrender.

Duke returned fire and the sea echoed broadside against rolling broadside, white smoke billowing over the sleepy waves. An unequal combat. As was common at this period, the Spanish rate of fire was far slower than that of the British, so although *Duke* was smaller she was effectively more powerful. With *Duchess* drawing ever closer, it soon became clear to Captain Pincherty that either he must sink or surrender. He struck his colours before the morning was over.

The privateers had won - but not without paying a price. Rogers was shot in the upper jaw by a bullet from a Spanish musket. The bullet had penetrated through his left cheek and had removed a large chunk of his upper jaw and several teeth. His throat swelled up. He was in agony for weeks after and only able to give orders in writing. Things got better some time later when he swallowed something, as his book records with eighteenth-century phlegm: 'I got out a Piece of my Jaw-bone that lodg'd there since I was wounded'.[289]

In 1709, there were two Manila ships and *Nuestra Señora de Begoña* was only the smaller of them. On Boxing Day, a second and much larger vessel, *Nuestra Señora de la Encarnacion Disengaño* came into view. She was a giant of 900 tons, more than three times the size of the *Duke*, bucketing south with the wind in her sails, a much tougher proposition. Among her six hundred passengers were 150 English and Irish, presumably catholic, ex-pirates who were carrying with them all their ill-gotten gains and who were determined to defend themselves whatever the price. This time, the fight went on all day and again on the following day, the privateers circling the giant ship like angry wasps but unable to come close for the kill. Barrels of gunpowder had been hung from the Spaniard's yardarms, ready to be loosed if the privateers should come alongside, and whenever the privateers drew too near they were driven back by 'fireballs' and 'stinkpots'. Boarding offered the only chance of success because canon-shot made little impression on the Spaniard's massive hull. The Manila vessels were built in the Philippines of teak sheathed in lanang timbers making them almost impervious to shot because the wood did not splinter and was 'heavy as stone'.[290] Captain Pincherty later told Woodes Rogers that he had once seen a Manila ship after it had been attacked by the Dutch 'had 90 Balls taken out of her Side, sticking there as it were a Wall of soft Stone'.[291]

After a dreadful forty-eight hours, the privateers returned to Puerto Seguro exhausted. In all, there were three dead and eleven wounded on the *Duke* and twenty dead or wounded on the *Duchess*. *Marquis* was unscathed. Carlton Vanbrugh was badly burned and Woodes Rogers, having directed the fight with his bandaged, broken jaw, had been wounded again. A flying splinter had cut his left heel, the 'Heel-bone being struck out and all wider my Ankle cut above thro'.[292]

It was time to go home. They might have failed to take the bigger ship, but the contents of the *Nuestra Señora de Begoña* were worth a duke's pension and they could honourably consider their voyage a success. Ransoms were organised for the release of the remaining hostages and an arrangement was made for payment of the money outstanding from Guayaquil.[293] The freed prisoners were transferred to a captured barque together with letters for England, letters which were eventually carried back to Europe on the Spanish *flota* across the Atlantic. Such were the courtesies of warfare in those days.

The privateers were now down to four ships: *Duke*, *Duchess*, the *Marquis* (*Havre de Grace*) and the captured Manila ship, renamed the *Batchelor* after Mr Batchelor one of the Bristol owners, each deep-loaded with booty. The intimidating Dr Dover, President of the Council of Officers and shareholder, wanted to be captain of the *Batchelor* but he had no seafaring skills. In Woodes Rogers's opinion, 'his Temper is so violent, that capable Men cannot well act under him, and himself is uncapable'.[294] There were fierce disputes and Rogers, being too sick and wounded to attend Council, was obliged to give his opinion in writing. Dover got his command but with two supplementary captains to help him and Alexander Selkirk as sailing master. Dampier stayed on the *Duke*. There was no Hatley of course. He was lost at sea.[295]

The four ships left Puerto Seguro to begin their long voyage across the Pacific on 12 January 1710. It was 11 March by the time they reached Guam, the men weak with illness and wounds, several dying on the way, and June before they reached Dutch Batavia (Jakarta). Batavia in those days was both eastern bazaar and haven of European order. Neat church steeples pricked the Javan sky but in its teeming, rickshaw-crowded streets, Chinese merchants, Indians, Dutchmen and neat-featured local Javanese with their sharp knives jostled together. Here *Marquis* was sold, 'eat to a Honey-comb by worms'.

Tensions among the officers continued. Dr Dover wrote to the owners in Bristol complaining that Rogers 'weak and thin' was 'a dead weight to all .. who Scorn's to lett his tongue utter anything buy Satyr agst. his Country and Owners so Swelled with pride yt He makes itt a Capitall offence for any officer or man to mention some of yor. Names too often punishing merit & too often advancing such as have prostituted their words and Consciences to his Exorbident desires ...'.[296] The men, however, backed Rogers.

At Batavia they encountered British ships for the first time since leaving home, all of them belonging to the East India Company which held a monopoly on British trade in that region by the terms of its founding charter of 1600. The captains were friendly but the East India Company and its directors were extremely influential back in London and Woodes Rogers had to be careful of more than Dr. Dover. The Company was very protective of its monopoly and it was important that none of his privateers should be seen to be trading with the Dutch even for necessary supplies since this would technically mean a breach of the monopoly. Carlton Vanbrugh put out some feelers but fortunately nothing came of them.[297]

From Batavia, the privateers made their way across the Indian Ocean to Cape Town, arriving on 28 December 1710, where Vanbrugh died of fever, and, on 6 April 1711, they left Cape Town as part of a Dutch convoy for the final leg, the long journey up the west coast of Africa. To avoid any possibility of contact with the enemy, they sailed up the west coast of Ireland, round the Hebrides and down the North Sea. At last, at 7.00 in the evening of 31 July 1711, they cast their anchors at the Texel, the mouth of the Zuyder Zee, out from the long, windswept sand dunes of the Dutch coast. It was the end of an extraordinary adventure. They were almost home – but not quite.

secret Peace Talks suited him

Peace negotiations between Britain, France and Spain had started in January 1711 while the privateers were at Cape Town. The talks were held in total secrecy and without the knowledge of Britain's continental allies. They were led by Queen Anne's Tory first minister, Robert Harley, later Earl of Oxford, friend and employer of both Jonathan Swift and Daniel Defoe. Harley was an attractive character. He drank copiously, loved dinner, collected books* and dabbled in literature. Secret peace talks suited him. He was congenitally secretive. It went with an almost pathological disinclination to state his positions clearly, one of his less endearing qualities. His speeches were vague and meandering to the point of incomprehensibility and his writing was a knotted mass of qualifications, subordinate clauses and subordinate subordinate clauses, often deliberately impossible to fathom.[298] He used Swift and Defoe, in the indirect and

---

* The Harleian collection formed the core of the early British Library.

deniable manner appropriate to his nature, as the two star members of a stable of propagandists who, from apparently independent positions, defended his policies to the general public. In particular, they were needed to undermine the Whigs and the Duke of Marlborough who were opposed to any peace deal behind the backs of the European allies.

It was said that, in those days, honest Church-of-England Tory squires, the type of men who were the backbone of Harley's new government, called their good dogs after Tories and their bad dogs after Whigs. Harley, an ex-Whig and an ex-Dissenter, was basically a bad dog and an unlikely leader for such men. Because of this, his attempt to secure a peace very nearly failed. By the beginning of March, when the privateers were coming towards the end of their stay at Cape Town, he confided to Swift that his rival at the head of government, 'whoring-flagged-when-he-left-town'[299] Henry St-John, later Viscount Bolingbroke, was manoeuvring among the Tory squires in parliament to remove him from power. But then, luckily as it turned out, on 4 March 1711, Harley was stabbed by a renegade former French priest by the name of Marquis de Guiscard. Guiscard, a disreputable character who always went around with a bottle of poison and a dagger in his pocket, had been expelled from France 'for misconduct' but was now suspected of spying for the French government. Called before a cabinet council set up to investigate him, Guiscard had leapt forward and stabbed Harley with a penknife. Fortunately the blade was deflected by Harley's embroidered stomacher and only grazed his breast bone. Harley fell back, 'smelt whether his guts were pierced' and then defended himself with a chair when Guiscard tried again. When it was all over, Harley, ever the collector, withdrew the blade and wrapped it in a handkerchief together with the handle which had broken off and was lying on the floor. He later hung a portrait of Guiscard on his wall.[300]

The assassination attempt transformed Harley's prospects and thereby the peace process. Suddenly he was a popular hero. Crowds enveloped his sedan chair as he was carried home. Complementary odes were published in the city's journals. He stayed in bed for six weeks, milking his convalescence for all it was worth, during which time Guiscard died of the sword wounds he had received from St. John and others. His pickled body was put in a trough for the public to view at a fee of two pence a look.[301] On 26 April 1711, by which time the privateers were sailing north up the Atlantic Ocean, Harley was back in parliament and working on the next step in his elaborate preparations for peace. Shortly before they arrived at the Texel, he pushed through a bill setting up the South Sea Company.

Harley's purpose in setting up the South Sea Company was to regulate government finances without having to have recourse to the Bank of England which was widely seen as a Whig institution and therefore potentially hostile towards his peace plan.♣[302] In early 1711, the government owed around £9,000,000 in 'unfunded' debts because of the war. The largest part of this was £6,000,000 in debts accumulated by the Royal Navy. Marlborough's army on the continent was also spending large amounts, as much as £1,500,000 per year. Harley's South Sea bill ordered that all these debts were to be forcibly converted into shares in the new South Sea Company while, in return, the government undertook to pay £568,276 10s annually to the company, equivalent to six percent interest on the debts. The new company was to have a monopoly of trade to the South Sea as soon as a peace treaty was signed, and the £568,276 10s per year income from the government would be used to finance its trading efforts[303].

On paper everyone was a winner. The government had unloaded its debt and its former creditors now held a negotiable asset in the form of shares in a possibly very profitable enterprise. The creditors were a mixed bunch:

> *We are a wretched motley crew,*
> *More various than the weather,*
> *Made up of debtors old and new,*
> *Jumbled and rocked together;*
> *Tars, soldiers, merchants, transport, tallies,*
> *Chaned in a row like slaves in galleys.*
>
> *We furnished beer, we guns and balls,*
> *We ships or money lent,*

♣ The Bank was established in 1694 with the backing of the then Whig Junto.

110

With hemp enough to serve them all;
O may it so be spent.
And since his payments are so few,
Give Caesar what is Caesar's due.[304]

The bill granted to the South Sea Company:

The sole trade and traffic, from 1 August 1711, into unto and from the kingdoms, lands etc. of America, on the east side from the river Arinoca, to the southernmost parts of Terra del Fuego, on the west side thereof, from the southernmost part through the South Seas to the northernmost part of America, and into, unto and from all countries in the same limits reputed to belong to the Crown of Spain, or which shall hereafter be discovered.[305]

It was a big monopoly. In time, enthusiasts confidently predicted, the South Sea Company could outgrow the East India Company. South America was calling out for British products, they said. The inhabitants of Chile and Peru were desperate for worsted hose, Cheshire cheese, sealing wax, clocks and watches - and slaves. All would be underpinned by the slave trade, which Britain already dominated in other parts of the world. All that was needed was peace and the company could start trading. Plans were mooted for an initial, large trading expedition. The Directors of the East India Company, whose monopoly was supposed to run to the Straights of Magellan, were furious.

Home at last

As a consequence of this, when *Duke*, *Duchess* and *Batchelor* (formerly *Nuestra Señora de Begoña*) cast anchors off the Texel on the evening of 31 July 1711, the South Sea was very much in the public mind but, unfortunately, it was also very much in the mind of the directors of the East India Company. Shortly after the privateers' arrival, a letter reached Woodes Rogers from the Bristol owners warning that the Company was 'incensed against them' and that it was not safe to return to England.[306] The directors of the East India Company suspected that the privateers had traded with the Dutch while at Batavia. This was sufficient grounds to act against them.

111

So near and yet so far. Letters came and went. A period of crippling frustration. July faded into August and August into September. The North Sea was flat, Holland was flat, the men were flat - and starting to become mutinous. They had to be carefully watched when they went ashore. All those on board could do was sit and wait for the outcome of meetings held in London. In August, John Hollidge, one of the Bristol owners, came over to Holland and almost the entire complement of all three ships signed affidavits at his request stating that nothing had been bought or traded at Batavia except things urgently needed for the voyage.[307] To back them up, the Amsterdam agent of Anne's First Minister, Robert Harley, wrote that 'our brave South Sea Adventurers' had sold 'not one Pin's worth'[308] of their cargo in Amsterdam and Harley himself wrote to the East India Company in support.[309] Harley spun his web. On 10 September, the charter incorporating the South Sea Company was signed and sealed and, on 27 September, preliminaries for a peace agreement between Britain and France were at last signed in London.

Britain was effectively out of the War of the Spanish Succession although the official peace was still nearly two years off.

On 2 October 1711, after more than two months in limbo off the Dutch coast, but with the East India Company still making threats, the owners felt that they could wait no longer. After a false start when, despite Selkirk's best efforts, *Batchelor* (the renamed Manila ship) was driven back by high winds, the three ships crossed the Channel with a British naval escort - in case the French should choose to ignore the spirit of the recent agreement. On a calm, clear night, three years and two months exactly since they set sail from King Road at the mouth of the Avon, *Duke* and *Duchess* cast anchor in the Downs, out from Margate on the Kent coast.

They were home at last.

Next day *Batchelor* was escorted round the Kent coast and into the protective waters of the Thames. London was abuzz with the news. Journals such as the *Daily Courant* and the *London Gazette* had reported their crossing of the Channel and their movements up the coast[310]. Bewigged gentlemen in the coffee houses had followed their progress in the papers. It seemed very appropriate, the South Sea being so topical, that a Manila ship should have entered the Thames, the first since Thomas Cavendish's triumphant return in 1588, when he was towed up river his ship rigged with sails of blue damask and his men all dressed in silk,[311] actually in silk grass but no one knew the difference.

There was no such triumphal progress for *Duke*, *Duchess* and *Batchelor*. *Batchelor* was moored at Erith, just up from Dartford, then a small, busy port now a soulless suburb, the old town comprehensively destroyed in the 1960s and 70s. It was near enough to London that they could have smelled the stench of the great city on a west wind, product of innumerable carriage horses, coal fires, unresolved sewage issues, Smithfield meat market and the sheer number of infrequently washed citizens. But no sooner was *Batchelor* at anchor than agents of the East India Company rowed out and threw a note of seizure onto her deck. Attempts to take her by force were beaten off at first and, on 14 October 1711, she was joined by *Duke* and *Duchess*, but, by 17 October, the crew of the *Batchelor* succumbed and she was under the control of the East India Company.[312] Meanwhile press gangs circled. A gentleman called Stephen Creagh, himself formerly a shareholder in two privateers, had been appointed agent by many of the men while they were off the Dutch coast. On their behalf, Creagh now had to pay 'fees of protection' and other charges for the release of 'most of the men impressed at Wapping'.[313] For the miserable men, there was one scrap of silver lining however. Seizure of the *Batchelor* had spurred the owners to come to an accommodation with the East India company. In return for £6,000 from the profits and a smallish bribe, the *Batchelor* was released and the East India Company waived all further claims. They even lent a skilled warehouse man to help in sorting the goods.

The ships were moved upstream and at last came to rest at one of London's docks. The hectic townscape beyond would have been familiar to many, if not most, of the remaining sailors, Wren's new churches pricking the sky and St. Paul's, completed three years earlier, towering above, its great bell almost inaudible during the busiest hours because it was drowned in the ceaseless roar and jangle of coaches, carts and hurrying people. Warehousing started on 11 December 1711 while agents - for the officers and men on one hand and for Woodes Rogers and the owners on the other hand - watched closely. Trust was minimal. Even a small part of the loot could have set someone up for life. There was even an agreement over who should look after the keys to the wharehouse. Apart from the goods stored on the *Batchelor* and the other goods stored in their own hulls, on the *Duke* there were three large chests of plate, jewels, money and gold dust and on the *Duchess* there were four large chests of plate, gold, pearls and precious stones.[314]

Disregard to the ordinary Things

Lawyers and agents hovered like vultures, but so did the literary men in their frenetic quest for novelty, so different to the slow world of ships. It was Richard Steele, co-editor and author of the *Tatler*, who was first to spot the potential literary plunder. During that difficult autumn, Woodes Rogers found time from his endless problems to meet Steele at a London coffee house,[315] perhaps at Steele's regular near the Inns of Court.[316] Rogers was already writing up his journals into a book and Steele may have offered advice. In return, it was probably from Woodes Rogers that Steele first heard of Alexander Selkirk's rescue from Juan Fernandez Island and it may have been Steele who pointed out the dramatic potential of Selkirk's ordeal. Steele went on to meet Selkirk on several occasions, or so he claimed. He wrote an account which was eventually published (late 1713), taking up a whole issue of his then journal, *The Englishman*.[317] He described Selkirk's experiences with rats, cats and sea lions then turned to the man himself:

There is a strong but cheerful Seriousness in his Look, and a certain Disregard to the ordinary things about him, as if he had been sunk in Thought ... after a few Months Absence, he met me in the Street, and though he spoke to me, I could not recollect that I had seen him; familiar Converse in this Town had taken off the Loneliness of his Aspect and quite altered the Air of his Face.[318]

It was two years since Selkirk's rescue and Selkirk had spent almost the entire time since then on crowded ships. Steele must be forgiven a certain poetic licence.

A cold winter came on, a winter of ink. There was a writing race between Woodes Rogers and Edward Cooke, Second Captain of the Duchess. Rogers's ability to keep writing during this period is particularly impressive given the problems which confronted him, but perhaps not surprising from someone who could lead a boarding party with a broken jaw and bone stuck in his throat. Meanwhile, on 11 January 1712, Stephen Creagh laid a complaint on behalf of the men in the Chancery Court. He accused the owners and captains of irregularities and accused Rogers of fraud against the owners.[319] Rogers eventually went bankrupt so this was unfair but the sailors' impatience was understandable. As yet, little or no money had been forthcoming from the voyage. Some men were destitute.

Edward Cooke won the writing race. His *A Voyage to the South Sea and around the World*, rolled off the printing press first, in March 1712, complete with quality illustrations, a dedication to Robert Harley and a plug on the title page:

Wherein an Account is given of Mr Alexander Selkirk, his manner of living and taming some wild Beasts during four Years and four Months he liv'd upon the uninhabited Island of Juan Fernandez.

Disappointingly, there was just a paragraph about Alexander Selkirk inside the book itself. Someone else, the publisher perhaps, must have alerted Cooke to potential interest in the Selkirk story at the last minute or perhaps Cooke had learned that Woodes Rogers was going to make something of it. If anything, Cooke seems to have disliked Selkirk. His second volume, brought out to a more leisurely timescale, refers to the 'Man found on the Island' in more detail but is dispassionate in tone if not faintly disparaging[320] in contrast to the colourful and affectionate account given in Woodes Rogers's book which was soon to follow.

Cooke propagandised for the South Sea trade. His book contained descriptions of all the ports along the Pacific coast of South America and as far north as Acapulco, with plans of harbours and copies of seized Spanish charts, almost a guide book for future British traders. Meanwhile the South Sea Company was planning its next move. In January 1712, both Cooke and Woodes Rogers were consulted about a major expedition for when the war was over.[321] There would be a fleet of twenty-one warships, three of them of seventy guns or more, fire ships or bomb ships, forty transports, hospital ships and four thousand soldiers. Rogers both advised and considered sailing on the expedition. Selkirk would probably have sailed too.[322]

Woodes Rogers's *A Cruising Voyage round the World*, was published a few months after Edward Cooke's book. It is far more entertaining but like Cooke's book it has its propagandist side. Its introduction mirrors, to a remarkable degree, arguments laid out in a proposal which Daniel Defoe had sent to Robert Harley on 23 July 1711, the day the privateers cast anchor at the Texel. In this proposal Defoe had suggested that the South Sea Company should set up a settlement at Valdivia to use as a trading hub for the Pacific.[323]

But if Woodes Rogers was indebted in some way to Defoe for his introduction, he more than repaid the debt. His book had a plug on its title page similar to that on Cooke's title page but less misleading: '... an account of Alexander Selkirk's living alone four Years and four Months in an Island', but Rogers did not make the mistake of short-changing his public. Within was a long description of 'Alexander Selkirk a Scotch Man' and Selkirk's ordeal covering several pages with plenty on goats and sea lions and on taming feral cats and on Selkirk's state of mind.

Here at last were the real riches resulting from the cruise of the *Duke* and *Duchess*, riches which Daniel Defoe would shortly exploit.

William Dampier, sadly, was not part of all this. He was sixty-one years old and his writing days were over. He had other troubles. In July 1712, Selkirk testified against him in a court case brought by the owners of the *St. George*, who felt that they had been cheated during the voyage of 1702-7 and hoped to get their hands on some of the profits from the *Duke*.[324] Selkirk gave written evidence claiming that Dampier 'behaved himself the whole Voyage very ill & very rudely & very vilely both to his Officers and to his Men'.[325] Selkirk is described as 'a material witness ... in a short time going a long voyage to some remote Isles beyond the Seas',[326] probably a reference to the forthcoming great expedition of the South Sea Company. However, that expedition depended on peace with Spain and peace was slow in coming. The goods destined to be sold began to rot.

It was all rather odd. When negotiating the preliminaries for peace the previous summer, Harley had backed off from demands for a British base in Latin America or perhaps on Juan Fernandez Island. With the South Seas trade, he had settled for a fifteen percent reduction on tariffs on British goods to Spain and on the transfer of the *asiento* (the right to supply slaves to Latin America) from France to Britain for a period of thirty years.[327] In the final peace treaty, signed the following spring (1713), the Company was granted the right to trade just two ships per year direct to South America.

There was trouble ahead.

CHAPTER 7

Lima and the Ancient Mariner

the Ruin of me

William Dampier and Alexander Selkirk were back in England but what of Simon Hatley, lost on the other side of the world? After having been separated from his shipmates off the Galapagos, Hatley had sailed for four days, first among the Galapagos islands and then out in the Pacific, standing towards the land, without food or water, vulnerable to attack, in the oppressive tropical heat by day and with the cold stars to remind him of his isolation at night. He kept to sea as long as he could but finally one of the men died and the others rebelled, forcing him to head to the mainland and captivity, a pitifully short end to his first command:

The reason of my having no provision was the ruin of me, for after I had lost company with them, I kept the sea looking for them ... until one of the men that I had died of hunger, then the rest forced me to go ashore on the Maine ... [328]

They touched land somewhere just south of the equator in the province of Quito in what is now Ecuador. It was late May 1709. The most likely spot is the long, sandy beach of Canoa a few miles south of the

118

headland of Cabo Pasado, abode of howler monkeys and, nowadays, of huge, somnolent bulls belonging to the local *estancia*. For a few miles south from Cabo Pasado there are steep, limestone cliffs so that Canoa is the first place where a ship can be safely run aground. Today it is a pleasant resort village where a scattering of beach cafés sleep beneath rattan sun-shades. Then it was a wild place, home to a settlement of 'savage people', half-Indian/half-black, struggling at the margins of colonial society. The population of eighteenth-century South America was a fraction of what it is today and European culture had penetrated less profoundly into the spaces between the towns and the huge estates or *encomiendas*. The forest lands, the wild mountains, the lonely beaches, the rocky headlands existed in a sort of limbo. There were successful settlements of escaped slaves in some of the more remote places and the Indians just to the north of the equator were still completely 'untamed'.* It was at such a wild and abandoned spot that Hatley had chosen to come ashore, perhaps hoping to find food and water undetected. Unfortunately, he and his men were spotted by a local Indian who raised his neighbours. These locals showed an utter lack of regard for the terrible hunger and thirst of the English sailors. They tied their hands, whipped them and hanged them so that they must 'unavoidably have lost their lives, had not a Padre who lived in the Neighbourhood, come time enough by good Providence, to cut 'em down, and save them'.[329]

Thanks to the priest, the captive 'pirates' were kept alive and taken to Lima, over a thousand miles to the south. The first part of this journey was equatorial, probably through Guayaquil, passing through rolling hills, where fat-trunked trees now tower above the surrounding vegetation. Thomas Stradling had made a similar journey a few years before after having been captured following his escape attempt in the canoe[330]. Hatley and his men were taken down the coast[331], possibly on mule back which was Hatley's mode of transport on another such journey[332]. Less than a month had passed since the British attack on Guayaquil and moves were already under way to prosecute the unfortunate *Corregidor*, Don Iéronimo Bosa, and to tighten up the defences. South of Guayaquil and what is now Ecuador lay the

---

* As late as the 1960s, some north American Protestant missionaries were murdered by native Indians along the Esmeraldas coast a little further to the north.

coastal desert of northern Peru, white as snow by moonlight and dull ochre in the light of day, punctuated by low scrub bushes and the occasional settlement. Tough and monotonous to travel through, even more so in chains.

a most delicious Place

After a further three or four weeks of travelling, Lima came in sight. It lay on a gentle slope about six miles inland from the port of Callao. The first thing a traveller saw on approaching was the ornate towers of its churches, seventy-nine in all, rising above the city wall and with just a hint of something Arabic about them from the influence of the many builders of Muslim origin who had worked there. The city's population was around 30,000 according to the Frenchman Amadée Frezier, who was there in 1711,[333] but this is conservative. It was a beautiful place, he said, the perfect location, suspended between the mountains and the sea. It was also unimaginably rich. In 1682, when the Duke of la Plata came to take up his viceroyalty, it is said that the main streets were paved with silver ingots to an approximate total value of 320,000,000 French pounds sterling, a quite incredible sum.[334]

Hatley entered Lima from the north, passing first, under curious eyes, beside a shady walk of orange trees 'the beauty of those Trees always green, the sweet Odour of the Flowers lasting almost all the Year, and the Concourse of the Caleshes* daily resorting thither at the Time of taking the Air, make that Walk a most delicious Place[335]', a powerful contrast with his own wretched state. After that came the spacious, outer suburb of Malambo and then the stone bridge which spanned the Río Rímac, a 'torrent' from the mountains running between the northern side of the wall and Malambo. On most days of the year this torrent was, and still is, more of a slow ooze, but when the snow thaws in the mountains then it becomes a torrent indeed.

Frezier and other travellers waxed lyrical about the climate. It never rained in Lima although each morning, for eight months of the year, a cool, grey mist, hung above the streets and often a fine dew would settle on people's clothing. For water, the river was tapped just outside the wall and

---

* A type of coach.

an excellent and inexhaustible supply was funnelled down skilfully-dug covered channels beneath the main streets to feed the fountains and gardens of the town. There were imperfections: as a result of the lack of rain, Lima would have been very clean if all the streets had been paved, but most of them were unpaved and 'consequently are full of mud and soil'.[336]

The streets themselves were long, straight and wide so that, from the centre, the city seemed to stretch endlessly in all directions and to meet the hills and the sky, always grey in the mornings and clear blue in the afternoons. They were punctuated by squares, thirty-two in all, mostly situated at the front of the churches. The streets and squares were busy with life, crowded with beggars and coaches as well as long trains of mules bringing goods from the hinterland, the semi-frontier world of Indians and *encomiendas* beyond the walls. The huge quantity of mule dung produced by these mule trains and by the mules that pulled the hundreds of coaches soon dried in the rainless air and hot sunshine of the afternoons. It turned to a fine powdery ochre, dust and formed part of the distinctive smell and feel of the city.[337]

Hatley and his men would have found themselves led through a bewildering, brilliant, cauldron of humanity. The faces of the people jostling in the squares and along the streets reflected the wide racial and social range of South American society, a complete spectrum. There were Indians in brightly-coloured textiles, their wide, bronze faces those of the ancient Incas, there were Spaniards and there were all shades of racial mixture in between. Colour was of great significance since shades of whiteness were also shades of privilege. Mustees were the children of Spanish fathers and Indian mothers. Fine mustees were the children of mustees and Spaniards, terceroons had yet more Spanish blood. Mulattoes were half Spanish/half black African. And so on. Lording it over the rest were the Creoles, American born but of pure Spanish blood and, above them, the Spaniards born in Spain.[338] To be white was to hold the ticket to a life of indolence. Race was an obsession. Later in the century, the government offered certificates of whiteness, *credulas de gracias de sacer*, in return for a fee. The more doubt there was about the blood of the supplicant, the higher the fee. All this an echo of the obsession with

121

limpieza de sagre, pureness of blood, back in old Spain - although in Spain the main fear was of Jewish or Muslim blood left over from the *Reconquista*.

Whatever their colour, all Limanistas were united in their love of fashion. Even the beggars, it was said, were the best-dressed beggars in the world.[339] Colonial society both male and female was given over to display, all people delighting in 'unreasonable luxury in their clothing'.[340] Visitors remarked on it. The women, in their ankle-revealing silk skirts, free of hoops or stays, were 'insatiable as to pearls and Jewels, for Bracelets, Pendants and other Ornaments',[341] 'generally beautiful enough, of a sprightly Mien, and more engaging than in other Places'.[342] The men dressed in the most expensive cloth, bedecked with jewels even to their hatbands. And both sexes were festooned with lace, as much as they could afford. In order to display this peacock finery, over a thousand carriages paraded through the streets in the afternoons, so dense that traffic jams formed. The shiny gold and silverwork of the coaches and the elaborate liveries of the drivers and footmen dazzled the eye despite the dust and dirt.

nothing scandalous

And in the midst of this shimmering metropolis what of Hatley? A brief moment of attention as he and his men threaded through in irons and under guard? A woman crossing herself against the evil eye? They were taken to the prison on the Plaza Real, now the Plaza de Armas, the central plaza of the city, two blocks down from the river and the city wall.[343] This was the hub of Lima. It was about the size of a rugby pitch and at its centre stood a magnificent brass fountain with basins at each of the four corners. By custom slaves were the only people allowed to draw water from it, which they supplied to the neighbouring buildings and businesses for small coins, having no other means of subsistence.

The prison was on the west side along with courts of justice and the Council House, all fronted by a long, high-arched arcade. Opposite were the cathedral and the bishops palace. The viceroy's palace was on the north side and along the south side was a row of shops, also fronted by a high arcade. Visitors remarked on the *mudejar* (Hispano-Moorish) style of much

122

of the architecture, product of masons from Andalusia where Moorish influence was strongest. It was an exuberant, over-elaborate style by English standards, 'earthquake baroque' as it has sometimes been called. Hard materials were avoided in construction. Builders used soft materials and these were easily sculpted into rich ornamentation. Sadly, of all these magnificent buildings, only the cathedral is still standing. All the rest of Hatley's date have been destroyed in one of the many earthquakes which plague Lima, to be rebuilt with varying degrees of success by later generations.

Into prison they went and the gates clanged shut. At least there were other British sailors there to greet them. Thomas Stradling and ten to a dozen of his men, together with some of Dampier's from the *St. George*, had been stuck there since early in the war.[344]

It must have been both frightening and tantalising to be so near the centre of a great city, unable to flee and unable to take part. Outside the life of Lima went on its tempestuous, frivolous way; inside there was the tedium and despair of indefinite imprisonment: 'none of us have any likelihood of going home'.[345] Every evening, a mere wall's-breadth away, the crowds would gather under the arcades around the well-lit plaza, so many people that until late at night it was as busy and crowded as at midday. Groups of girls walked arm in arm, sweet scented jasmine in their hair, on the left side for married women on the right side for the unmarried. The admiring men walked to and fro among them or perhaps just leaned against the walls to watch. Some brought chairs so that they could enjoy the spectacle at their ease.[346]

Lima excelled in flattery and flirtation. Seduction was in the air. 'Among them is nothing scandalous; so far from it, that it is a Disgrace not to keep a Mistress'.[347] Even the priests and the members of religious foundations made 'no scruple of it'. Of these there were a huge number, over a million in Spanish America as a whole and a higher proportion than elsewhere in Lima itself.[348] Many of these monks and nuns lived lives of great luxury, employing huge numbers of Indian servants and paid little or no attention to their vows of chastity. As the saying went: 'a priest without children is a priest without balls'.[349]

Young, unmarried Creole girls were strictly chaperoned and consequently unavailable, many being deprived of education and protected from the skill of reading for fear of their being corrupted by forbidden books, but liaisons with married women were a different matter. For a joke, in Cartagena, on the coast of what is now Colombia but culturally similar to Lima, towards the end of the century, a married man bet that he could send the entire city into a state of panic without exerting himself. He simply came home early without allowing time for his wife's lover to leave. The result was a chain reaction of prematurely abandoned trysts, of escaping lovers clambering over walls and out of windows, each returning early to their matrimonial homes and setting off more mayhem.[350]

All this a mere wall's-breadth away. Hatley managed to smuggle out several letters according to Woodes Rogers[351] although only the one remains, that dated 6 November 1709, the official copy now lodged in the National Archives. It shows that he and some of the others had a very rough time. Life revolved around two grim addresses: the prison and, far grimmer, the House of the Inquisition.

the Inquisition

The House of the Inquisition stood on the south side of the Plaza del Inquisition three blocks away to the east, now the Plaza Bolivar. The present building dates from 1736, that which Hatley knew was partially destroyed in an earthquake that year, but the existing building gives a vivid impression of what the earlier one must in part have been like, particularly as it has been converted into a museum for that purpose. Behind the classical pillars, handsome wooden doors give on to the inner hall with, beyond it, the *sala de la audiencia*, the imposing court room, the holding rooms and torture chambers, all conveniently arranged. The polished tiles, the sleek wooden doors, the sensible layout, all testify to the efficient way in which the Holy Office went about its business. In a room to the side which was used as a holding cell, the graffiti by prisoners can be read on the exposed plaster, including a skull and crossbones, emblem either of death or piracy, and the words, in English, 'there is no hope here'.[352]

There were other subsidiary offices, also with full time officers, in regional centres of the viceroyalty but the Lima office was the head office of the Inquisition in Peru. Founded on the continent in 1569, the Inquisition's job was to defend the purity of the Catholic faith, to root out heretics, including Protestants, crypto-Jews, Muslims and witches and to prevent the dissemination of ideas and books which undermined the Catholic faith. This fearsome, bigoted, authoritarian institution wielded immense power. To enter its clutches was to enter a surreal, Kafkaesque world. The Inquisitors made routine use of torture to extract confessions and, what was perhaps more frightening, the accused had no idea what he or she stood accused of, nor of who was doing the accusing.[353] A single accusation, perhaps spoken perhaps in writing, and the hapless victims could find themselves thrown into prison for many years, some never to emerge again. Witnesses, who often included members of the victim's own family, were summoned, interrogated and sworn to secrecy. The victim was completely in the dark, often literally so, while the Inquisitors wove their sinister web around him. All the tricks of the interrogator were available. Early on, the unfortunate was often offered pardon in return for a full confession, but later, if that failed, he was often tortured. Robert Louis Stevenson, author of *Treasure Island*, passed through Lima in the late nineteenth century and left a description of the torture room as it then was. In the middle stood a table about eight feet long by seven wide. It was fitted with an iron collar for the victim's neck and straps connected to ropes for the limbs. By turning a wheel the torturers could tighten the ropes thus stretching the victim's naked body. There was a pillory in one corner, positioned so that the victim could be whipped without being able to see his tormenters. A whole selection of whips hung on the walls, some with knotted thongs and some with thongs of wire. There was a chain-mail tunic with points 'about an eight of an inch long' pointing inwards and leather straps to tighten it. All this along with tongue pincers, thumbscrews and devices for crushing fingernails. Today there are life size effigies in the basement depicting some of these torments along with story boards, but the dusty, rusting implements Stevenson saw *in situ* must have made a more profound impression. He smuggled out a souvenir.[354]

In spite of all this, the Inquisition in Lima was actually a mild affair compared to its vicious parent back in Spain.[355] The first execution took place in Lima in November 1573, four years after it was founded, when Mathew Salado, a French Lutheran, was burned to death in an auto-da-fé in the Plaza Real,[356] but in the 237 years of its active existence only thirty-two people were 'relaxed', the official euphemism for executed, twenty-three of them for Judaism. Only three were English sailors, Walter Tiller, Edward Tiller and Henry Oxley, all executed in 1592 and members of Thomas Cavendish's first expedition to the South Sea. Other English sailors were executed in Lima but not by the Inquisition. They were mainly sentenced to death for piracy by the civil courts.

As the years went by, the South American Inquisition grew still milder and, by Hatley's time, the worst was almost over. All bar one of the executions of Jews, heretics and others performed by its order had taken place in the sixteenth and seventeenth centuries, the last of these in 1664. The last execution of all, by that time an aberration, was in 1736 when Señora María Francisca Ana de Castro, a beautiful woman and a native of Toledo, was executed for Judaism.[357] The process of change had accelerated shortly before Hatley's arrival, at the start of the War of the Spanish Succession, under the influence of the new French Bourbon king of Spain, Philip V. The first Bourbon-appointed Viceroy arrived in Lima in 1709, dying there while Hatley was still in prison, and attempted to shine a tentative beam of light into the medieval mindset of his realm. Don Manuel de Oms y de Santa Pau, a former Spanish ambassador to the French court*, was a passionate admirer of French culture. He founded a liberal literary academy along French lines which met weekly in the vice-regal palace. Among its elite membership he diplomatically included a senior Inquisitor who dabbled in poetry.[358] Don Pedro José Bermudez, poet and Inquisitor, may well have been one of Hatley's judges.

Hatley would have been unaware that the Inquisition was becoming less severe. The terror and cruelty of it were part of bulldog protestant

---

* De Oms was the first to tell Prince Philip that he was to be the next king of Spain - with the words, 'from this moment there are no Pyrenees', a saying commonly attributed to Louis XIV.

mythology, part of the *Leyenda Negra*, the 'Black Legend' of Catholic, Spanish cruelty and intolerance. Once he was there, nothing in his own experience would have led him to change his opinion. Within four months of his arrival under guard, he had already been subjected to a terrifying ordeal, 'plagued by the fathers' as already mentioned, to force his conversion. He and one of his co-prisoners were hanged on a gallows until almost strangled before being cut down. The second time that year. His neck must have been getting sensitive.

He held out. November faded into December. Christmas came and went, celebrated in a grand mass on Christmas Eve in the cathedral across the plaza and, sometime during this period, Thomas Stradling escaped for the second time, was captured by a French ship and taken to Britanny.[359] Hatley and the others remained and were subjected to yet further pressure.

Life outside continued - the traffic jams of jangling coaches, the laughter, the music, the flirtations. In February came the carnival leading up to *Mardi Gras* (Fat Tuesday), the maddest and most gloriously frivolous day of the year, when shrieks of laughter, fireworks and all the sounds of joyous mayhem would have penetrated the thickest walls. It was customary to stockpile egg shells throughout the year, filling them with water which was sometimes scented or dyed with indigo and carmine before they were sealed with wax. When morning came, sleepers were woken with broken eggs and flour paste on their faces. The Limanistas, servants and masters alike, dressed in white from head to toe and made their way out into the streets to give battle. Special projectile tubes were erected on some of the balconies and the iron grills removed to give a clear field of fire. Others, less sophisticated, just sloshed water down onto those below from buckets. Wise men and women took umbrellas but that was poor protection, indeed almost a provocation. All were fair game. Mock sieges took place, usually the women defending a balcony and the men attacking from below. Whole gangs of young people roamed the streets armed with pumps and syringes large enough to throw water into the interiors of houses. Church bells rang, fireworks blazed, the walls reverberated with shouts and laughter, the streets were drenched as were the people. At night, everyone dried off and changed and many ventured forth to dance till dawn, when the bells started ringing for the great procession with yet more fireworks.[360]

One suspects that the sounds of revelry may have done more to encourage thoughts of conversion than the bullying of the fathers. For Hatley and his fellows, the world had shrunk to four walls, iron shackles and the grim journey of three blocks to the House of the Inquisition. Gradually, the remorseless pressure had its effect. In January, Thomas Esterlin, twenty-seven years old from London, joined 'our Holy Mother Church'.[361] In May, Philip Brewer, twenty-two years old, converted, and in October Jacob Gils, a thirty-year-old Dutchman. Finally, on 11 November 1710, Hatley himself stood in the *Sala de Audiencia* before the black-robed inquisitors, by his side his Father Interpreter 'Joranto', possibly an Irish priest. If it was like its replacement on the same spot, this was a long room where the light probed down from deep, high windows with a richly-carved wooden ceiling lost in shadow and a dais at the far end where the Inquisitors sat in judgement. He would have knelt before them on the tiled floor and through his interpreter and instructor he admitted all the 'errors of the Protestant sect' and was reconciled with 'our Holy Mother Church'.[362]

His ordeal was not yet over however. In two more *audiencias*, on 24 November and on 2 December 1710, he was made to acknowledge his errors in connection with a certain small charm. It seems almost incredible that officials of this most fearsome arm of the Spanish Empire should have stooped to deal with such trivia but this is what they did and it was rather typical. In England, men were designing steam engines, building iron bridges and working out the movements of the planets; in the Spanish Empire they were concerned with magic. Hatley was obliged to declare his belief in the efficacy of a magic trick for catching thieves which had been performed by a sailor while he was at sea. A key had been hidden in a prayer book which contained Psalm 49, which key was supposed to move when the name of a thief was mentioned. Simon agreed that such things were the work of the devil and produced a piece of paper on which was written Psalm 49 as a demonstration of his former superstition.[363]

A sop for the inquisitors? Who knows? On 2 December 1710, the business was finally over. Through his interpreter he confessed to all his former errors of belief and asked to be instructed in the mysteries of 'our Holy Faith'. He was instructed to receive the Eucharist three times in a year at the discretion of his instructor. He was to pray, kneeling down, the Our Father, the *Ave Maria* and the Creed. He was also ordered to hear mass on Sundays. He was then reconciled for a second time, absolved of his sins and dismissed.

Perhaps he thought they were mad. His experience allows us a small glimpse into Spanish Catholicism in this period, the result of astonishing levels of superstition and credulity and of an almost complete inability to distinguish form from substance. In the Spanish world, immense care was taken over the minutiae of religious observance while flagrant transgressions of the most basic aspects of the faith were passed over in silence. It was a matter of great concern, for instance, that, after Holy Communion, not a crumb of the host, which was treated with the most extreme reverence, should remain stuck in a dental cavity or elsewhere in the mouth. The sick would be handed a glass of water afterwards and the priest would ask: *'Ha pasado su Majestad?'* – 'Has his Majesty gone down?'[364] The same priest who might well accept a favour afterwards. In Spain it became common practice to kneel when a priest passed by in his sedan chair, even though the morals of priests were commonly despised. An Englishman in Cadiz who did not want to get his knees dirty was accused of being a heretic when he did not kneel. He was quick to kneel after that.[365]

The conversion of Protestant sailors contributed in a small way to this belief industry. Their souls had been saved from eternal damnation. It was an act of grace and therefore things associated with it carried divine power. Woodes Rogers relates the experience of a sailor called Boyce who joined the privateers at Guayaquil having been a captive of the Spanish for several years and forced to convert. Boyce had been baptised in Mexico Cathedral by the abbot who put salt in his mouth and poured oil on his head during the ceremony. The oil was then rubbed off with small pieces of cotton cloth and the pieces of cotton were distributed among the faithful as precious relics[366]. If Hatley underwent something similar, perhaps there were Ancient-Mariner relics briefly in circulation in Lima. Coleridge could have made something of that.

For the sailors the choice was stark: convert like Hatley or either stay in prison or be put to work in semi-slavery in the mines or one of the *obrajes*, workshops where chained Indians, debtors and convicts were forced to toil, usually in appalling conditions. Converts however were freed. Usually they were taken on as servants by some wealthy citizen who acted as mentor and would gain virtue thereby as well as the value of the new servant's labour. Converts could do well. There were a number of English converts in Latin America at this time who had no intention of going home, even if the opportunity presented itself. Woodes Rogers cites, among others, a Thomas Bull, formerly a clock maker from Dover, who had been in Latin America for eighteen years and was living in Tabasco, in Mexico, in 1709, 'grown very rich'.[367]

Simon Hatley did not grow rich, at least, there is no evidence for it. He did however learn Spanish, that much is certain. He was a young man. Perhaps he learned it from a *señorita*.

Graffiti on the wall of the House of the Inquisition, Lima

130

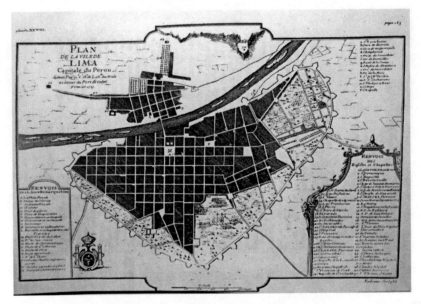

Plan of Lima 1711[368]

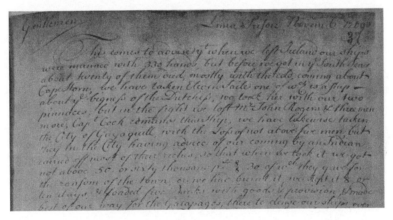

Start of Simon Hatley's letter from Lima Prison, 1709

South American costume, mid-eighteenth century

CHAPTER 8

◆◆◆◆◆◆◆◆◆◆◆◆◆◆◆◆◆

Gentleman Venturers

divvying up

Hatley emerged from the hall of the *Sala de Audiencia* in December 1710. Two and a half years later, on 13 July 1713 when Robert Harley got his final peace treaties, he was free to leave Peru. He would have had little difficulty in finding a ship, probably to Spain and from there to England. Skilled sailors could always work their passage home. Sometime in late 1713, he stepped foot on English soil after an absence of more than five years and walked once more beneath the grey skies of home. He was twenty-eight years old.

He came back to a mess.

Nine public auctions of the loot from *Duke*, *Duchess* and *Batchelor* had been held between February 1712 and May 1713,[369] although the dross, ranging from chests of cloves to 'one old looking glass', was still on offer when Hatley got back.[370] The sales were held at the Marine Coffee House, in Castle Court, a cramped, grey tunnel of an alleyway off Birchin Lane, now in the heart of London's financial district near the Bank of England. Simpson's Tavern, a slightly later building, now occupies the site. The total value of goods sold was £147,975 12s 4^1/$_2$d.[371] A very large sum - but less so once it was divided up.

On the face of it, the voyage had been a success but like so many privateering voyages it ended in a swamp of litigation. Carlton Vanbrugh and William Bath, the owners' agents on the *Duke* and *Duchess*, had both died before they could get home and after their deaths record keeping had been erratic. Suspicions festered in the absence of clear-cut information. Representatives of the officers and crew accused the captains of selling chests of treasure while the voyage was still in progress. The owners, equally hard-done-by after the exactions of the East India Company, refused to recognise claims for 'storm money' by those who had taken part in the attack on Guayaquil.[372] Woodes Rogers went quietly bankrupt.[373]

It was August 1713, nearly two years after the return of the *Duke* and *Duchess*, before the Master in Chancery felt able to authorise payments to the crew. These were calculated at £42.6s 0d per share, the original contracts having been based on a choice of wages or 'shares instead of wages'.[374] Most men had opted for a combination of the two and they felt cheated by the settlement. They had captured a treasure ship. It should have been like winning the lottery. They had expected a return of around £1,000 per share so £42.6s 0d felt like an insult.[375] And there were other complications. Notices of the judgement were posted at Wapping, Limehouse and other places frequented by sailors, but many of the crew had since sailed on other voyages, died or borrowed against their shares. A few, such as Simon Hatley were listed as 'lost'.[376]

Hatley was eventually paid £180 10s 2d after deductions for purchases on board and for his contribution to the 'Chatham Chest', a pension fund for seamen.[377] £180 was a small sum compared to Woodes Rogers's £1,530 but it was better than nothing, enough to buy a house or two in Woodstock for instance. In addition, by a general order of the court of May 1714, he was granted £40 'storm money' for his part in the taking of the *Havre de Grace/Marquis*. To put it in context, wages of merchant seamen ranged from as little as £1 per month to the £2 16s, noted in Edward Cooke's book, fluctuating considerably according to demand. In normal circumstances an ordinary skilled seaman might have expected to be paid between £24 and

£46 10s for the sixteen months that Hatley was at sea, a junior mate perhaps twice that amount.[378]

Queen Anne died that August. Towards the end she had grown very fat and swollen, her health destroyed by the burden of multiple pregnancies and by a reign almost entirely dominated by war. She had retained the beautiful, bell-like speaking voice for which she was renowned but it was captive in a bloated and unsightly body. A special apparatus of ropes and pulleys was necessary to raise and lower her between floors at Windsor Castle, an apparatus originally constructed for Henry VIII.[379] She was buried in a huge, almost-square coffin in Westminster Abbey.

In her place came George I, Elector of Hanover. George harboured ambivalent feelings about his new kingdom. He resented that, in negotiating separately for peace, Britain had left her continental allies, including Hanover, in the lurch and because of this he nursed a particular grudge against the Tories, the party which had backed Robert Harley's peace negotiations. His protuberant, china-blue eyes fastened with animosity on Robert Harley, architect of the peace, and within a year of George's accession Harley was in prison in the Tower. At around the same time, Henry St. John fled to Paris disguised as a servant, where he became a Jacobite.

Times were hard. There was no need for privateers now that war was over. The Royal Navy contracted in size. As many as 40,000 sailors found themselves unemployed.[380] There was a surge in piracy. Unemployed men of the *Duke* and *Duchess* hung around the dockside bars and nursed their grievances. The litigation rumbled on. In August 1715, nearly four years after their return to England, the men petitioned the Lords that they had been badly treated by the Master in Chancery who, they said, had refused to listen to their earlier accusations of fraud. Some also seem to have fallen foul of their agent, Stephen Creagh, who had threatened them with a whip.[381]

The officers also had their problems. Selkirk does not seem to have responded well to the brief moment of fame resulting from the publication of Edward Cooke's and Woodes Rogers's books. He had held the same number of shares as Hatley, quite generous considering he was rescued well

135

into the voyage, and had received a similar sum of money.[382] He had met Richard Steele and possibly Daniel Defoe,[383] had sat in fashionable London coffee houses and had tasted the interest of well-placed and famous men but perhaps it was unpleasant to be the object of their curiosity. There was a universe of difference between his sailor's life in remote and dangerous places and the domestic hustle and bustle of Britain, a difference that they could never fully comprehend. In September 1713, he was charged with assault in Bristol.[384] He was probably drunk. He moved back to his home town of Largo to stay with his family and bought a house, but he was unable to settle down there, and soon there was another violent incident.[385] He moved to London.

In part, the interminable legal actions were a result of the sheer complexity of the financial mess which grew up after their return: percentages, wages, bribes, expenses, shares, storm money, advances and purchases on credit were all in the pot together. It was a nightmare for those who tried to sort things out. William Dampier died in March 1715 in his house in Coleman Street in Old Jewry in the City of London without receiving the full payment of his potential £4,551 in combined wages and share of the owners' profits. And still things rumbled on. As late as 1717, £1000 was paid to his estate.[386] An account dated 10 August 1717, even later, addressed to Stephen Creagh and Woodes Rogers was still attempting to tie up the loose ends. It summed up 'purchase taken, wages and shares and also storm money'.[387]

And by that time, the peace showed signs of unravelling.

so inestimable a Jewel

The main function of the South Sea Company at its formation had been to raise money for the government but, on paper at least, it was also meant to be a genuine trading company. It had to keep up the appearance of trade in order to encourage further investment and not to be exposed as the purely financial, speculative engine it really was. For the directors, trading proved to be considerably more difficult than raising money, in large part due to the recalcitrance of the Spanish. The Spanish authorities were as hostile to foreign, Protestant penetration of their markets after the war as they had been before and during it. Defoe had predicted this in his *Essay on the South Sea Trade* of 1711:

> *Unless the Spanish are to be divested of common sense, infatuate, and given up, abandoning their own commerce, throwing away the only valuable stake they have in the world, and in short, bent on their own ruin, we cannot suggest that they will ever, or for any equivalent, part with so valuable, indeed so inestimable jewel, as the exclusive power of trade to their own plantations.*[388]

The Spanish did almost everything possible to frustrate the South Sea Company. Three company slave ships sailed in 1714 carrying 1,230 Africans in the usual vile conditions, but they were not allowed to land their hapless cargo and the slaves were eventually sold in the West Indies.[389] Subsequent years brought larger shipments and more thousands of slaves but always bureaucratic difficulties and never any decent profit. The same sorts of prevarications and delays plagued the two general trading ships per year allowed under the treaty, although, to be fair, some of the problems were self-inflicted and speak volumes about the South Sea Company's inefficiency as a trading concern. In 1714 one of the first two ships was loaded exclusively with woollens, hardly a suitable product for the tropics. There was no annual trade fair at Cartagena that year and the woollens were still in Cartagena two years later, unsold and 'subject to the moth and other vermin which abound there'.[390]

The Spanish monarchy had been humiliated by the Treaties of Utrecht. As well as being forced to grant trade concessions to the South Sea Company, they had lost Gibraltar, Minorca, Sardinia and their territories in Italy. If it had been up to the Spanish king, Philip V, nothing much might have happened, but lazy and depressive Philip was easily dominated by his forceful Italian wife, Isabella Farnese. In the stilted, gloomy world of the Spanish court, Isabella began to plot revenge. She considered the loss of Spain's Italian territories to be an insult to the Spanish crown.[391] In November 1717, Spanish forces invaded Sardinia, now controlled by the Austrian Emperor, and once that was conquered they moved on to invade Sicily, formerly under Spanish control but now also an Imperial territory. On 2 August 1718, Britain, Holland, France and Austria finalised a

'Quadruple Alliance' in order bring Spain back into line. Nine days later, on 11 August 1718, the British fleet under Admiral Byng destroyed the Spanish fleet off Capo Passaro to Spanish complaints of 'barbaric behaviour'[392] because the two countries were not yet formally at war.

our caesarian and imperial Flag

War was coming anyway, a short war of almost medieval pointlessness caused by dynastic pride and very little else. It is perhaps no coincidence that, around this time, Daniel Defoe sought relief from current affairs in a new venture. He had been using fictional elements in his writing for some time. In 1714, he had fallen in with an eccentric publisher by the name of Samuel Keimer who gave him a further push in this direction. Keimer was a French Prophet. He wore yard-long green ribbons, symbol of the sect, and an unfashionably full beard in accordance with the requirements of *Leviticus*, and inside each ribbon was sewn a slip of parchment, on it the words 'Jonathan of the Tribe of Asser' - his sect name - so that God would be able to identify him as one of the Elect on the Day of Judgement.[393] Keimer's mind was open to fantasy. Defoe experimented with the use of dialogue and character to support his arguments. He wrote a number of semi-fictional political pamphlets for Keimer, what might be described as 'faction'. They included 'secret histories' in which a semi-fictional narrator sees behind the scenes of recent important events. The secret histories pushed the envelope of fiction. The most successful of them, published in 1717, was *The Minutes of the Negotiations of Monsr. Mesnager*. Here the narrator is an under-secretary to Louis XIV, a real man although the words which he speaks are Defoe's alone. By means of Monsr. Mesnager, Defoe manages both to criticise the Peace of Utrecht and simultaneously to defend his former protector Robert Harley, an achievement given that Harley was the architect of the treaty but possible because it was largely fiction. And in 1718, between pamphlets and articles, Defoe took his interest in fiction to its logical conclusion. He began work on what is reckoned by many to be the first true novel in the English language - *Robinson Crusoe*.

Meanwhile, others were prepared to pursue their fantasies in reality. Unwilling to wait for a formal declaration of war, a group of unscrupulous London merchants, the 'Gentleman Adventurers' Association', made plans for a new 'cruising' expedition to the South Sea. Their objective was plunder pure and simple with barely a fig leaf of patriotism to justify it. Their ships would sail under a commission from the Austrian Emperor since the Austrian Empire and Spain were already at war in southern Europe.[394]

The principle partner in the Gentleman Adventurers' Association was a wealthy, ex-Royal-Navy purser by the name of Edward Hughes. There would be two ships, the *Success*, 350 tons and thirty-six guns, and the *Speedwell*, 200 tons and twenty-two guns. Hughes chose a former shipmate to be overall commander and to captain the *Success*. This was Captain George Shelvocke, then aged forty-three. Shelvocke, from a Shropshire farming family,* was a skilled navigator who had joined the Royal Navy at the age of fifteen and had risen to the rank of lieutenant. He had at one time been shipmates with Edward Hughes.[395] In 1713, at the end of the War of the Spanish Succession, he had been stood down along with many others and times had been difficult ever since. Shelvocke, forty-three years old, corpulent and a cripple from gout, was almost destitute when Hughes invited him to stay at his country house that summer in 1718 in order to discuss plans. Hughes advanced £20 to tide him over.[396] Shelvocke could scarcely believe his luck.

The Gentleman Adventurers set out to recruit a team of senior officers with experience of the South Sea and of buccaneering or privateering ventures. The Second Captain of the *Success*, serving under Shelvocke, was to be the former buccaneer John Clipperton, last heard of in 1704 in the Gulf of Nicoya when he mutinied against William Dampier on the *St. George*.[397] Clipperton's subsequent marauding voyage round the world was ample qualification. The Captain of the smaller *Speedwell* was a gentleman by the name of Robert Mitchel, of whom nothing more is known but the Second Captain, serving under Mitchel, was to be none other than Hatley,

---

* He was christened 1 April 1675 at St. Mary's Church, Shrewsbury, and had served with Admiral Benbow, himself a Shropshire man.

now aged thirty-three and risen to become a senior officer. Hatley's experience on the *Duchess* and his knowledge of the South Sea and of Peru would be very useful. Hughes's intention was to follow the successful formula of the voyage of the *Duke* and *Duchess*. To this end, he arranged for copies of Woodes Rogers's book, reprinted the previous year, to be placed on both vessels.[398] It was intended that the senior officers should confer frequently, as had been the practice under Woodes Rogers, in order to avoid dissension.

That autumn, before he set sail once more, Hatley travelled the winding road to Woodstock, where nearby Blenheim Palace was now rising like a wedding-cake from the chaos of its building site. His father had died in 1712 while Simon was in prison in Lima and Simon had inherited numbers 46-8 and 50 High Street, the three rental properties at the top of High Street.[399] He was to come into full possession of them on the death of his mother. However, on 29 September 1718, 'Simon Hatley, Mariner, Gent.', and 'Mary Hatley, Widow', his mother, signed an indenture conveying numbers 46-8 and 50 to his sister, also Mary, and her husband Blagrove Gregory, the son of another family of prominent Woodstock aldermen. Hatley and his mother received £140 in return.[400] There is no hint in the documents as to why he needed this money. Perhaps he intended to invest it in the coming voyage or in some other voyage, perhaps he was buying South Sea stock, perhaps he was just plain broke. One thing is certain - it marked a break in his association with his home town. Woodstock with its provincial preoccupations, its suffocating local hierarchy, its Tailor-of-Gloucester, paned windows and its pretty stone houses (his brother William still at number 6/8 High Street),[401] may have seemed dull after London and the prospect of another major voyage to the South Sea. With his father dead, his mother very old and due to die shortly and his property sold, Hatley's connection with home was growing faint.

That November 1718, Shelvocke crossed the English Channel in *Speedwell*, the *Success* remained moored in the Thames in the process of fitting out. He moored in the neat harbour of Ostend, where the tall, gothic spires of the Cathedral still loom over steep, gabled rooftops reconstructed after more recent wars. He was to purchase alcohol for the voyage and to

140

collect his commission from the Austrian Emperor in Vienna. It authorised him to sail: 'well fitted and furnished with arms, through any seas far and wide, to follow any such as are enemies of Our Most August House ...'[402] and, after various stipulations and conditions, 'We allow to the above-mentioned Capt. George Shelvocke the free use of Our Caesarian Flag, Arms and Ensign'. The imperial flag would come in useful but one more bit of window dressing was needed in order to emphasise the voyage's Austrian credentials and thus minimise accusations of piracy. *Success* was renamed the *Prince Eugene* and *Speedwell* was renamed the *Starhemburg*.

The prospect of command after years of destitution seems to have gone to Shelvocke's head. He behaved like a child let out of school. The owners had instructed him not to raise the Imperial flag and not to fire off his guns. Shelvocke proceeded to hoist the flag, break open the wine and brandy, entertain on board and to fire off five barrels' worth of gunpowder. In addition, he recruited ninety Flemish sailors and six officers when he had been advised to keep the numbers down to sixty men with three officers. All this took longer than it should have and when he returned to the Downs he found that the *Success/Prince Eugene* was there before him ready to sail and Hughes and two other of the owners were waiting at nearby Deal and very concerned at his late arrival. Hughes was so put out by Shelvocke's behaviour that he decided on a complete alteration to the structure of command. The Flemish sailors were sent home with two months' wages, Mitchel disappeared from the scene, Shelvocke was demoted to captain of the *Speedwell/ Starhemburg* and Clipperton was made Captain of the *Success/Prince Eugene* and overall commander.

It was late autumn and the leaves had fallen from the trees by the time Hughes and his partners returned to London. *Speedwell* and *Success* then made their way round the damp, autumnal coastline to Plymouth, to the Devon coast where the grey bulk of Dartmoor looms behind. They arrived in Plymouth's snug harbour in November and loading got under way immediately, the laden carts at the quayside, the creak of capstans and pulleys, the shouts of the men. But they were late. The original plan had been to catch summer in the South Atlantic so that the weather would not be too fierce when they rounded the Horn. Shelvocke's delay at Ostend had prevented this. There was one advantage however - late in the year, Spain confiscated all the assets of the South Sea Company in South America and on 28 December, Britain declared war. It was now possible for the Gentleman Venturers to arrange for a new commission directly from the British government, a more convincing arrangement than that with the Emperor. The new commission was made out to the name of John Clipperton.

Shelvocke's demotion had poisoned the atmosphere and Clipperton, 'a blunt, rough, free-spoken Sailor, [who] had not much the Air of a Gentleman',[403] did nothing to mend matters. He made it no secret that he would have preferred Hatley as captain of the *Speedwell*, Simon being 'much such another as himself'[404] according to Shelvocke. By this, Shelvocke meant that both Clipperton and Hatley were buccaneers rather than regular navy men, with all that that implied in terms of lax discipline and possibly piracy. Shelvocke believed that the navy was 'the only nursery for Sea-Officers' and claimed that Clipperton was 'a stranger to regular discipline'.[405] Tension between irregulars such as Hatley and Clipperton and navy men such as Shelvocke went back a long way, to Pepys's deliberate creation of a gentlemanly officer class for the Royal Navy back in 1677 with the introduction of lieutenants' exams. The irregulars for their part saw themselves as the equals of naval officers, or ex-naval officers, but with more initiative and freedom of spirit. The worst thing that Clipperton could say of a man was 'that he had serv'd in the navy.[406,407] Indiscipline was far from the sole preserve of irregulars. Ever since Pepys's reforms there had been complaints of drunkenness and of naval ships in port cluttered with the gentlemen captains' hangers-on: 'near twenty landmen has his footmen, tailor, barber, fiddlers, decayed kindred, volunteer gentlemen or acquaintances'.[408]

Factions formed among the officers. Clipperton took to visiting Hatley and the other officers of the *Speedwell* and together they would ridicule Shelvocke. Shelvocke claimed, histrionically, that Clipperton told the officers they 'would soon have an occasion to toss me overboard'.[409] Shelvocke did not cope well. He grumbled and was petulant. He said that Clipperton was not fit to be 'given in the charge of a collier'. He criticised the owners publicly. Eventually a stern reproof arrived from London and he was obliged to write a series of grovelling replies. Reading between the lines, what he describes in his book as his 'ill state of health' was probably caused by drink. His love of the bottle was remarked on. William Betagh, Captain of Marines on the *Speedwell* (and, as an ex-naval purser, a man who should have been a natural ally) decided that his captain was a drunk with a 'particular affection for strong liquors'.[410]

Provisioning proceeded tortoise-slow and winter drew in. Gradually the ships filled up with the usual provisions: casks of bread, biscuit, salt beef, suet, cheese, flour, oatmeal, dried peas, water casks and ammunition. Animals were herded into pens on deck. More crew were recruited. But the window of opportunity for a summer passage round the Horn had long passed. Winter was almost over and snowdrops were peeping through the soil when *Speedwell* and *Success*, now shorn of their Imperial names, set sail for the South Sea in 'fresh gales and squally with rain'.

Somewhere, thousands of miles to the south, an albatross was wheeling in the wind.

CHAPTER 9

◆◆◆◆◆◆◆◆◆◆◆◆◆◆◆◆

t𝔥e Albatross

Journey of Discontent

The ship was cheered, the harbour cleared,
Merrily did we drop
Below the kirk, below the hill,
Below the lighthouse top.

Coleridge, at the outset of *the Rime of the Ancyent Marinere*, probably had in mind the little port of Watchet in North Devon where he began to write his poem. Although *Success* and *Speedwell* set sail from Plymouth, the rituals of departure would have been roughly as Coleridge describes them. Privateers left port with flags flying, often to the cheers of onlookers and firing their guns in salute.[411]

It was 13 February 1719. *Success* and *Speedwell* set their course for the Canary Islands, the first *rendez-vous* point should the two ships become separated. Unfortunately, a storm hit them four days out. Neither ship was yet fully seaworthy and the storm raged continuously for two days. *Speedwell* was in particularly poor shape. Her eighteen-pounder guns were mounted between decks when they should have been stowed low down in the hull for better balance. There was no room below because she was

144

carrying the entire stock of alcohol for both ships, a curious oversight. By the evening of Thursday 19 February 1719, the wind howling, she had all her sails taken in and was being tossed like a toy under 'bare poles'. As midnight approached, she was hit by a monster wave which smashed down out of the roaring blackness. It broke off her stern and quarter dead lights, plates fitted over the portholes, and the water poured in. Men prepared themselves for death in the dark chaos. Many of them were landsmen and had never known anything like it before.

With the dawn came some slackening of the wind. Older hands shook themselves and looked around, but there was no sign of *Success* on the heaving, grey circle of the sea. Shelvocke pointed to some flotsam which drifted close by and suggested that she had gone down in the storm and this was the remains of her.[412] He ordered the topsails to be set but, instead of renewing his course for the Canaries and the *rendez-vous* point, he turned north-west for several days. He had no evidence that the *Success* had sunk and it is hard not to conclude that he was trying to lose her. The two ships would not see each other again until nearly two years later, in January 1721 in the Pacific.

The storm had been a bruising experience. Men who had joined in light-hearted optimism now realised that they were in for something dangerous. Seventy of them rebelled and demanded that the ship turn to windward and home. It took all the officers fully armed to bring them under control. Shelvocke was an odd mixture of deceit, courage and weakness. Instead of punishing the ringleaders, as Woodes Rogers would have done, he resorted to his favourite remedy, brandy all round, finding that 'the dram being once or twice repeated, proved the best means of entirely oversetting their wicked intentions'.[413]

Relationships between second captains and captains were often difficult. The second captain of a ship (or her first mate) was nearly always an educated man and a skilled navigator. He had to be able to assume command if the need arose and was therefore a potential threat to the captain's authority. Shelvocke now blamed the mutiny on Hatley. There was a furious row between them on the open deck in front of all the men. Hatley criticised Shelvocke's seamanship. He claimed that his greater

145

knowledge of the South Sea made him more fit to command and that he had secret orders from the owners and from Captain Clipperton to that effect.[414] In response, Shelvocke ordered the crew to address Hatley as plain 'Mr Hatley' from then on. It is likely that both men were drunk or at least well oiled. All ships ran on alcohol but *Speedwell* was awash with the stuff. Shelvocke's favourite tipple was hypsy, a mixture of wine, water and brandy which he consumed 'in a wanton manner' believing it to be an antidote for gout.[415]

Having tarried off the Bay of Biscay, *Speedwell* came in sight of the peak of Teneriffe on 17 March 1719. *Success* was already long gone. By the time *Speedwell* left the Canaries ten days later, having taken her first prize, a small Spanish ship of no great value, *Success* was on the point of leaving the next *rendez-vous*, the Cape Verde Islands. If Shelvocke's intention was to rid himself of Clipperton, he had already succeeded.

From the Canaries *Speedwell* sailed sullenly south. All arms were locked in the bread room in case of mutiny. They sold the prize at the Cape Verde Islands but then were mistaken for pirates, which was not so far from the truth. Turner Steven, the gunner, went so far as to suggest that they tear up their orders and sail round Africa to the Red Sea, there being 'no harm in robbing those Mohometans'.[416] On Monday 20 April 1719, after various dismissals and desertions, they began the long Atlantic crossing, the weather varying from light breezes to 'sometimes great squalls of wind and rain, with thunder and lightning', 'the most uncertain weather imaginable'. For Hatley it must have been forty-one days of discontent, either out on watch or huddled in the great cabin drinking hypsy and listening to Shelvocke.

On 4 June 1719, they came in sight of Cape Frio on the Brazilian coast east of Rio de Janeiro, and the next day they saw a merchant ship out from Rio come butting through the waves towards them. Perhaps Shelvocke and Hatley were drunk, perhaps Shelvocke thought only of his recent destitution, perhaps Hatley had invested his money in the voyage and wanted a swift return. What is certain is that they acted foolishly. The strange ship was Portuguese. The Portuguese were long-standing allies of Britain and any aggressive act towards her involving profit was piracy.

Nevertheless a musket was fired across her bow to bring her to and Shelvocke raised 'Our Caesarian and Imperial Flag' which he still had on board. The emblem on the Austrian Imperial flag was a black eagle on a yellow field and from a distance it could be mistaken for a skeleton on a light background, a common flag of pirates. Hatley, suddenly Shelvocke's 'best busker',[*][417] rowed across in the ship's boat, his men armed to the teeth with muskets and pistols.

Despite the protestations of innocence in Shelvocke's book, it is clear that Don Pedro, the Portuguese captain, was under the impression that he was being attacked by pirates. On seizing a ship, it was common practice for a pirate leader to enquire of the common sailors if their captain was 'an honest fellow that never abused any sailors'. Don Pedro feared 'blooding and sweating', the process by which a merchant captain 'on the ill report of his men' was forced to run the gauntlet naked through the pirate crew, each pirate armed with a sail needle to prick him in the buttocks, back and shoulders, after which he was placed in a sugar cask swarming with cockroaches, covered in a blanket and left to 'glut the vermin with his blood'.[418]

Whatever transpired, Don Pedro was remarkably generous. Hatley returned to the *Speedwell* with fresh fruits, three or four dozen boxes of marmalade, other sweetmeats, Dutch cheeses, a large quantity of sugar, a dozen pieces of silk flowered with gold and silver, several dozen Chinese plates and basins, and a small Japanese cabinet. More importantly, he took a purse containing three hundred gold Portuguese *moidores*, worth around £400, six each for the boat's crew, ten for the boatswain, eighty to a hundred for Hatley and the rest for Shelvocke.[419] Hatley's share was worth between £108 and £135, a significant sum in those days, enough for instance to buy a modest property in southern England.

The Portuguese captain sailed off and *Speedwell* continued south-west, along a land 'very woody and many small rivers also many wild parrots, paroquets and maquaws'[420]. They sailed past Grande Island where *Duke* and *Duchess* had provisioned, and past Santos, port for Sao Paulo,

---

[*] Busker - one who cruises for prey on the high seas, from the Spanish *buscar*, to search.

147

once captured by Cavendish. Brazil was little known in eighteenth-century Britain. Beneath the carpet of trees extending a vast distance inland, the *Paulistas*, Indian/Portuguese slave traders based at Sao Paulo were at that time extending the frontiers ever deeper into the jungle, a brutal process which had started in the sixteenth century. They marched behind holy banners in *bandeiras* sometimes many thousands strong. On a raid into the Jesuit colonies of Paraguay, set up as a haven offering protection from the *Paulistas*, one *bandeira* netted fifteen thousand Indian slaves, tying them to long poles for the return journey to Sao Paulo. Indian slaves were worth around thirty to forty dollars compared to well over a hundred dollars for Africans so quantity was important.[421] The last raid took place in 1750.

Shelvocke was heading for St. Catherine's Island about three hundred miles further along the coast, basing his decision on the account in Amadée Frezier's book. Frezier described a safe anchorage, good, pure water and 'wholsome Air', the only slight disadvantage being an infectious distemper called *Mal de Biche*, which caused a headache 'attended with a *Tenesmus*, or continual desire of going to Stool without doing anything'.[422] The cure - a 'Plaister of Gunpowder ... applied to the Fundament'.

At 11.00 in the morning on 20 June 1719, *Speedwell* let go her anchor in about six fathoms of water in the channel between St. Catherine's Island and the mainland. At first sight, it was a tropical paradise. The shore was clothed in 'a continual Grove of Trees which are all the Yeare green', woods 'extremely fragrant, from the many aromatic trees and shrubs with which they abound'.[423] There were small sandy bays and only a scattering of ramshackle houses further along the shore.

The locals, when they made themselves known, were a mixed bunch of fugitives and free spirits who had fled to St. Catherine's from other parts of the wild lands of Brazil. They maintained a precarious existence without any formal authority apart from a 'captain' of indeterminate status. There was no resident priest and there were only a few 'tame' Indians. The locals wore 'tyger skins' when they ventured into the woods, as a form of stocking to cover their legs because the woods were so thickly tangled.[424] Their staple diet was monkey.

There was wildlife in profusion, above all - birds. Vespucci had described the birds of Brazil back in 1504:

What shall I say of the number of their birds and the variety of their plumage, colour and song and their many species, and their beauty? I do not wish to expatiate on this for I doubt that I would be believed ...[425]

Early maps of the area of the South America near St. Catherine's Island referred to it as the 'Land of Parrots'. St. Catherine's Island itself was brilliant with them. Parrots were valued by sailors both as food and as exotic pets. In the sixteenth century, a French ship paid for its passage home with a cargo of six hundred parrots and they doubled in value during the voyage because they had learned to swear in French.[426]

It is hard to visualise this land of parrots now. It has become a city, 'Florianopolis', named after Floriano Peixoro, the 'Iron Marshal', President of Brazil 1891-94. Its total population, including surrounding satellites, exceeds 800,000 people and it straddles both the island and the mainland. It has an airport, hotel chains, shops and nightclubs. At night, the glow of its lights almost blots out the moon.

The English sailors set to work, sticky with sweat in the semi-tropical heat, fanning out across the island, the carpenters to fell trees for planks and the coopers to trim casks ready for fresh water, the remainder stowing guns low down preparatory to the dangerous ordeal of the Horn. But all was not well. For all his posturing, Shelvocke's grip was weak. During those weeks in 1719, things got completely out of hand. Perhaps it was the hot, close air, perhaps it was an outbreak of *Mal de Biche*, perhaps it was drink. Hatley, if Shelvocke is to be believed, behaved particularly badly:

He was bad enough to act any unhandsome part, especially if one may be allowed to judge of a man by his actions, for, at this place, from our first arrival, he began, and continued to comit such outrages, that I had daily complaints of his abusing their women in the grossest manner; and further, that he, and a gang that used to go about with him to buy fresh provisions, had threatened to ravish old and young, and set their houses on fire; nay and actually burnt one, which the inhabitants had permitted us to use as long as we had occasion for it.[427]

149

A far cry from the 'poor Mr Simon Hatley' described by Woodes Rogers - except that the building, used as a temporary workshop by the coopers and sail-makers, was burned by Second Lieutenant Randal and not by Hatley at all.[428] Hatley may or may not have undergone some sort of moral deterioration at St. Catherine's Island and Shelvocke was happy to libel him to that effect, but on the other hand, Shelvocke was equally happy, so it seems, to take Hatley's advice. He gave orders for the stern of the *Speedwell* to be entirely cased in thick plank with only two small 'skuttles' to let light into the great cabin. When *Duchess* had rounded the Horn in 1709 with Hatley as Third Mate, it will be remembered that it was the stern of the ship which was smashed in by a wave thus endangering the lives of the officers.

To the south of *Speedwell's* anchorage at St. Catherine's Island, the channel between the island and the mainland narrowed to a gulf between tree-lined banks. To the north-east it widened to the open sea. Very early on Thursday 2 July 1719, as the sky grew grey above the eastern horizon, the English sailors woke to see a large ship at anchor just off 'Parrot Island' to the north-east, a green speck of land almost attached to the shoulder of the main island about five miles off. As the sun rose, bleaching sea and sky, Shelvocke sent the ship's launch to investigate.

The strange ship was the *Ruby*, formerly an English man-of-war and now under French command. She was returning from the South Sea where she had been employed to deter illegal traders. Next day, with her guns run out just in case and ready for action, the *Ruby*, moved further into the channel and let go her anchor close by the *Speedwell*. The French captain, M. la Jonquière was nervous. Many of his sailors had fallen sick during their passage round the Horn and he also had a large quantity of treasure on board as well as twenty wealthy Catholic priests. Shelvocke, unaware of *Ruby's* problems but acutely aware of his own and of the state of simmering near-mutiny among his crew, ordered the *Speedwell* into a similar state of preparedness. Alone in the wilderness and with all the huge expanse of Latin America to choose from, two heavily-armed ships confronted each other across a few short metres of water. It was absurd. La Jonquière was first to break the ice. He sent over his launch with that very powerful missile, an invitation to dinner.

The French dinner was a big success. At the return dinner however, when la Jonquière and his officers were guests on the *Speedwell*, the simmering discontent among the British sailors boiled embarrassingly into the open. While the officers sat carousing in the great cabin, Hudson the boatswain, backed up by a gunner and the master carpenter, protested loudly outside that they too should have been invited. In the ensuing fracas, Hudson flailed out, hitting William Betagh. Mr Adams, the surgeon and one of Shelvocke's relatives, was also hit. Order was only restored with the assistance of the French officers.

One sweltering day blended into another. Shelvocke blustered and drank hypsy, contemptuous of all but a few favourites. Parrots wheeled in noisy flocks. The men sweated and toiled. The locals looked on. One day, another strange ship poked her nose into the channel, saw *Ruby* and *Speedwell* and left again. La Jonquière, suspecting that she might be the *Success* and that he was about to be outgunned, weighed anchor, fired a five-gun salute and slipped away. Ten days later, the strange ship reappeared. She was not the *Success* which by this time was in the Pacific, she was a French ship, the *Sage Solomon*, forty guns and a 160 men, on her way to the South Sea to trade illegally. M. Girard, her captain, had come to St. Catherine's intending to wait there until full summer in the southern hemisphere before attempting the passage of the Horn. His men dug a garden for lettuce and 'salading'.

By the end of July 1719, *Speedwell* was ready to sail but, on the 31st, just as he was preparing for departure, Shelvocke received a letter from his crew. Enclosed with it were new articles signed by all the *Speedwell's* petty officers and thirty-six of the best foremast-men. In the letter, the men complained that the original ship's articles signed at Plymouth had been mysteriously altered. Mr Godfrey their agent had examined them and had discovered that there was now three times as much writing in them as previously 'written by several hands and interlin'd in a great many places'.[429] The new articles enclosed with the men's letter clarified the previous terms but also insisted that all plunder and loot should be divided

151

at sea rather than back in England on their return. The old ghosts had come back to haunt them: 'If what we shall have the fortune to make this voyage should be carried to London, we should never receive the half thereof; for it is known to all, how the people on board the ships *Duke* and *Duchess* were treated ...'

Shelvocke was in no doubt who was behind the letter and the new articles. Simon Hatley, he claimed, had become 'a mighty favourite of the people' and was 'the chief person concerned in this affair.[430]

Actually, all the senior officers were in tacit agreement with Simon and the ship was effectively in a state of mutiny. Preparations for departure came to a stop. After a few days Shelvocke received another letter. This one was signed by all the crew and officers except for a few of the most senior men such as Hatley. The letter appointed Mathew Stewart, one of the mates, to be agent for the crew. The entire ship's company confronted Shelvocke on the quarter-deck and, having no choice, he and all the senior officers finally signed the new articles.

That was Shelvocke's story, but nothing about George Shelvocke was straightforward. In affidavits sworn by members of the crew before his brief trial for piracy in 1722, it is stated that the new articles were initiated by Shelvocke himself and that, in them, Shelvocke was to receive an additional five percent originally allowed to Edward Hughes, the chief owner, in lieu of expenses.[431] His complicity may have run even deeper. Mathew Stewart, the new agent for the crew, had started the voyage as steward to Shelvocke himself, serving in the great cabin, and Shelvocke for some reason had promoted him to mate over the heads of other, better-qualified young sailors.[432] It seems that Stewart was Shelvocke's man and was used by Shelvocke to manipulate the crew.

More was to follow. Having secured the new articles, Shelvocke proposed his relative, Mr Adams, to be the officers' agent and bullied the officers into agreeing. Most radically, he proposed himself to be agent for the owners and demoted the former agent, Mr Hendrie, to ship's purser and 'agent for prizes' a vague title of his own invention. He thereby deprived Hendrie of twenty shares in the potential profits, allocating them to himself.[433]

Qui bono? As a result of the 'mutiny' on St. Catherine's Island, Shelvocke had gained complete control of the distribution of money and plunder.

No sooner had this drama finished and it looked like the *Speedwell* would be able to sail, than another began. On 3 August 1719, a Portuguese man-of-war arrived at the anchorage, the *St. Francis Xavier*, forty guns and 300 men, bound for Macao in China. There were now three warships in the narrow waters, each ship bristling with guns and armed men. It was time to be away. On Thursday 6 August 1719, *Speedwell* weighed anchor ready to fall down the channel during the night in preparation for departure for the open sea the following morning, not a moment too soon as far as the locals were concerned. Unfortunately, three of her crew chose this moment to desert. The ship's pinnace and a body of men commanded by one of the mates were despatched in pursuit.

Evening was drawing on when the men in the pinnace landed on the island. They walked about six miles inland to one of the local 'plantations'. It was midnight by the time they arrived, the woods dark as pitch and night-birds calling. Understandably, the inhabitants of the plantation took fright on finding themselves visited by a body of armed men appearing out of the darkness. According to Shelvocke, they suspected that it was Hatley 'come to take leave of them in the manner he had threatened'.[434] The English sailors found no deserters and returned peacefully through the woods in the early hours of the morning, but just as they were climbing back into the pinnace they were ambushed. A crowd of locals broke out of the undergrowth shouting 'kill the dogs!', 'kill the English dogs!'[435] Muskets crackled. Three of the sailors were wounded.

Speedwell had no choice but to return to her anchorage. Next day Hatley rowed over to the *St. Francis Xavier* with a letter of complaint. He had been on board before, to explain about the encounter with the Portuguese merchant ship off Cape Frio, an explanation which, thankfully, had been accepted. As he climbed aboard this time, he found that the 'Captain' of the island, a man by the name of Emmanuel Mansa, had got there before him. Mansa was apoplectic with rage. He accused Hatley of all manner of outrages including that of calling him, Mansa, a cuckold, a bad insult in that part of the world. Mansa attacked Hatley and the Portuguese sailors joined in. Hatley was only saved from a lynching because the French captain, M. de la Rivière, and some of his officers together with the ship's priest intervened.

De la Rivière was friendly, or at least he wished to avoid trouble. He obligingly blamed the locals. He sent a letter to Shelvocke the following morning apologising for the attack and asking that the English refrain from taking their revenge:

Those people are without knowing King or Prince ... are wild, and hidden in the woods, if you should seek revenge upon them. It would risk your men to very butchery.[436]

The two captains exchanged further visits. Finally, and at long last, *Speedwell* was able to weigh anchor. De la Rivière came on board for breakfast, staying 'a full tyde's work down the harbour with us' before saying his farewells.

It was 18 August 1719. 3,500 miles of open sea lay ahead.

the Horn

They followed the long 'desert coast' of Argentina, keeping it never more than a hundred miles or so to starboard, racing through hard, squally weather, through continuous shoals of seals and penguins, clouds scudding over, white puffs against the blue. Shelvocke may have been a crook but he had literary talent. His sense of wonder increased with every mile they sailed and this is vividly reflected in his account. It is not surprising that Coleridge was inspired. Around *Speedwell's* masts and rigging, black and white 'pintado' birds clustered screaming in the wind, their wings 'chequered like a draught board'. With them, huge albatrosses, suspended motionless in the rushing air, their wings 'extending to twelve or thirteen foot'.[437] To Shelvocke, everything seemed excessive, overwhelming. As they passed the estuary of the River Plate the sea became so clogged with seaweed that they had 'much trouble to clear ourselves'. By September 1719, when they were level with Puerto Deseado, the surface of the sea was flecked with 'an abundance of things like white snakes, perhaps the spawn of the larger sort of fish'.

154

It grew colder. The sea seethed with vast numbers of 'whales, grampuses, and other fish of monstrous bulk'. Their fetid breath when they breached 'came close to stifling us' and it was almost impossible to avoid bumping into them with each rise and fall of the waves.

About a month after leaving St. Catherine's Island, *Speedwell* was at 50° south, past Puerto San Julian and approaching the Strait of Magellan, which Shelvocke sailed past. He was aiming for the Strait of le Maire, the channel between the easternmost point of Tierra del Fuego and Staten Island, so named by the Dutchman William Schouten in 1615. It was now very cold. Looming over them were 'continuous chains of mountains, one with another, perpetually hid by snow' which culminated in the 'Three Brothers', gatekeepers to the opening of the strait, and behind them 'a slender peeked mountain appearing like a column of snow' which leaned its head south-east to the Antarctic Ocean and the emptiness beyond. On the other side of the strait as they rushed towards it, Staten Island seemed to float like 'a huge white cloud'.

The Strait of le Maire is about twenty miles through and eighteen miles across at its narrowest point. It is perhaps the most dangerous waterway in the world. Here tide and the prevailing wind do battle for supremacy so that sometimes the surface of the water seems to boil like a cauldron with huge bubbles. Sometimes vast waves maintain themselves in terrifying stasis, held up by the conflicting pressures and ready to crash down and vent their pent-up energy. Anson, passing through in 1780, described how his men were in perpetual danger of being dashed to pieces. Dampier wrote of his ship being 'tossed like an eggshell'.[438]

Once given over to the tidal flow at the mouth of the strait, *Speedwell* was swept into it with incredible rapidity - until half way through when the tide turned and she was swept back out the way she had come in with equal rapidity. The character of the waves could change from one moment to the next. On her second attempt, she laboured 'in the most violent manner' her bowsprit and stern dipping alternately under the water 'insensible to the guidance of her helm'. At last, around midnight, the tide shifted once more and carried them through, hurling them into the Antarctic Ocean where they were driven yet further southwards with a 'brisk gale'.

Speedwell was driven by winds that raged 'tempestuously without intermission'. South of the latitude of Cape Horn, which was still to the west of them, the Southern Ocean circles the Globe without land of any kind to obstruct the waves. Huge swells, sometimes a quarter of a mile from wave crest to wave crest, 'dogs before their masters', start their life here to roll indefinitely outwards.[439] *Speedwell* was forced as far south as 61°, not far off the Antarctic Continent, in 'continual mists' and in constant danger of icebergs. On 1 October 1719, a sailor by the name of William Camell cried out that his hands were numb and he could not hold himself. He fell from the rigging and drowned.

There were no more teeming whales, no grampuses, no Pintado birds. Nothing. Just fog and wind, horizontal sleet as hard as gunshot and 'gloomy, dismal clouds'. They were utterly alone. 'No sight of any fish of any kind, since we were come to the Southward of the Streits of le Maire'.[440] Until –

> *At length did cross an Albatross*
> *Through the fog it came;*
> *As if it had been a Christian soul,*
> *We hailed it in God's name.*

Except that in Shelvocke's account, no one hailed the 'disconsolate, black albatross' which appeared out of the sky to hover around the *Speedwell* that October in 1719. It merely hovered about for several days like a lost soul until Hatley, depressed, took a gun and, after missing several times, shot it 'hoping for better weather thereby'. Through the mists and half-truths of Shelvock's account one can surmise that Hatley had entered some sort of abyss of the emotions.

> *"God save thee, ancyent Marinere!*
> *From the fiends that plague thee thus -*
> *"Why look'st thou so?" - "with my cross-bow*
> *I shot the Albatross."*

156

There has been much discussion as to what type of albatross was shot by Hatley/the Ancient Mariner. Several varieties inhabit the air between the Horn and the Arctic landmass. The Wanderer has the largest wingspan but is more white than black, the Black-Browed has dark wings from above but looks white from underneath, the Light-Mantled Sooty is more grey than black. They all have something to distinguish them from Coleridge's albatross except one, the Dark-Mantled Sooty. It was a Dark-Mantled Sooty, commonly about the size of a large goose, which had the misfortune to die that day.

Contrary to what is implied in Coleridge's poem, there was no taboo at this period against killing albatrosses. In fact, they were quite frequently cooked and eaten although sailors complained of the oily fishy texture and taste of their flesh.[441] Sometimes a triangular, wooden frame was baited and trawled behind a ship in such a way that an albatross attempting to take the bait would be snared by the beak.[442] The legend of the taboo was Coleridge's invention. It is also due to Coleridge that the albatross became a symbol of the Southern Ocean.

On the southern point of Cape Horn Island some four hundred miles to the north of where Hatley fired his shot, on a lonely promontory 1,400 feet above the icy, crashing waves, where once, so it is claimed, Sir Francis Drake had cast himself down 'upon the uttermost point groveling',[443] there stands a monument created by the Chilean sculptor José Balcells. Seen from the north, its two triangular bronze halves form the shape of an albatross. On a nearby granite marker is carved a poem by Sara Vial, the friend of Pablo Neruda.

I am the Albatross that lingers for you at the end of the earth.
I am the forgotten soul of the dead sailors
that crossed Cape-Horn
from all the seas in the world.
They did not die in the savage waves,
today they fly on my wings
to eternity,
in the cradle of the Antarctic winds.[444]

157

The albatross died in vain. *Speedwell* rounded the Horn battling northward through continuous, brutal, stormy weather. By the end of October 1719, she was off the coast of southern Chile and provisions were running low. Nerves were more frayed than ever. The unfortunate Mr Hendrie, formerly the owners' agent and now demoted to purser, was excluded from the officers' mess and William Betagh was locked in the arms chest for a while, accused of mutiny for having demanded extra rations.[445] Shelvocke said Betagh had a 'voracious appetite', an accusation which Betagh strongly denied. Shelvocke may have been irritated by Betagh's habit of reading on deck in preference to drinking 'hugger-mugger' in the great cabin with the other officers.

It was midday, 14 November 1719, when they at last saw the mountainous coast of southern Chile. By that time they were down to seven butts of water. They headed for the large island of Chiloe, just off the coast at latitude 44° south, having unsuccessfully attempted various anchorages to the south of it. A French sailor on board advised that they would be able to raid the two ports of Chacao and Calbuco. The first is on the Island of Chiloe itself, the second nearby on the mainland. Poor advice since both ports were no more than villages with very little worth plundering.

Today, Chiloe Island is a kingdom of mist and rain, said to be the abode of witches and spirits. It stands apart from the rest of Chile. Bright, liquorice-allsort, shingled houses cluster in neat, green valleys up inlets which sparkle when the sun breaks through. All along its eastern coast you can see, across the water, the sugar-cone volcanoes and mountain peaks of the Andes stepping northward, high as clouds.

On Monday 30 November 1719, *Speedwell* entered the channel which separates the mainland from the north of the island. Her decks were cleared for action and she was flying a French flag, ready to attack Chacao. It was 'rainy thick weather'[446] and the wind was blowing fresh. However, the tide flowed so strongly that she was forced to cast her anchor in shallow water just off the mainland to wait for it to change. The wind increasing, the tide flowed outwards with 'prodigious rapidity' and the channel, about a mile wide at its narrowest point, became a foaming torrent. The anchor cable frayed and broke and they were in imminent danger of foundering when, at the last moment, the tide turned and swept them through. Visibility was so bad that they passed right by Chacao without seeing it and continued round the island down the eastern, inland shore.

Two wide bays down from Chacao there is a distinctive, large, pyramidical rock, set slightly apart from the eastern coast of Chiloe but connected to it. On fresh mornings when the sea sparkles and the seals dive, it seems to rise like a giant and ghostly figure above the foam-haze. Shelvocke described how beyond it and a little further south they came to a sheltered inlet. It was here in all probability, where the small fishing village of Quemchi now sleeps by the water, that *Speedwell* put in that Monday in 1719. Nowadays Quemchi is a peaceful place where dogs wander and fishing boats bob by the quay. There are two restaurants and a church. Back then there were no houses at all, just a cross on the hill behind.[447]

Next morning, Second Lieutenant Randall set out in the launch to find Chacao and Hatley took the ship's boat to find a watering place. He found a good spot with the help of the local Indians. It had plentiful wood and water and was within the protective range of *Speedwell's* guns. Unfortunately, that evening the Indians informed them that they were ordered to have no dealings with the strange ship and could trade no provisions. The Spanish authorities were wary of the Indians and enforced their orders with rigor.

Most of southern Chile was not at this time under the control of the Spanish. The Mapuche Indians of the mainland, formerly known as the Araucanians, had kept the Spanish at bay for nearly two hundred years, ever since the first attempts at conquest back in 1540. They had taught themselves to fight in European formations, to ride horses and wield pike and lance, also axes and broadswords, and they marched into battle to the beat of drums.[448] The Mapuche controlled most of the mainland up to the River Biobio, well to the north of Chiloe, but the Indians of Chiloe, although partly Mapuche, had been subdued by the Spanish quite early in the process of colonisation. Only seven years before, 'made desperate by the cruelty of the Spaniards' they had rebelled killing over sixty of their oppressors. The Spanish colonists, aware of their vulnerability, had exacted a bloody revenge, killing over two hundred Chilote Indians in return.[449]

Indian from Chiloe in pursuit of a bull

Unable to trade for provisions, Shelvocke tried to negotiate with the local Spanish governor. He adopted the identity of a Frenchman, 'Captain Janis le Breton'. A Spanish captain arrived from Chacao in a *piragua* and stayed all night on board without apparently discovering the deception. But the Spanish remained wary. They left their letters beneath a white flag on a small island at the entrance to the inlet. After several days of this and the negotiations seeming to be stuck, 'Janis le Breton' became frustrated. His letters to the governor became aggressive and his sailors began to take provisions by force from the local Indian plantations. Thanks to these more aggressive tactics, by 17 December 1719, *Speedwell* was ready for the sea once more, her decks cluttered with penned livestock and her hold stocked with maize, wheat, barley, potatoes and fresh water.[450] In another way though she was empty-handed. No amount of looking on the bright side could disguise the fact that this first attempt on a Spanish target had been unsuccessful. At 4.00 in the morning on 17 December 1719, 'Janis le Breton' weighed anchor and slipped away like a thief in the night.

The Bay of Concepción, 350 miles north of Chiloe, is a deep bite out of the coast of Chile across a narrow headland from the modern city of the same name. The northern approach to the bay is partially guarded by the small island of Quiriquine and its water, several miles wide, provides an anchorage for quite large ships. To the south, there are low, salt flats, almost level with the sea, where cows and horses graze and on hazy days when sea and sky blend into one, the high-hulled, empty ships seem to float above the animals grey on blue, more like airships than ships of the sea.

Speedwell rounded the headland on the evening of 23 December 1719 in the indolent, mauve dusk. Immediately on arrival, the ship's boats were lowered and Hatley set off in the pinnace, well manned and armed, to surprise any shipping which happened to be there. He returned the next morning having captured the *Solidad d'Anday*, a barque of 150 tons. He then took a small ship of 25 tons carrying fruit from the Island of Quirquine for the market at Concepción. This small ship, renamed the *Mercury*, would play a part in his story.

By morning, the Spanish had been alerted to the presence of the intruder. Up to ten thousand people lined the shore like a circus audience, watching in impotent rage as Hatley chased yet another small ship almost up to the town, which then lay on the south-east shore* where the modern town of Penco is now situated. He only gave up the pursuit when he came within range of the Spanish eighteen-pounder guns which were mounted on a rickety platform by the harbour. The Spanish fired two shots and he was

---

* It was moved to its present location in 1751.

161

forced to retire. The Spanish were actually very poorly prepared. The fort was in ruins and the rickety gun platform was about all the fixed defence there was,[451] which was hopelessly negligent when one considers that in former years Concepción had twice been sacked by the Mapuche and had been attacked by the Dutch as well.

Nothing ever went straight for the *Speedwell*. The following day, Lieutenant Randall set out in the newly-named *Mercury* to track down a ship reported to be at anchor six miles to the north. The potential prize was hauled up on land and Randall made the mistake of landing in order to take her. The landing party was ambushed, three of the sailors were cut down as they waded back to the *Mercury* and two others were wounded and taken prisoner. So far the privateers had taken three ships for very little reward and had lost five men. Not a very good score.

Next day however, as dusk was settling, their luck changed and they captured a big ship as it entered the bay. This was the 300-ton *St. Fermin*, loaded with linen, rice, sugar, molasses and five to six thousand Spanish dollars worth of money and silver plate. Her captain, Don Fransisco Larraín, was rowed to Concepción to arrange a ransom for his ship, worth a potential further sixteen thousand Spanish dollars[452]. But, as at Chiloe, negotiations were frustratingly unproductive. The Spanish governor was polite but so noncommittal that, on 1 January 1720, William Betagh was put ashore to negotiate in person. He carried a copy of the commission and of the Declaration of War and he was accompanied by one of his marines. Their reception was hostile. The locals were particularly incensed by the marine's busby which was very tall. The marine was very short and squat and he looked so ridiculous that the inhabitants took the busby to be a deliberate parody on the Pope's mitre.[453] Betagh and his marine were jostled and taunted as they walked through the streets. The situation was explosively tense. 'Great bodies of horse' were posted along the shore. That night on *Speedwell* the men stayed under arms and a net was spread seven foot out from the gunwale to deter boarders.

Betagh returned with a Flemish Jesuit, a Spanish lawyer, an Englishman and a Scotsman, both presumably Catholic residents in Chile, more like the ingredients of a joke than serious emissaries for a negotiation.

Money was offered but not enough. Negotiations remained deadlocked. The Spanish governor allowed the two captive English sailors to return to their ship as a goodwill gesture but no ransom came. Shelvocke's tone became bullying:

I could not longer be so unjust to my country and myself as not to complain of the outrageous mean act of stripping my two wounded men as they were passing through the town to come on board ... this could not be term'd a handsome return for the tender usage his fellow subjects met withal from me ...I would have patience till the next morning, when, if he deceived me again, I gave him my word and honour the St. Fermin should be in flames by noon.[454]

Tender usage? An unusual description for theft at sea.

The morning of 6 January 1720 came and went. The sails of the *St. Fermin* were loosened for better combustion and towards the end of the afternoon, no ransom being forthcoming, she was put on fire, the cotton sails making 'a prodigious blaze'. *Speedwell* and *Mercury* put out from the bay while behind them great billows of smoke drifted across the water. They set sail north-west towards the Islands of Juan Fernandez, the next *rendez-vous* point with *Success*.

For once the gods smiled. *Speedwell* and *Mercury* raced through summer seas. Five days after they left Concepción, the ragged backbone of Mas a Tierra, now Robinson Crusoe Island, appeared over the horizon and by 12 January 1720, *Speedwell* was at anchor off Cumberland Bay, where Selkirk had been rescued. There was no sign of *Success* - by this time she was at the Galapagos Islands,[455] the next *rendez-vous* point - but carved into a tree trunk in a prominent position by the shore were the words 'Captain John' and 'W Magee'. Magee was the name of the surgeon of the *Success*, a friend of Clipperton. It was a message from John Clipperton to show that *Success* had called there as arranged. He had avoided using his surname for fear of alerting the Spanish, his name was known to them from his previous adventures with Dampier. A futile precaution because he had since raided all the way up South America and the whole coast was in a state of alert. A more-detailed message buried beneath a cross set up nearby had already been removed by the Spanish.[456]

The stay at the Juan Fernandez Islands was uneventful. On 15 January 1720, *Speedwell* and *Mercury* set sail once more, heading further north. By Friday 5 February, they were in sight of 'El Morro', the 'Snout' of Arica, the massive, arid headland which juts into the sea above that town. A poor choice. Although Arica was port for the silver mines of Potosi, the immense wealth which had passed through over the years had left little impression. In 1720, the town looked like little more than a heap of ruins spread along the sea shore at the edge of a mountainous desert. The houses were 'covered only with mats', bundles of sedge placed vertically and bound with leather thongs or strips of cane.[457] Only the largest houses and the church were built of bricks.

Lieutenant Brooks took *Mercury* ahead into the harbour. It was protected by the headland and by the little island of Iquique,* now called Guano Island, which lies just off the headland and is now connected to it by a causeway. At that time, Iquique was snowy white with deposits of guano (bird dung) in places yards deep, although nowadays it is just bare, grey rock. Back then it stank when the wind was in the wrong direction. The guano came from the immense numbers of seabirds which lived there, so many that at times the sky was darkened by their wings. The guano was mined by a small population of Indians and black slaves who lived on the island. Up to twelve ships per year were loaded with the stuff which was sold as fertiliser on the mainland and further afield.

Mercury captured a guano ship, the *Rosana*. No use except for ransom and unpleasant to be in. Next day, *Speedwell* rounded the island and took a small ship loaded with dried fish. There was no element of surprise. By the time *Speedwell* entered the harbour, the shore was lined with groups of men, armed and ready to fight. Shelvocke moved four guns across to the *Mercury* and the two ships sailed menacingly as close to the shore as they dared. Touch paper was lit, canon roared and cannon shot ploughed up the shore. It did little damage to the defenders. Contrary to expectations, they stood their ground protected by a hastily-erected breastwork of stones. Shelvocke sent ashore an Indian prisoner from one of the prizes with threats and a demand for ransom. The Indian made it through the crashing breakers

---

* Not to be confused with the modern city of the same name further south.

and, with considerable courage, returned with a message. The defenders 'cared not a fig for any such *boracho*',[458] in other words 'drunkard', the most contemptuous name they could think of for an Englishman. Shelvocke should have known better. This was not the first time that the citizens of Arica had driven off sea-born marauders. In 1681, pious Captain Watling, Dampier being one of his party, had attacked the fort at Arica, placing a hundred Spanish prisoners in advance of the line of buccaneers. Despite this, the Spanish had opened fire and Watling and his men had been driven back through the angry town through a 'hail of missiles from every window and doorway'.[459]

Speedwell and *Mercury* sailed on. A feeling of unease, if not exactly of desperation, was developing, a feeling of being driven off. They called into the port of Ilo further up the coast. There were four ships in the harbour. Three of them were small Spanish merchantmen but the fourth was the French ship, the *Sage Solomon* last seen at St.Catherine's Island. *Sage Solomon* had taken on reinforcements from the town so she that was very well manned and she was prepared to fight. She fired off four guns as a warning. Britain and France were allies. It would have been unwise to attack. *Speedwell* was driven off yet again.

The men were restless, Shelvocke scheming, the officers confused. Unknown to them, on 17 February 1720 as they were sailed north from Ilo, peace was declared between Britain and Spain. It would be some time before the news reached South America but technically, (although ignorance of the peace was an established defence), from that time on all attacks could be seen as acts of piracy.

my Heart as dry as Dust

Towards the end of February, somewhere out from Paita, Hatley took over command of the *Mercury*. He had travelled overland from Lima along that coast before, he said,[460] and he knew that many small vessels, some of them richly laden, traded down to the capital from the various small towns along the way. He suggested to Shelvocke that he sail close in to the shore in order to intercept some of these ships, leaving *Speedwell* to continue further out to sea. The *rendez-vous* was to be the Island of Lobos del Mar, where *Duke* and *Duchess* had recuperated before attacking Guayaquil.

Hatley would be free of Shelvocke, if only for a while, but, perhaps more importantly, Shelvocke would be free of Hatley. Fresh provisions were loaded into the *Mercury* and the pinnace was detailed to accompany her. Hatley received a copy of the commission and a crew of fifteen men, seven of them officers. The proportion of officers to men was absurdly high. Among them were William Betagh, Captain of Marines, and other quite senior, skilled and valuable sailors such as the boatswain, who were important for the smooth running of the larger ship. It is possible that Shelvocke deliberately parted with these officers and with Hatley thus unburdening himself of most of those whom he saw as a threat to his authority. This was William Betagh's opinion.[461]

On 26 February 1720, *Mercury*, Hatley commanding, stood towards land and *Speedwell* continued north well out to sea. Hatley was taking a risk. He was in enemy waters and the *Mercury* was just a small, coastal vessel with a shallow draft. Betagh described her as a 'lighter'. They had built a deck on her at the level of the gunwale and provided oars and a mast but she was not really designed for deep-sea sailing. In this unwieldy vessel Hatley and his men cruised for twelve days, calling twice at Lobos del Mar without any sight of the *Speedwell*. To start with all went well. They captured a small barque laden with chocolate which they ransomed, and off Capo Blanco at the opening of the Gulf of Guayaquil they took a 200-ton pink.

The pink was a deep-sea ship with seventy men on board. Hatley and his men had shown courage in taking her. Hatley landed the Spanish captain and some of the 'gentleman prisoners' and transferred most of his crew to her, leaving three to man the *Mercury*. He then kept his position off Cabo Blanco for several days hoping to meet up with the *Speedwell*. Early on 9 March 1720, a sail at last appeared far off, and *Mercury* and the pink headed towards her, the English sailors relieved that they were about to be reunited with their companions even if it meant putting up with Shelvocke once more. Unfortunately, as the morning wore on and the two ships gradually approached each other, realisation dawned that the strange ship was not *Speedwell*. By mid morning they were quite close and it became obvious that she was a warship and therefore almost certainly hostile. It was too late to turn and run. Hatley decided to bluff it out.

The strange ship was the *Brilliant*, part of a squadron of three ships fitted out in Lima to track down the privateers, and she was much more powerful than the tiny force which Hatley had at his disposal which was spread between two ships, one of them not much more than a fortified barge. Hatley rested his hopes on his captured pink having already been checked out by the *Brilliant* a few days previously, as he had been informed by the Spanish captain before he landed him ashore. *Brilliant* might therefore be unlikely to check her out again. If Hatley could give the impression that the pink was still under Spanish control, maybe he could escape capture.

Mercury kept well back. All the English-looking sailors on the pink were sent below decks, leaving just a few Indians and Blacks above to pretend to be the sort of crew which might be expected on a Spanish vessel. Morning faded into afternoon by which time *Brilliant* was close enough to fire a warning shot. Had they heard anything of the English privateers? the Spaniards shouted across. No they hadn't. Why were they not further on their way to Lima? Because of the currents, Hatley replied.

The captain of the *Brilliant* seemed to swallow this but, just as the sailors on the *Brilliant* were 'getting her tacks aboard' ready to leave, John Sproke, he who had presented the mutinous articles to Shelvocke back on St. Catherine's Island, suddenly emerged from below decks with two other of the English sailors. English sailors wore their bellbottoms long, to just above the ankle, whereas the French and Spanish wore them further up the calf. A French sailor on lookout at the masthead of the *Brilliant* spotted them:

'Par Dieu, Monsieur!' he called out. *'Ils sont Anglais!'*[462]

The game was up. The captain of the *Brilliant* immediately ordered a broadside of round and partridge shot to be fired at close range. It did little damage except to Hatley who was slightly wounded in the head. All the English sailors were taken captive and the *Brilliant* set off after the *Mercury*, nearly sinking her with a murderous volley of twenty-five guns although she put up no resistance. The three English sailors on board joined the others already captive aboard the *Brilliant*.

For Hatley, there must have been a feeling of ghastly inevitability about his capture. He had twice ventured into the South Sea and had twice been stopped. If subject to religious sentiment, he may well have concluded that Divine Providence was against him and that God in his wisdom did not want him to enter the South Sea at all.

The English 'pirates' were disembarked at Paita, then only around seventy-five houses,[463] the nearest port for overland transportation to Lima. It was common practice to disembark there because the journey south overland was quicker than the journey by sea against the prevailing wind. Today, most passenger transport goes along the Panamericana through Piura about fifty miles inland from Paita, which has rather lost its *raison d'être* as a result. But, perhaps because of this, despite earthquakes, el Niño and other disasters, Paita is the least changed of all the ports along the Pacific seaboard of South America which were once attacked by the buccaneers and privateers, a small, hot bowl of humanity scooped from the bare mud hills just as it was in Hatley's day. It is a charming old town and the old ghosts still watch from shadowed corners. There is still, at a crossing under a piece of corrugated iron, the figurehead from Captain Edward Davis's pirate barque, which went down in a storm in the harbour in 1685 and was fished from the water soon after by the inhabitants. 'La Figura' looks down on Paita's sleepy streets with staring, pagan eyes. Once she looked down on carriages and mules; now she looks down on a dusty miniature universe of family-run shops and motorcycle rickshaws. Paita is a world apart.

The English captives were sent six hundred miles on muleback down the coastal road to Lima and prison. Hatley, in pain from the wound to his head, was singled out for rough treatment.[464] When the Spanish sailors had rifled through his possessions they had found a purse containing ninety-six Portuguese *moidores*, money taken from the Portuguese ship off Cape Frio all those months before. His possession of the *moidores* marked him out as a pirate even though the supposed act of piracy had not been committed against a Spanish ship. His former imprisonment put him in double danger.

168

By May 1720, he was back in the prison in the Plaza de Armas* and this time he was kept chained and in solitary confinement. He had taken the purse of *moidores*, he was the commanding officer and he was therefore the guilty principal. William Betagh, who was better treated than the rest and had travelled south aboard the *Brilliant*, found him there on 1 June when he too was briefly imprisoned. Now that all the English sailors were under one roof, the 'court of judges' charged them as pirates and they were threatened with execution. But times had changed. Spain had no interest in exacerbating tensions with Britain. The Viceroy and Archbishop, Don Diego Morsilio,[465] intervened and they were released - all except Hatley.

William Betagh got out first as a result of the good offices of a French captain then resident in Lima, who vouched for his behaviour.[466] Betagh kept an eye on the English sailors. Some were lodged in the hostel of a convent and several converted to Catholicism in order to benefit from the largesse of a local patron. There were no threats of forcible conversion. Times had changed. Betagh loved Lima. The women were beautiful, the air was neither too hot nor too cold:

If the general bent of human nature be for constant happiness and freedom from pain, the man of pleasure must go to Peru, and make Lima his temporal paradise.[467]

The English sailors used to meet in a pub which was kept by John Bell, an Englishman who had a black wife. One night the sailors got drunk, quarrelled and smashed up the statue of a saint. They landed up in the clutches of the Inquisition. However, in a judgement which was liberal even by modern standards, they were excused punishment because they had acted under the influence of alcohol. Later, John Sproke and some of the others got in more serious trouble. They had been sent to the port of Callao to help fit out a French ship, the *Flying Fish,* but while there they plotted to commandeer a small ship and sail her to Panama and thence travel overland to the Caribbean, Sproke commanding, in a repeat of Thomas Stradling's epic escape attempt earlier in the century. They had stockpiled guns and

---

* The unfortunate Don Ieronimo Bosa, governor of Guayaquil at the time of *Duke* and *Duchess's* attack, was being held elsewhere in the prison at this time. He did not come to trial until 1730 when he was in his forties. He was fined - Little (1960) 102.

were almost ready to leave when they were caught. They narrowly escaped execution but were again released.

Only the Simon Hatley, the repeat offender, remained inside. He was chained in his cell. The authorities wanted him either sent to the mines or executed and they attempted to use the case of the Portuguese ship off Cape Frio to bring this about, even though the 'crime' took place outside Spanish jurisdiction. Close by in the Plaza de Armas, the warm nights of flirtation, the parading carriages, the laughter and music; inside darkness, boredom and fear.

He had re-entered a nightmare.

St. Catherine's Island, 1711

Chacao, Chiloe Island, seen from the channel

170

A *Indienne du Chily broyant du mays pour en faire de la farine.*
B *Indien en Poncho et Pohuna.*
C *Indienne en Choñi et yqüella.*
D *Indien jettant le laqs au taureau pour l'arreter.*

Indians of Chile

Bay of Concepión, view to the east of Iquique Island

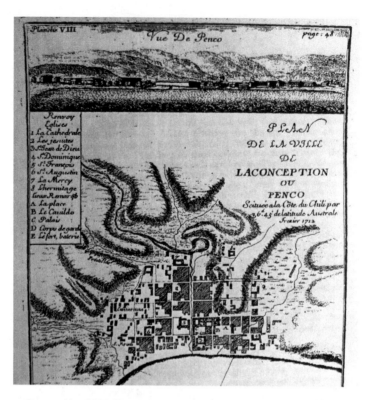

Concepción, 1711 (Penco is an alternative name for old Concepción)

The Snout of Arica

Arica, Guano Island, today - devoid of guano

Paita, Calle de la Merced, 1836

173

La Figura, figurehead of Captain Edward Davis's ship raised from
Paita Harbour in 1685

CHAPTER 10

Crusoe and Gulliver

the life of a Man you knew

The Life and Strange Surprising Adventures of Robinson Crusoe, of York, Mariner was published on 25 April 1719, about three months after *Speedwell* and *Success* set sail from Plymouth. By the end of the year it had run through three editions and had already been translated into two languages: Dutch and German. Daniel Defoe made over a thousand guineas out of it.[468] Even before Queen Anne's death, he had felt sufficiently confident of his finances to move his large family into a fine, new house in Stoke Newington with rambling rooms and four acres of garden. *Robinson Crusoe* put the seal on his success.

Robinson Crusoe may have drawn its original inspiration from Alexander Selkirk's experience as a castaway and from the experiences of mariners such as Simon Hatley and William Dampier, but it is thick with Defoe's own religious and political preoccupations. In a sense it is less a fictional biography and more an allegorical autobiography, that, by means of fiction, describes Defoe's own emotional and spiritual history. In the sequel, *Serious Reflections during the Life and Surprising Adventures of Robinson Crusoe*, published the following year, Defoe admits as much. He describes his book as the 'life of a man you knew ... whose misfortunes and infirmities perhaps you had sometimes unjustly triumphed over ...'[469] Crusoe has many of Defoe's personal characteristics, in particular an awe-inspiring capacity for hard work, without which Crusoe could never have survived on his island as he did, and an almost supernatural resilience after major setbacks.

To begin with, Crusoe disobeys his father's command to become a lawyer. He is determined to go to sea instead. Defoe's own relationship with his father was similarly tinged with guilt. James Foe, the steady tallow chandler who died in 1706, had had to put up with a lot. It cannot have been easy being the father of a son, however brilliant, whose life was a tale of unpaid debts, bankruptcy (for the huge sum of £17,000 in 1692), prison (on various occasions), endless controversy and the pillory. Even the change of name from Foe to Defoe may have been hurtful.

If Hatley read the book after he returned from prison in Lima in 1723, which is very possible given his own connection with Selkirk and the South Sea, he could not have failed to see a parallel with his own life. Indeed *Robinson Crusoe* may have made uncomfortable reading. Simon, like Crusoe, had failed to follow in his father's business, choosing to go to sea rather than to be a haberdasher of hats in Woodstock. Like Crusoe, he had suffered danger, solitude and hardship. What thoughts had passed through his mind while chained in the prison cell in Lima? Crusoe's sentiments may have been disturbingly familiar:

I had been well instructed by Father and Mother; neither had they been wanting to me, in their early endeavours, to infuse religious Awe of God into my Mind, a Sense of my Duty, and of what the Nature and End of my Being requir'd of me. But alas! Falling early into the Seafaring Life, which of all Lives is the most destitute of the Fear of God, though his Terrors are always before them; I say, falling early into Seafaring Life, and into Seafaring Company, all that little sense of Religion which I had entertain'd, was laugh'd out of me by my Mess-Mates, by a harden'd despising of Dangers; and the Views of Death, which grew habitual to me...[470]

For 'Seafaring Company' read Shelvocke and a bowl of hypsy.

176

Robinson Crusoe sets out on his first voyage from Hull in 1651. He is shipwrecked in a storm, sets out again, is captured by Algerian pirates and becomes the slave of a Moor. He escapes, is helped by a Portuguese captain off the coast of west Africa and sails with him to Brazil where he settles and soon becomes a successful, if lonely, tobacco planter. It is now 1659. Greedy for greater success, he arranges with some other local planters to set out on an expedition to Africa to purchase and smuggle black slaves who are in poor supply in Brazil. The ship is caught in a violent storm and wrecked off the mouth of the River Orinoco. He is the only survivor. This is where the famous part of the book begins. With great labour, he rescues various useful artefacts from the wreck, sets himself up in a cave and builds a fenced enclosure. Gradually he makes things comfortable. He hunts, grows corn, tames goats. His persistence is heroic. It takes him forty-two days to make a plank, months to enlarge his cave, two years to make a *piragua*. Finally the world intrudes once more. Some cannibals arrive with their victims. He hides while they eat and one escapes whom Crusoe rescues and calls 'Friday'. He teaches Friday English and Christianity. More cannibals come. Crusoe and Friday kill several and rescue two prisoners. One of them is Friday's father and the other is a Spaniard. Friday's father sets out for the mainland to rescue some other Spaniards castaway there but meanwhile a British ship arrives. It has been captured by mutineers. Crusoe and the captain regain control of the ship and sail off to England, taking Friday with them and leaving three of the mutineers behind. It is 1686. Almost twenty-eight years have passed since he was first washed up on the island.

This is a book with a happy ending. On his return to civilisation, Crusoe finds that his Brazilian estate has prospered in his absence and he is now a wealthy man. In 1694 he revisits his island, which has now become his 'Collony'. The Spaniards from the mainland, having first subdued and then reformed the English mutineers (an interesting reversal of religious stereotypes), have done well. They have captured some cannibal men and women from the mainland and there are now children. Crusoe promises to send more women from England.

Crusoe, for all his faults and his contemporary blindness to the evils of the slave trade, is an upright, if initially wilful, citizen, which is rather more than could be said for Alexander Selkirk, nor for William Dampier or Simon Hatley. In *Robinson Crusoe*, there are no buccaneering raids, no episodes with Portuguese ships off Cape Frio, no drunken brawls in Bristol, and the smuggling of slaves into Brazil would not have been considered a serious misdemeanour by his readership. Through his ordeals, Crusoe learns to acknowledge and accept God's providence. When at last he becomes truly repentant of his former errors, the world takes on a benign appearance and he is reconciled with his lot. Of particular appeal to Coleridge who rated *Robinson Crusoe* very highly, Crusoe becomes reconciled with the natural world, itself evidence of God's goodness. His island, at first a desolate, isolated prison, becomes in time his 'beloved' island:

The most pleasant Place in the World, and all the Happiness my Heart could wish for, was to be but there again.[471]

Coleridge admired this 'vision of a happy nightmare'[472] as he described *Robinson Crusoe*. His own Ancient Mariner is also reconciled with nature, although there are differences in keeping with the character and times of the two authors. Crusoe's road to enlightenment takes twenty-eight years and a great many pages and is the product of hard work; the Ancient Mariner's takes a few weeks and, as might be expected from his impractical but inspired creator, enlightenment comes suddenly when the Ancient Mariner sees the beautiful water snakes:

Oh happy living things! No tongue
Their beauty might compare:
A spring of love gushed from my heart,
And I blessed them unaware:
Sure my kind saint took pity on me
And I blessed them unaware.

The self same moment I could pray;
And from my neck so free

The Albatross fell off, and sank
Like lead into the sea.

the Death of Selkirk

When *Robinson Crusoe* was published, Alexander Selkirk was renting a house on Pall Mall. He was married (possibly), to Sophia Bruce, the daughter of a crofter from near his home town of Largo, and he was working as mate on the *Enterprise*, a coastal ship which ran between the Channel ports.[473] It must have been strange to see his ordeal used for another man's profit. There were descriptions in *Robinson Crusoe* which were very familiar. He would have recognised Crusoe's building of a shelter, and the goats undoubtedly came from Selkirk's own experience as related by Woodes Rogers.

Selkirk was unable to settle down. The following year, November 1720, found him in Plymouth. There he met a woman called Frances Candis, the owner of a pub frequented by sailors. On 12 December 1720, he married her, possibly bigamously, in St. Andrew's Church and made a new will disinheriting Sophia.[474] He had signed on with HMS *Weymouth*, bound for West Africa, to protect slave ships and other merchant vessels from the pirates who infested those waters.[475] Shortly after the marriage ceremony, he set sail.

By March 1721, HMS *Weymouth* was off the coast of Gambia and was ready to begin work, but she ran aground on a sandbank in the mouth of the River Gambia and her voyage became beset by difficulties. Sickness struck. The African coast was dangerous for European sailors, who lacked immunity from the many tropical diseases which lurked there. Indeed, mortality among the crews of slave ships was in roughly the same proportion to their numbers as among their poor, slave cargoes. Benin is further east but the saying held good all along that coast:

Beware and take care,
Of the Bight of Benin.
Of one that comes out,
There are forty go in.[476]

179

By June, many of *Enterprise's* men were in a wretched state from a virus carried by mosquitoes which had previously fed on sick monkeys.[477] They began to die and more of them died every day. By late November, it was Selkirk's turn. At 8.00 pm on 13 December 1721, he died, bleeding from his eyes and mouth. He was buried at sea. He was forty-nine years old. In retrospect, his death coming so soon after the publication of *Robinson Crusoe*, it is as if once Defoe breathed life into Crusoe, it was time for Selkirk to leave.

Return of the Voyagers

Selkirk had been dead for several months when, after their very separate adventures over the circle of the earth and over a period of more than three years, the survivors of *Speedwell* and *Success*, all except Hatley, sailed back to Britain, arriving in the summer of 1722 not actually simultaneously but within surprisingly few weeks of each other.

John Clipperton returned in June 1722. He had circumnavigated the globe, suffered mutiny, removal from command and imprisonment in Macao. He was without the *Success* which he had been obliged to sell at Batavia[478] and his state of mind was erratic. A life of drink and buccaneering had taken its toll. He was destitute. He died 'heart-broke ... at his long run of misfortune' in the family home in Galway a few days after his return.[479]

George Shelvocke returned in July 1722, casting anchor at Dungeness on the evening of 30 July where he hired a small vessel to take him to Dover. From Dover he travelled immediately to London to see the owners and to give an account of his adventures.[480] His voyage had not been easy. He had lost the *Speedwell* off the Juan Fernandez Islands in late 1720, had seen his authority as captain seep away until he was captain only by sufferance of his crew, effectively under the 'Jamaica Discipline', almost a pirate. He had built a new ship[481] at the Juan Fernandez Islands which he named *Recovery* and he had celebrated the Pretender's birthday with a bonfire, the men wearing roses made of paper and rags and drinking punch, vinegar, sugar and water because they had no alcohol.[482] He and his men

180

had then sailed north on their 'bundle of boards', capturing a larger Spanish vessel to which they transferred, naming her *Happy Return*.[483]

In the spring of 1721, off Panama, Shelvocke had at last met up with the Clipperton in *Success* and together they had cruised unsuccessfully for the Manila Ship. They had separated soon after, the two captains quarrelling over division of the spoils. But now came the high point of Shelvocke's voyage. After leaving the *Success*, he had gone on to capture a rich 200-ton Spanish merchant vessel, *La Concepción de Recova*, in the Gulf of Panama (20 May 1721), after a fierce battle of more than two hours.[484] From Panama, laden with loot, he had sailed north, taking further prizes, to the coast of California and from there had made the Pacific crossing to Canton China, anchoring at Wampo on 18 November 1721.

Canton, sweltering and humid, was China's premier port for foreign merchants at that time. Thirteen European trading stations lined the river, teeming with the life of junks and tall European ships. Above each station a large national flag hung from a high flag post.

Once *Happy Return* was safely anchored, Shelvocke's men had deserted him in droves, seeking berths on other ships. One of them, David Griffiths, in a boat loaded with his loot and baggage, was pursued by a Hoppo or customs man whom he shot dead with a musket fearing that the Hoppo was going to fleece him. (Griffiths was drunk.) His crime caused considerable difficulty. It was the Chinese authorities' practice when a crime was committed, to kidnap someone of the same nationality until the real culprit was given up.[485] Several innocent English traders suffered before David Griffiths was led away. Shelvocke meanwhile had to leave the *Happy Return* which had disintegrated during the Pacific crossing and was beyond repair. Along with a remaining handful of men, he sailed on an East Indiaman to Batavia and thence home via the Cape of Good Hope. Of over a hundred who sailed from Plymouth in 1719 aboard the *Speedwell*, eighty-four were dead, taken prisoner or otherwise lost by the time he arrived at Dungeness.[486] Just sixteen made it home with him.

the Bubble bursts

The homecoming of the men of *Speedwell* and *Success* was very different from the homecoming of the men of the *Duke* and *Duchess* eleven years earlier. *Duke* and *Duchess's* return had been the subject of intense public interest, a timely return once they were out of the clutches of the East India Company, coinciding as it did with the founding of the South Sea Company. But by 1722, the world had changed. The South Sea Company had crashed in September 1720, at about the time that *Speedwell* was slipping south along the coasts of Patagonia towards her encounter with the albatross. Attitudes towards the South Sea among the general public had altered for the worse.

The disaster had begun to develop in the latter part of 1719 and into 1720. During that period, South Sea stocks rose in value from £128 (at the beginning of 1720) to over £1,000 by July, cleverly encouraged by the directors of the company.[487] Around the time of Hatley's unfortunate adventure off Cape Frio, the value of the stocks was rising so rapidly that different prices were being paid at the two ends of Garraways in Exchange Alley, the labyrinth of lanes in the angle between Cornhill and Lombard Street where trading took place. Speculation thereafter became frenzied. Defoe marvelled at how greed had turned decent men into gamblers: 'the Biting, the Sharping, and Circumventing one another … is like a Contagion'.[488] When asked for his opinion about the good sense of this speculation, Isaac Newton is said to have remarked that he could calculate the motions of the heavenly bodies, but not the madness of people.[489]

The signs of impending disaster were clear enough to those who had eyes to see. On 7 July 1720, John Law, the Scottish banker responsible for similar speculative frenzy in Paris, had to take refuge in the Palais Royal, his coach attacked by an angry mob many of whom had been reduced to poverty when the value of stocks in the Mississippi Company plunged.[490] Back in England, people in the know became cautious. The Marlboroughs began to sell their stock, Robert Walpole was gradually unloading his considerable holdings,[491] converting the cash into land in Norfolk. Shamefully, even the directors of the South Sea Company sold stocks and bought property.[492] Among the general public, optimism continued however. On 22 August 1720, Pope wrote to Lady Mary Wortley Montague urging her to buy into a new subscription.[493] Even Walpole planned further investments. But at the very end of August, when *Speedwell* was nearing the Straight of le Maire, the Bubble burst. The value of South Sea Company stocks evaporated almost overnight as investors at last woke up and realised that if any proper return were to be made on the huge sums invested, the company would need to turn in a trading profit of something in the region of £15,000,000 per year,[494] a figure from fairyland.

The Bubble burst during St Bartholomew's Fair, London's annual descent into joyous anarchy which had been extended to last a fortnight during the reign of Charles II. Centred around Smithfield, the streets were crowded with stalls and booths. Prize-fighters, wire-walkers, musicians, acrobats, puppets, freaks and wild animals competed for the attention of the festive crowd. The contrast between joy and personal disaster could not have been more extreme. As in France, thousands, including incidentally several prominent French Prophets for whom presumably a short-term gamble was more sensible than long term planning, found themselves suddenly destitute. Such was the despair, so it was said, that a man was knocked down in Exchange Alley for laughing at a joke.[495] The crisis continued for nearly a month until, in late September, the Bank of England stepped in and bought up the stock together with the East India Company.[*] Small wonder that when Shelvocke and the rest returned in 1722, talk of the South Sea produced faint interest at best. It was yesterday's news, a thing better forgotten, and they were yesterday's men.

an Evidence for Hughes

William Betagh had written to the owners of the *Speedwell* from Lima after his release from prison there.[496] He had outlined his concern regarding George Shelvocke's honesty and informed the owners about the changes to the original articles, changes which the mutinous ship's company had agreed to at St. Catherine's Island off Brazil in July 1719. Betagh was back

---

[*] The South Sea Company continued to trade, if half-heartedly, for many years, only surrendering the *Asiento* in 1750 in a supplement to the Treaty of Aix-la-Chapelle. It was not finally abolished until 1854 - Carswell (1961) 268.

in London in October 1721,[497] before Shelvocke and Hatley. He became agent for Edward Hughes, the leading owner, and when Shelvocke arrived in London, on 1 August 1722, to meet the owners, Betagh pounced. Shelvocke was hoping, in Betagh's words, 'by a genteel donation'[498] to pacify any resentment the owners might feel towards him for the loss of the *Speedwell* and the meagre profits they could expect. Instead, the owners had Betagh's letter of accusation read aloud in Shelvocke's presence and Shelvocke was unceremoniously arrested and locked up in the 'Woodstreet Counter', a small prison in the heart of the City of London. He was joined there over the following days by twelve of his crew, one of them, William Burrow, eighteen years old, very ill from smallpox.[499]

The day following Shelvocke's arrest, the insidious Mathew Stewart, who had been promoted by him to mate back on St. Catherine's Island and had possibly acted as his accomplice during the events which took place there, was arrested at Dover. An account book was found on Stewart's person.[500] This book contained damning evidence. Written in Stewart's handwriting was a list of the total proceeds from the capture of *La Concepción de Recova* in the Gulf of Panama in May 1721 - proceeds which Shelvocke had made no mention of to the owners and never confessed to subsequently. In his book, Shelvocke described the *Concepción de Recova* as containing only: 'Flour, Loaves of Sugar, Bales of Boxes of Marmalade, Jars of preserv'd Peaches, Grapes, Limes *et cætera*'.[501] William Betagh, in his own book written in reply, explodes in indignation:

Now, Be it known to ALL MEN, *That, that et cætera was A hundred and eight thousand six hundred and thirty six pieces of eight ...*[502]

Stewart's account book told the real story. Along with the foodstuffs admitted by Shelvocke, the *Concepción* had been carrying cash to the value of 98,104 Spanish dollars, of which 11,325 dollars were for Shelvocke alone, the rest to be divided, or already divided, among the thirty-two surviving members of his crew in proportions consonant with the revised articles.[503] There may well have been much more. The owners were incensed and determined to have justice. William Betagh visited several of the returned sailors at their homes and lodgings in London and persuaded

184

them to 'be an evidence for Hughes and the rest of the owners against Captain Shelvocke' in return for suspension of proceedings against them. These affidavits, now lodged in the National Archives,[504] confirm Betagh's account and add extra incriminating details. In parallel to their action over the prize money, the owners attempted to have Shelvocke tried for piracy for the incident off Cape Frio, backed up by complaints by the Spanish ambassador in London, the Marquis de Pozzo Bueno.[505]

They reckoned without George Shelvocke. He may have been a crook but he was a clever crook. He managed to get out on bail on a Sunday and succeeded in avoiding acceptance of writs issued against him by the owners. He approached an unnamed brother-in-law who acted as intermediary with two of the owners who were parties to the action against him, perhaps persuading them that there was really very little money left over and that they had better cut their losses. Bribes were paid, presumably out of some of the proceeds from the *Concepción*. These two owners pretended to come to a settlement and since they were parties to the action 'a sudden stop was made to the prosecution'.[506] Shelvocke got away with it.

Some of his sailors were less fortunate. Two months later, George Gill and young William Burrow were still in the Marshalsea Prison and very ill, William Burrow's life being 'despaired of'.[507] The action for piracy quietly faded. With regard to the piracy, the problem for the prosecuting authorities was that no one had ever seen any Portuguese *moidores* in Shelvocke's hand. The only person who had been in definite possession was Simon Hatley.

As for Hatley. He spent over twelve months in irons in his prison cell in Lima and did not return until 1723 having narrowly escaped hanging or the mines because of the incident with the Portuguese ship off Cape Frio. For once, fortune had, if only eventually, smiled. The act of piracy, if such it was, had been committed against a Portuguese ship rather than a Spanish ship and Spanish law was unclear as to how the Liman authorities should proceed. Having heard testimony of George Shelvocke's 'vile proceedings', they had decided that Shelvocke was 'the principal in the piratical story'[508] and Hatley had been freed, although with the cloud of the incident still hanging over him, there being no certain proof that anyone other than him had benefited from the generosity of the Portuguese captain. Certainly, no one other than himself had been found with *moidores* in his hand. The possibility of further legal action by the British authorities or by the Portuguese owners and captain must have weighed heavily.

almost to the disgust of his species

Jonathan Swift began writing *Gulliver's Travels* in late 1720 after the South Sea Bubble had burst and when *Speedwell* was off the Pacific coast of South America. He was likely spurred to start work by the overwhelming success of *Robinson Crusoe* the previous year. He wrote 'sitting like a toad in a corner of his great house',[509] in a muffled world of increasing dizziness and deafness, in the empty echoing uncarpeted deanery of St. Patrick's in Dublin where the only really homely room was his book-lined study on the ground floor. He had been toying with the ideas behind *Gulliver* for years. They had been born out of convivial meetings of the Scriblerus Club, during his glory days in 1713, in the rooms of his friend John Arbuthnot, doctor to Queen Anne, in St. James's Palace, London.

Membership of this small, select dinner club included Arbuthnot, the poets Alexander Pope, Thomas Parnel and John Gay and the politician Henry St. John (Viscount Bolingbroke). Robert Harley, Earl of Oxford and architect of the Peace of Utrecht, had been an occasional member and it was Oxford who first called Swift by the nickname 'Dr Martin' 'because martin is a sort of swallow, and so is a swift'.[510] From the Scriblerus Club had arisen the *Memoirs of Martinus Scriblerus,* written by John Arbuthnot with perhaps some parts by Pope but with ideas contributed by everyone and, with particular enthusiasm one suspects, given the final outcome, by Jonathan Swift. Martinus Scriblerus is a pedant who travels the world drawing wrong conclusions, considerable space being given to his upbringing which includes having the Greek alphabet stamped on his gingerbread. It was planned that on his first voyage he would be carried 'by a prosperous storm to a discovery of the ancient Pygmean Empire',[511] on his second voyage he would be shipwrecked in a land of giants, on his third voyage he would discover a 'kingdom of philosophers who govern by mathematics'[512] and on his fourth voyage he would come upon a land of

186

vile creatures 'almost to the disgust of his species'.[513] In essence these were the voyages of Gulliver although less compelling when written by Arbuthnot, perhaps because Arbuthnot picked rather obscure targets for his satire.

When Swift took possession of their story and sat down to write it as his own version, the swashbuckling age of the South Sea men was drawing to a close. 'My Cousin Dampier', referred to early on in Swift's book, had been dead for over five years, Selkirk was on the point of dying off the coast of West Africa and Hatley had already shot the albatross, the last of the acts which would connect the South-Sea men to the men of literature. *Gulliver's Travels*, as befits a book which rounds off an era, is something of an old man's book, famously 'written to vex the world rather than divert it'.[514] Swift was only fifty-three and had another twenty-five years to live when he started writing but he was old in the sense that he saw himself as at the end of the voyage, disappointed in his ambitions, fearful of deafness and of the senility which eventually engulfed him - 'I shall be like that tree, I shall die at the top'.[515]

Swift, for all his playfulness and kindness among friends, was not an easy man. There is a streak of misanthropy in his masterpiece. *Gulliver* starts relatively mildly, after the shipwreck on Lilliput, with a satire on the wars between European states and religions, works its way through a vast range of human foolishness, greed and pride and develops with gusto into a condemnation of the very essence of what it is to be human - if to be human is to be bestial, as Swift maintains. In emotional tone it is a very different book to *Robinson Crusoe*. *Robinson Crusoe*, a near-continuous commentary on Crusoe's thoughts and state of mind, is warm, personal, believable and very readable even today. *Gulliver*, by contrast, exhibits an absence of emotional depth. Coleridge, who admired Swift's wit and style, knew what was lacking, 'Swift was *anima Reabelaisii habitans in sicco* - the soul of Rabelais dwelling in a dry place.'[516]

But Swift wrote for his middle-aged friends and not for the common herd. His friends eagerly awaited completion. In December 1721, Henry St. John, Viscount Bolingbroke, by then back in England having flirted with Jacobinism in Paris, but not yet fully reconciled to his fall from power, wrote that he 'longed' to see the *Travels*. In January 1724, Swift was writing to his friend Charles Ford 'I have left the country of the Horses, and am now on Flying Island, where I shall not stay long, and my two last journeys will soon be over'.[517] In August 1725, he wrote again: 'I have finished my travels and am now transcribing them. They are admirable things, and will wonderfully mend the world'.[518]

He wrote part III, the account of Laputa (*la Puta* - 'the whore' in Spanish) the Flying Island last, perhaps because it was the least enjoyable section of the book for him to write, an attack on science and members of the Royal Society, the 'philosophers who govern by mathematics' - and attempt to distil sunbeams from cucumbers. Perhaps he was in a hurry to write about the Land of the Houyhnhnms, the Land of Horses, before Laputa because it was the part closest to his heart. Although originally destined to be Part III he quickly realised its power and moved it to come last. In the land of the Houyhnhnms we come across the Yahoos, based on Dampier's unfriendly description of Australian Aborigines.[519] Far more unpleasant than Dampier's Aborigines, the Yahoos are bestial, little better than animals, but they are people as is proved when a female attempts to mate with Gulliver. They are so bestial that when Gulliver returns from his last voyage, he is, as planned at the Scriblerus Club, full of 'disgust for his own species'. He prefers to sleep in the stable with his horses rather than with his wife whom he finds repulsive and who, he now realises, is a Yahoo like everyone else.

As soon as I entered the House, my Wife took me in her Arms, and kissed me; at which, not having been used to the touch of that odious animal for so many Years, I fell into a Swoon for almost an Hour ... I could not endure my Wife or my Children in my Presence, the very Smell of them was intolerable ...[520]

Was Swift onto something? Did some men choose the sea to escape the company of women and their fellow citizens? Happy marriages are conspicuous by their absence from the lives of the sailor authors and of their companions. Dampier got married but scarcely saw his wife again, Woodes Rogers's wife may have left him,[521] Selkirk beat up one woman and married another. Were Hatley, Selkirk and the others, with no wives at all or drifting from wife to wife rootless somehow lacking in a normal desire for domesticity, did they feel in some sense similarly to Gulliver?

Robert Harley, Earl of Oxford, died in 1724. He had survived his period in the Tower following the accession of George I and had defended himself with bravery against accusations of treachery. Shortly after his death, in November 1724, Harley's son invited Swift to come to England to write his father's biography with full access to all the Harley papers. 'There would be no one more welcome to me than yourself. You should live in your own way and do just what is most agreeable to you. I have houses enough; you shall take your choice'.[522] Swift's friends Pope, Gay and Arbuthnot joined the chorus, urging him to come over. But something held Swift back. He lingered in Dublin. It was not until March 1726 that he returned to London, carrying with him the completed manuscript of *Gulliver's Travels*. He returned to a hero's welcome. The friends read *Guilliver* and were enchanted. There followed long stays at Pope's house in Twickenham, a two-week holiday on horseback with Pope and Gay, dinners with the rich and powerful. Life was at it should be.

Swift's exile was over, or it could have been if he so chose. But he did not. Esther Johnson, 'Stella', to whom he may have been secretly married by this time, was seriously ill back in Dublin. He left towards the end of July 1726, worried beneath a pretence at calm, Pope accompanying him as far as Chester. Pope described the nagging sadness of the journey: 'I felt the extreme heat of the weather, the inns, the roads, the confinement and closeness of the uneasy coach ...'.[523] There were concerns about the government's reaction to a book which was so cynical of government. It was only after Swift was safely home that Pope arranged for the manuscript to be delivered to the printer 'dropped at his house in the dark from a hackneyed coach',[524] a suitable start to the maze of hints and denials of authorship which Swift subsequently delighted in.

Travels into several Remote Nations of the World, by Lemuel Gulliver was first published, in London, on 28 October 1726 and was, like *Robinson Crusoe*, an instant success. Any fears of government anger vanished almost overnight. It was too mad, too inventive, too brilliant, too excessive to be gagged. The common herd took to it with enthusiasm. Even its targets were

189

willing to forgive. The Princess of Wales loved it and took no exception if told that she was the model for the Queen of Brobdingnag. Even the Duchess of Marlborough, an old enemy, was impressed. The first printing sold out within a week and it was translated into Dutch and French before the year was out.

intirely a Deception

Sometime that same year, George Shelvocke's *A Voyage round the World by way of the Great South Sea* was also published, an absorbing tale of courage and resilience in which the long-suffering George Shelvocke overcomes all odds to complete his mission, although with less-than-satisfactory results due to circumstances and sailors beyond his control. It too was a success although not, of course, in any way on the scale of *Gulliver*. There is a Homeric and tragic quality to Shelvocke's book. The voyage is undermined before it begins, by Captain Clipperton (now, fortunately for Shelvocke, dead and unable to defend himself) who sets out to weaken Shelvocke's authority and set his crew against him. From this original betrayal all subsequent disasters spring. The crew becomes Shelvocke's burden throughout the voyage, incompetent and mutinous, as are his surly, disobedient officers, in particular Second Captain Simon Hatley and William Betagh, his Captain of Marines of 'unparalleled wickedness'.[525] Shelvocke pulls no punches. Raging seas, cruel Spaniards, noble savages, grasping priests, hints on navigation and business opportunities, exotic wildlife, war at sea, starvation and drought, all the palette of the sailor-authors, compete for the reader's attention - but always the real villains are the crew and the officers. *A Voyage round the World by way of the Great South Sea* is a thrilling adventure story but it gets its narrative power from the obsessive, carping malice of its author.

Shelvocke dedicated his book to the Lord Commissioners of the Admiralty, remarking, 'if your Lordships think my conduct in this expedition deserves censure, I shall humbly submit my self to your Lordships' just reproof'.[526] On the surface he appeared to face up to the 'various unjust Aspersions have been thrown upon me', meaning, of course, Betagh's accusations and the subsequent court actions, but these matters are never fully addressed. Pleas for understanding are offered instead. Readers, Shelvocke suggests, with remarkable cheek, should not 'lend a credulous ear to hearsay without considering the malice and dishonest ways that are conceal'd in the breast of the reporter'.[527]

On reading Shelvocke's book, William Betagh found that he had been systematically libelled, accused of sailing against his shipmates on a Spanish ship after his capture and disembarkation at Paita and of other treasonable activities (about which there may have been a grain of truth) as well as insubordination and attempted mutiny. He was outraged. He knew that the author was a crook. His reply, published in 1728, *A Voyage Round the World*, was also dedicated to the Lords Commissioners of the Admiralty and was meant to put matters straight, 'as his (Shelvocke's) pretended narrative is intirely a deception, and his whole conduct an indignity to his country, I thought it my duty to give your Lordships a genuine account of the man as well as our voyage ...'.[528] Betagh's book is a jumbled, poorly-written concoction, not nearly so entertaining as Shelvocke's but its equal in malice. Their Lordships may have wondered at having two such diatribes dedicated to them within the space of two years.

William Betagh's book sealed the end of an era. There were no further privateering ventures to the South Sea for nearly twenty years, when Commodore Anson and his squadron set off in 1740 with their compliment of five hundred marines, actually Chelsea Pensioners, of whom 'all those who had limbs and strength to walk out of Portsmouth deserted, leaving behind them only such as were literally invalids, most of them being sixty years of age ...'[529] The freewheeling days were over. Even piracy, which had exploded to the dimensions of a plague at the end of the War of the Spanish Succession,* by 1730 was reduced to a minor irritant. The unique circumstances which had allowed Dampier, Selkirk and Hatley to cruise so freely on the other side of the world would never be repeated.

Dampier and Selkirk were already dead. Woodes Rogers died in Nassau, Bahamas, in 1732 where he had gone initially to suppress piracy[530].

---

* There were as many as 2,500 pirates in up to thirty ships roaming the seas at any one time in the years 1716-22 . As many as six hundred pirates were hanged between 1716 and 1726 - Rediker (1987) 283.

191

Daniel Defoe died in 1731 in lodgings on Rope Makers' Alley in the city, broke once more and weighed down 'under the load of insupportable sorrows',[531] and Shelvocke died in 1742 in his son's house on Lombard Street.[532]

Crime does pay, sometimes. George Shelvocke, destitute when Edward Hughes offered him the position of commander in 1718, ended his days in ease and affluence and his son went on to become Secretary of the General Post Office and a Fellow of the Royal Society.[533] Shelvocke's memorial stone in St. Nicholas's Church Deptford, now destroyed, eulogised 'a gentleman of great abilities in his profession and allowed to have been one of the bravest and most accomplished seamen of his time'.[534]

Of Simon Hatley we know nothing after his return from prison in Lima in 1723,[535] the threat of a further trial for piracy hanging over him. We know only that, having arrived in London, he 'went immediately for Jamaica, never showing his face to any one of the owners: so that *Shelvocke* imagined there was no witness of consequence to reveal his craft and treachery'.[536] Port Royal was then a riotous haunt of pirates. It is tempting to imagine him with a pint of rum, recuperating in the company of 'Unconscionable Nan, Salt Beef Peg or Buttock-de-Clink Jenny',[537] but unfair. He was a sailor. After Jamaica he probably sailed elsewhere.

CHAPTER 11

Coleridge

the Road to Bristol

On 10th April 1794, Silas Tomkyn Comberbache, a dragoon, twenty years old, of medium height with longish, slightly curly, dark hair, pale skin and poor teeth, was discharged from the 15th Light Dragoons based in Reading 'being insane'.[538] It was an unlikely time for the army to be discharging anyone. The previous year, Revolutionary France had declared war on Britain, the start (for Britain) of the Napoleonic Wars.

The British army of the late-eighteenth century was undemanding about the quality of its recruits. As the Duke of Wellington famously remarked: 'Ours [our army] is composed of the scum of the earth - the mere scum of the earth.'[539] A touch of insanity such as that displayed by young Silas Tomkyn was a minor disqualification for the role of private dragoon, almost an advantage given what was expected of cannon fodder. But Silas was exceptionally unfitted to be a soldier even by the standards of the time, let alone a cavalryman. In the first place, he couldn't ride, in the second place he confessed to 'a complete indisposition towards bodily activity' and in the third place he was extremely absentminded. 'Reverie-ish and streamy'[540] was how he described himself.

Others saw beyond these faults. There was 'something awful about him,' wrote a contemporary, 'his equals in age and rank quailed before him'.[541] Silas Tomkyn Comberbache was an assumed name. The unsuitable dragoon's real name was Samuel Taylor Coleridge. He was a Cambridge scholar 'of brilliant understanding'[542] and one of the rising stars of his generation. Insane he was not, that was a device dreamed up by his brothers and by the army to get him out. But the episode in the dragoons and the absurd name did have a touch of lunatic absurdity about it, typical of the man who wrote the *Rime of the Ancyent Marinere* four years later.

To be sworn into the army under such an absurd name indicated an almost suicidal self-disregard. It was a ridiculously exaggerated step, taken with quixotic abandon, an act of penitence for guilty debts and feckless indolence at Cambridge, but paradoxically it had its positive side. It was such a lunatic and irresponsible thing to do that it became the start of what Coleridge later saw as a spiritual and intellectual voyage away from the conventional, a nautical conceit nourished by his wide reading of adventures and accounts of voyages of exploration, books such as those by Woodes Rogers and William Dampier.

That summer of 1794, having been released from the army thanks to his brothers and having completed the academic year at Cambridge in uncertain fashion, Coleridge set off on a walking tour. Walking was a demonstration of democratic principles.[543] All over Britain at that time young men dressed themselves in rough clothes, slung knapsacks over their shoulders and set out in search of the 'common people'. Some, such as William Wordsworth, ventured far afield. Wordsworth got as far as Italy in 1790, plodding back across a France in the throes of revolution, and returned again in 1791. Coleridge, wilder but less well-organised, settled for Wales. He set off on 15th June 1794, with a fellow student, a stalwart foil by the name of Joseph Hucks. His equipment consisted of a canvas knapsack and a specially-made walking stick, five feet long and carved with the head of an eagle on one side and a rough likeness of its owner on the other. Around the neck was fitted an Elizabethan ruff made out of tin.[544]

He ended up in Bristol, drawn there by a new friend, acquired while passing through Oxford. This new friend was Robert Southey, the son of an unsuccessful Bristol linen merchant. During beer-fuelled evenings in Oxford they had invented a new movement, 'Pantisocracy', from the Greek *pan-socratia* and meaning an 'all-governing society'. Coleridge preached Pantisocracy on all possible occasions. It was part philosophy and part a wildly impractical scheme to establish a communistic, rural community on the banks of the Susquehannah in North America. To more sober heads, it must have seemed that Silas Tomkyn was not as yet fully dead.

Coleridge arrived in Bristol on 5th August 1794. Through a friend of Southey a 'fellow citizen' by the name of Robert Lovell, already a convert to Pantisocracy and expecting to sail for America in the spring, he met the Fricker family, a widow and six daughters. Mrs Fricker had a dress shop. Lovell was married to Mary, the second Fricker daughter, Southey was after Edith, the third one, and the fourth, Sarah, was soon destined for Coleridge, initially for reasons of neatness as much as for love although that changed later. Sarah was bowled over by Coleridge, the cleverest of the Pantisocrats, with his 'poet's eye in fine frenzy rolling'.[545]

Things moved at a frantic pace. Having taken steps to secure their base as it were, Southey and Coleridge left the girls and Bristol behind them and set out on a tour of Somerset. They took in Bath and the Cheddar Gorge and, on 18th August 1794, they arrived near the little town of Nether Stowey, beneath the shoulder of the Quantock Hills about five miles from the north Somerset coast and the Bristol Channel.

They were there to visit Henry Poole, a fellow student of Coleridge at Jesus College, Cambridge, who was passing the summer at his family home. Henry, affable but too cautious to make a candidate for Pantisocracy, took his visitors to meet his cousin, Thomas Poole. Thomas, then twenty-nine years old, lived in a modestly substantial house on Castle Street, one of the two main streets of the little town, with his business premises at the back. He was the son of a prosperous tanner, and he himself was a solid, practical businessman with a broad Somerset accent, a most unlikely radical. But appearances were deceptive. Tom Poole was self-educated and benevolent in the purest sense of the word. During his life he founded the Stowey Co-

Operative Bank for local working people, the Stowey Women's Benefit Society and the Stowey Book Club, which circulated the works of Thomas Paine and Mary Wollstonecraft among others, and he later built the village school. Here was fertile ground. Poole summed up Coldridge (*sic*) in a letter. 'He is, I understand, a shining scholar ... his aberrations from prudence, to use his own expression, have been great.'[546] It was the start of a close friendship. Coleridge offered intellectual stimulation; Poole offered a rock to shelter by in stormy waters and also - Nether Stowey itself. It was at Nether Stowey that Coleridge wrote most of the *Rime of the Ancyent Marinere*.

The long, frantic summer drew to a close. By the time Coleridge returned to Cambridge that autumn, he had proposed to Sarah Fricker and was committed to emigration to the banks of the Susquehannah the following spring. His brothers thought he was 'deranged'.[547] Letters flowed fast and thick between the two founding Pantisocrats, hammering out the finer points of their programme. By February 1794, Coleridge, Southey and a fellow enthusiast by the name of George Burnett were ensconced in rooms at 25 College Street, Bristol, not far from the dockside where Simon Hatley had spent so much of his youth and where the *Duke* and *Duchess* had been fitted out. The scheme, on paper at least, was nearer to fruition. 25 College Street became the epicentre of a storm of proselytising activity, both for Pantisocracy and for other progressive movements.

But all was not well. There were disagreements. Southey, already trimming his sails to the wind (he feared for his inheritance)[548] proposed that it would not come amiss if servants were to undertake the basic drudgery; Coleridge thought all should be equal. Southey equivocated about the freedom and equality of women; Coleridge wanted to free them as much as possible. Coleridge was consistently more radical. Pantisocracy must either remain pure or it would be nothing at all. It was an ideal, a city on a hill where man could live in harmony with nature and with his fellow men. If not, it was just another failed emigration project - funds for the experiment were still almost nonexistent.

Today College Street is a wasteland of tarmac behind the 1930s Council House, but in the 1790s it was a Georgian terrace at the bottom of

Clifton Hill where terraces and crescents were sprouting up to provide homes for wealthy eighteenth-century Bristoleians away from the grime of the glass works and the docks. About three minutes up the hill from College Street lies Great George Street. No 7 was the home of a wealthy merchant by the name of John Praetor Pinney, and is now restored and open to the public as the 'Georgian House Museum'. Pinney's wealth came from sugar plantations on the island of St. Nevis. He was, or had been, a slave owner but had sold all but three of his plantations before retiring to Bristol. Although himself relatively humane, he had had few scruples in selling the largest of them to an owner notorious for brutality, whereat the slaves rebelled and were then ruthlessly suppressed.

Attitudes had changed since the time of Daniel Defoe, who betrays no misgivings in having Robinson Crusoe set sail from Brazil in order to acquire black slaves for his Brazilian plantation. Slavery and the slave trade had become discredited institutions when Coleridge and Southey came to call. Thomas Clarkson, founder of the British anti-slavery movement, described by Coleridge as 'the giant with one idea',[549] chose Bristol to begin his enquiries in 1787. Although John Pinney managed to square the less salubrious aspects of his career with his more progressive opinions, his sons, John and Azariah, were more idealistic. John, the eldest, had received the remaining three St. Nevis plantations together with more than two hundred slaves for his twenty-first birthday but he was a 'rabid Whig' who sought to salve his conscience by entertaining the more progressive thinkers in the city, including the two bright sparks from lodgings down the road. It was in the Pinneys' bright upstairs drawing room with views towards the Avon that Coleridge met the most important friend of his life and the next crucial figure in the genesis of the *Ancient Mariner*, a rising young poet from the north of England by the name of William Wordsworth, there to visit his friends, the younger Pinneys.

Pantisocracy, meanwhile, had run its course. In a final flight of fancy Coleridge suggested that they all move to one of the plantations on St. Nevis and set up a community of poets, making it 'more illustrious than Cos or Lesbos'.[550] In reality, Southey wanted out. On 1st September 1795 after a series of rows, he left College Street and returned to his mother's house in

197

Bath, feebly promising to rejoin Pantisocracy 'in about fourteen years'.[551] A month later, Sarah Fricker and Coleridge, the keeper of the flame, were married in St. Mary's Redcliffe, where sailors came to pray in the north porch at the beginning and end of their voyages and where a whalebone said to have been brought back by John Cabot in 1497 was displayed (and still is) above the entrance to the chapel of St. John the Baptist. Robert Southey and Edith Fricker were married there a month later but there were no mutual invitations.

Nether Stowey

Sarah was petite, twenty-one to Coleridge's twenty-three, blue-eyed and shapely and she adored him. The following March, after a brief, idyllic interlude in a cottage in Clevedon, they were living in Bristol, Sarah was pregnant and they were cramped, uncomfortable and short of money. In desperation Coleridge contacted Tom Poole down at Nether Stowey. Poole had helped out financially already, arranging for around £40 to be paid to Coleridge by various wealthy and admiring friends, a similar sum to be provided annually for the next six years.[552] Coleridge now asked for help with housing. Poole advised strongly against a move to Nether Stowey, partly because there wasn't a suitable house available and partly, one suspects, because he feared the responsibility of having a penniless poet on his doorstep. But Coleridge was persistent. Poole had something he needed. Visits to Poole's solid house afforded interludes of tranquillity away from a pressurized fight for survival back in Bristol. He needed the tranquillity in order to be able to think.

In September Sarah gave birth to their first child, Hartley. With the birth of Hartley, Pantisocracy, or something like it, was reborn if in a less ambitious form. Casting aside all other plans for making a living such as teaching or becoming a Unitarian minister, Coleridge, with splendid disregard for practicalities, threw himself on Poole's mercy, begging him to find a rustic retreat in the Quantock hills where his young family could live close to nature. 'I am anxious that my children should be bred up from earliest infancy in the simplicity of peasants'[553] he announced. Poole succumbed. He arranged for the tenancy of a run-down, thatched cottage at the top end of Lime Street, right in Nether Stowey itself, 'the hovel' as Coleridge enthusiastically described it.[*] There were two small downstairs parlours on either side of an entrance passage with a very basic kitchen at the back and, upstairs, three even smaller bedrooms. It was small and primitive but the garden was long and backed onto Poole's orchards and that was enough. Nearness to Poole had become something of an obsession. On 31st December 1796, Coleridge, Sarah and baby Hartley left Bristol in a wagon piled high with 'boxes of Books, and Chests of Drawers, Kitchen-Furniture, Chairs, and our Bed and Bed-Linen &c &c.'[554]

Coleridge and Wordsworth had started corresponding and exchanging manuscripts soon after their first meeting at Great George Street. Their respect for each other increased rapidly. In early April 1797, William, on the spur of the moment, made a detour via Nether Stowey while on his way from Bristol to Racedown Lodge in Dorset where he was living with his sister Dorothy (free of charge, courtesy of his friend and landlord the younger John Pinney). Spring was late and cold that year and as he walked west he passed through a grey landscape just shaking off the frosts of winter. He arrived at Lime Street to find Coleridge much in need of company. It was a meeting of huge importance to both men. They talked until deep in the night in Poole's 'great windy parlour' and when Wordsworth left the next morning their friendship was sealed.

Coleridge got back to work. Wordsworth went back to Racedown Lodge. On 5th June, he was out working in the garden, tending his carrots, cabbages and turnips when Dorothy famously looked up and saw a figure vaulting the gate at the far side of the home field before the road. Next thing Coleridge was running through the field towards them all tousled and hot from walking. It was a moment none of them ever forgot: 'He did not keep to the high road, but leapt over a gate and bounded down the pathless field, by which he cut off an angle.'[555]

There followed a fortnight of walking and talking and reading poetry. Horizons expanded under Coleridge's magic volubility. Coleridge was possessed by a new idea, or rather an old one revisited. Pantisocracy would be reborn, it would be St. Nevis in Nether Stowey, the banks of the

---

[*] It is now a charming, small museum.

Susquehannah beneath the Quantocks - a poets' colony in rural Somerset. There was no time to lose. The Wordsworths must move to Nether Stowey immediately.

While the Wordsworths had been growing vegetables at Racedown, Coleridge had been growing them at Nether Stowey. Both he and Sarah were fond of Nether Stowey and their little thatched nest at the edge of it. Despite Poole's fears, they had been accepted if not exactly welcomed by the locals. Sarah with her baby was in and out of the Cruikshanks round the corner who had a baby the same age, and Tom Poole's mother, widowed since the death of Tom's father, was gratifyingly sympathetic towards her son's and Coleridge's political opinions. As for Poole, whose care for the Coleridge household was downright paternal though his spelling of the name was eccentric, he had previously written a poem which says it all: 'Hail to thee, Coldridge, youth of various powers!..'.[556] Coleridge was able to make use of Poole's library. Poole had a gate cut through the fence between the two properties. All Coleridge had to do was walk up his back garden, through Poole's orchard and past his tanning workshops then up an iron outside staircase to Poole's 'book parlour'. On starry nights he and Sarah would leave Tom Poole's house and walk home together, he with his arm around her, the full rural idyll with literary embellishments. Coleridge kept pigs, ducks and geese and even helped with the cooking. He wrote to Wordsworth: 'I raise potatoes and all manner of vegetables; have an orchard; & shall raise corn with the spade enough for my family.'[557] It sounded wonderful, it was wonderful, but Silas Tomkyn had a hand in it all. There were financial worries and Coleridge who had once confessed, if over-self-critically, to a 'complete indisposition towards bodily activity' was hardly destined to be a gardener.

In moving to Nether Stowey, Coleridge had stepped yet further down the road from conventionality. He was acting out a conscious attempt to live in harmony with nature, difficult in any age and eccentric by the standards of the late eighteenth century. The ideas behind this program for natural living had been brewing for some time. Back in 1794, he had written *To a Young Ass*: 'I hail thee BROTHER - spite of the fool's scorn',[558] which would have been simply loopy if it had not contained a strong (and typical)

200

streak of self-mockery.[559] At least, at Nether Stowey the problems of donkeys were relatively abstract, but on the other hand there were mice. The little cottage was plagued by them. 'It irks me to set a trap,' he told Cottle. 'By all the whiskers of all the pussies that have mewed plaintively, since the days of Whittington, it is not fair … foul breach of the rites of hospitality! I mean to assassinate my guests!'[560] There is an echo of this in the preface to the *Rime of the Ancyent Marinere*: 'How the Ancient Mariner cruelly and in contempt of the laws of hospitality killed a Sea-Bird.'[561]

Coleridge, for all his excesses, held to an essentially decent type of religious belief both in his youth and later when he returned to the bosom of the Church of England. There was nothing eccentric about Unitarianism in the eighteenth century. The most advanced thinkers of the age were Unitarians, including the Wedgwoods, Erasmus Darwin and Joseph Priestley. Coleridge drew most heavily on Priestley. Priestley described a God who was omnipresent and immanent in all nature, the life force behind everything, 'his power is the very life and soul of everything that exists'[562] as he put it in his book *Matter and Spirit*, a concept which had profound resonance for Coleridge. It became bound up with his attitude to poetry - that a 'poet's *Heart* and *Intellect* should be *combined, intimately* combined & *unified* with the great appearances in Nature'.[563] These were the sort of things he was thinking about as he dug his potatoes.

On 28th June, Coleridge returned triumphantly to Nether Stowey bringing Wordsworth in tow. A few days later he set off back to Racedown to collect Dorothy, in a cart borrowed from Tom Poole, returning with the Wordsworth books and baggage over 'forty miles of execrable road'.[564] The cottage on Lime Street was crowded, but Sarah responded gamely. There is a description of her two days later, doing the household chores while Dorothy sits with Coleridge correcting one of his poems. Then on 7th July, Coleridge's old school friend, Charles Lamb, appeared. Conditions were now pretty cramped and everyone, Sarah and Hartley possibly excluded, spent as much time as possible outside walking on the Quantocks. At least the omnipresent Deity had a sense of fair play - he arranged for Sarah to accidentally spill boiling milk on Coleridge's foot putting him out of action for several days.[565]

Things continued to move at a giddy pace. The Wordsworths were at Lime Street for just a fortnight and within that fortnight they found a house, Alfoxden Park, just outside the village of Holford about four miles away. The absentee landlord was a ten-year-old boy, Langley St. Albyn. He was at boarding school in Bristol and his grandmother, Mrs Lancelot St. Albyn, who was ultimately responsible for the property, relied on her local agent to look after it for her. Tom Poole drew up an agreement which was duly signed by William and the agent and the Wordsworths got the whole thing with stables, coach house, park and furniture for a mere £23 per year, taxes included. The St. Albyns had let their house to a radical poet and were completely unaware of having done so. The Wordsworths had to pinch themselves. It was almost too good to be true. Dorothy was in raptures. 'A large mansion in a large park with seventy head of deer around us,' she wrote. 'It has furniture enough for a dozen families like ours.'[566] They moved in on 16th July 1797.

Today, Alfoxden Park is a charming, slightly eccentric hotel. There is wire-netting on the gate at the entrance to the park and sheep roam among the flower beds. Although it was the St. Albyns' family home for centuries, the Wordsworths' brief stay has superimposed itself. The bedrooms have names such as 'Dorothy', 'William' and 'Mariner'. It faces south towards the steep slope of the Quantocks with woods crowding down beyond the lawn. Its back is towards the Bristol Channel. In the Wordsworths' day there were 'nine lodging rooms, three parlours and a hall'.

the bright-eyed Mariner

There followed a rich summer. The two households were in each other's company almost daily in one form or another, often walking back late at night along the four miles of leafy lane between them. Through the tree trunks they would have glimpsed the white sails of ships moving stately as priests up the wide expanse of the Channel, perhaps waiting for a gust of wind or hurrying before a breeze to catch the tide which would take them up the Avon to Bristol. Those night walks with the owls hooting and the fireflies flickering became part of their common memories. For Coleridge and Wordsworth, and indeed Dorothy who kept a precious journal, it was a time of intense creative activity. Wordsworth looked back on it nostalgically in the *Prelude*:

> *That summer when on Quantock's grassy hills*
> *Far ranging, and among sylvan combs,*
> *Thou in delicious words, with happy heart,*
> *Didst speak the vision of that ancient Man,*
> *The bright-eyed Mariner ...*[567]

Together they tramped the hills and lanes, notebooks in hand, sometimes just Coleridge and William, sometimes William and Dorothy, sometimes all three. The Wordsworths were an odd couple. He wore out-of-date striped pantaloons and a brown, twill jacket and carried a camping stool; she was brown as a berry with clear, grey eyes, in old clothes and out in all weathers, not caring a fig for what the neighbours might think. Coleridge was almost drunk with it all.

But even as the summer unfolded, passing from May-blossom to poppy-time to heather-time on the hilltops, the worm was already in the fruit. After Charles Lamb left Stowey to return to London, he was replaced almost immediately by another friend, John Thelwall, small and plump with close-cropped hair, a notorious radical and atheist. He had been arrested, although unsuccessfully prosecuted, for treason and was in retreat from 'patriots' who broke up his lectures and threatened his livelihood.

On Sunday 23rd July, the Sunday following the Wordsworth's move to Alfoxden, there was a housewarming dinner in the hall there. The guests included Poole, Thelwall and the Coleridges, fourteen in all. When it was over, Thelwall, wearing a white hat, then the mark of a radical, stood up and held forth with 'such passion that James was frightened',[568] James being a local man hired to wait on the diners.

What was the world coming to? Treasonable men in white hats giving passionate speeches? Strange walks in the countryside, often at night, with campstools and notebooks? Could it all have something to do with the French invasion - advance planning and that sort of thing? And the young 'French' couple at Alfoxden who were not married but claimed to be brother and sister, with a child, Basil, they said was not theirs? The Wordsworths were looking after the two-year-old illegitimate son of William's school friend, Basil Montague, himself the illegitimate son of the Earl of Sandwich.

Rumour fed rumour. The government in London was alerted. Tensions were high because of the war. In February, French frigates had sunk several merchant ships off Illfracombe in Devon. They had then landed 1,200 French soldiers in Pembrokeshire and the orders of their commander, it was discovered after his surrender, had been to capture and destroy Bristol.[569] A government agent by the name of James Walsh was sent down to Nether Stowey to investigate. Walsh set up his base at the Globe Inn, Stowey, on 15th August. He proceeded to track the poets through the woods and fields, showing 'truly Indian perseverance',[570] and took down notes from the locals. It was ridiculous of course and Coleridge dined out on it for years, referring to the 'Spy Nozy affair'[571] because poor Walsh had mistaken a reference to the philosopher Spinoza, when taking down one of their conversations. Not so ridiculous was old Mrs St. Albyn's reaction when she got wind of what was going on. She wanted the undesirables out of her house. Nothing Tom Poole could write to her could convince her otherwise. She was adamant: the lease on Alfoxden would not be renewed after it expired the following July. From September, just two months after the Wordsworths moved in, there was a time limit on the *annus mirabilis*.

Coleridge was starting to write some of his best poetry. The long years of reading, the philosophical concerns, the religious concerns, all came together. He had a prodigious memory. Back in the days of Silas Tomkyn, while waiting for his discharge from the dragoons, he had spent a long evening with a bar-room bore listening to alcohol-fuelled theories of 'heaven and hell. 'My memory,' he wrote to his brother George, 'tenacious and systematizing would have enabled me to write an Octavo from his conversation'.[572] Now this extraordinary facility of recall began to bear fruit. In October[573] when the leaves were beginning to turn gold and the bracken to rust, he set off on a long walk west along the coast, and as the evening drew in and the moon rose over Exmoor he took shelter in a farmhouse near Culborne, high at the head of a wooded combe, past woods rich with 'wild deer, foxes, badgers and martin cats'. It was there that he wrote *Kubla Khan*, fifty-four lines composed 'without any conscious effort', perhaps his greatest poem. 'The fragment, with a good deal more, not recoverable, composed in a sort of Reverie brought on by two grains of Opium taken to check a dysentery, at a Farm House between Porlock and Linton, a quarter mile from Culborne Church, in the fall of the year, 1797.'[574]

He had been reading and rereading Purchas' *Pilgrimage*, published 1614, possibly a copy borrowed from Southey but not returned. Samuel Purchas, 'a man of many words',[575] was successor and one-time assistant to the great Elizabethan propagandist for exploration, Richard Hakluyt. His *Pilgrimage* is a vast compendium of accounts of voyages and observations of travellers from Biblical times down the end of the sixteenth century, an early anthropological survey of what was then known of the world. Like Hakluyt, Purchas was eager to inspire his fellow countrymen to set sail and take benefit of the globe. As he advertised it to his readers in the introduction, in the flowery Tudor cadences so beloved of Coleridge: 'a world of travellers to their domestic entertainment, easy to be spared from their smoke, cup or butterfly vanities and superfluities, and fit mutually to entertaine them in a better school to better purposes'.[576] In Book 4, Chapter 13, there occurs the following passage:

In Xanadu did Cublai Can build a stately Pallace, encompassing sixteene miles of plaine ground with a wall, wherein are fertile Meddows, pleasant Springs, delightful Streames, and all sorts of beasts of chase and game, and in the midst thereof a sumptuous house of pleasure, which may be removed from place to place ...[577]

Here was another side to the poetic equation. Coleridge had supposed that a poet's heart and intellect should be 'intimately unified with the great appearances of nature', but here heart and intellect were unified with the *words* of other writers, 'all other men's words are the poet's chaos' as he later put it. In *Kubla Khan* he took the episode from Purchas' *Pilgrimage* and combined it with other writings as well as his own observations of nature, to create a creation myth from a traveller's tale. Kubla Khan, god-like, conjures his pleasure-dome into existence:

In Xanadu did Kubla Khan
A stately pleasure-dome decree:
Where Alph, the sacred river ran
Through caverns measureless to man
Down to a sunless sea ...

A person from Porlock interrupted him before he could finish, or so he claimed.

Wordsworth and Coleridge were now in each other's company most of the time. Their friendship was all-consuming, even Tom Poole was sidelined. It was an attraction of opposites: Coleridge fluid, garrulous, endlessly inventive, Wordsworth tall, steady and very ambitious. They wrote very differently. Coleridge liked to compose 'in walking over uneven ground or breaking through the straggling branches of a copsewood; whereas Wordsworth always wrote (if he could) walking up and down a straight gravel walk ...'.[578] Inevitably they discussed a collaboration. Early in November Coleridge took both William and Dorothy along the route towards Porlock and beyond, staying the night at Lynmouth and walking four miles further to a dramatic, dry valley above the coast, the Valley of the Rocks. It was here that they dreamed up the outline of a gothic ballad to be called *The Wanderings of Cain*. Wordsworth was to write the first canto, Coleridge the second, and whoever finished first was to write the last one. Back at the inn, Coleridge completed his canto in record time but Wordsworth got stuck. Coleridge found him with 'that look of humorous despondency fixed on his almost blank sheet of paper, and then its silent mock-piteous admission of failure ...'[579]

Around a week later, on 14th November at four o'clock in the afternoon, they set out again, intending to have another go. They left Alfoxden in fading light and climbed up through the steep woods and out onto the open top of the Quantocks, onto the 'Great Track' an ancient way that leads across the hills to West Quantoxhead and from there descends to the coast. The route they took is little changed today. Oak and beech woods crowd the lower slopes but from the tops the whole expanse of the Bristol Channel is laid out like a garden pond, the islands of Flat Holm and Steep

Holm like half-submerged behemoths in mid-stream towards Bristol, the ships in mid-stream, and on the far side the white flecks of Welsh houses just visible along the shore. They chose to leave at four to see the sunlight fade to moonlight over the silent water. While they walked they talked, plotting their new collaboration, another gothic ballad. Publication was to pay the expenses of an extended walking tour along the coast.

By the time they had crossed the hills 'through a dark and cloudy evening' and started to descend the steep slope of West Quantoxhead towards the further valley and with the prospect of a warm inn at the little port of Watchet ahead of them, some of the outlines of their poem were already established, but a focal point was still lacking. Wordsworth, chastened by his experience with *The Wanderings of Cain*, was already taking a back seat, but he did make a crucial suggestion. 'I myself suggested,' he remembered many years later, 'for example, some crime was to be committed which would bring the Old Navigator, as Coleridge always delighted to call him, the spectral persecution, as a consequence of that crime, and his own wanderings. I had been reading in Shelvocke's *Voyages* a day or two before that while doubling Cape Horn they frequently saw Albatrosses in that latitude ..."suppose," I said, "you represent him as having killed one of these birds on entering the South Sea, and that the tutelary Spirits of these regions take upon them to avenge the crime."[580]

Thus it was that Hatley's shooting of the albatross in the Southern Ocean in October 1719 became the focus for Coleridge's masterpiece. The 'melancholy fits' and the hint of superstition suited Coleridge's gothic purposes perfectly. Here at one stroke was the central image he had been looking for, a direct development from *The Mark of Cain*. Cain is the original Wandering Jew, one doomed to wander eternally in expiation of a crime, a theme very much in the air in 1797. There had been a play, *The Wandering Jew*, put on at the Drury Lane Theatre that spring. Cain slays his brother Abel and is sentenced to be a fugitive and vagabond upon the earth, branded by an undefined 'mark' to stop people killing him and so to prolong his punishment. Shelvocke's account inspired a new twist, the 'mark' is now also the victim of the crime, an innocent bird:

207

Instead of a cross, the Albatross
About my neck was hung.

From there, there was only one further step. Coleridge took Cain/The Wandering Jew and made him into the central figure of what is effectively a green legend, a parable about man's careless abuse of the natural world. In the Bible Cain shrugs off his crime, asking God, 'am I my brother's keeper?' but in Coleridge's poem the brother in question is an animal, 'My Brother the Ass', the mice in the kitchen. It is only when the Mariner finds it in his heart to love the natural world, which happens when he is gazing on some water snakes, that the dead albatross falls from his neck:

Oh happy living things! no tongue
Their beauty might declare:
A spring of love gushed from my heart,
And I blessed them unaware.
Sure my kind saint took pity on me,
And I blessed them unaware.

The selfsame moment I could pray;
And from my neck so free
The Albatross fell off, and sank
Like lead into the sea.

And the myth is finally summed up:

He prayeth best, who loveth best
All things both great and small;
For the dear God who loveth us,
He made and loveth all.

It was dark by the time the three friends swung down West Quantoxhead and along the two miles of winding lane to Watchet. At the Bell Inn, about a minute from the harbour and still there, by the guttering light of a candle, the first lines of the Ancient Mariner were put to paper. Wordsworth bowed out: 'Our respective manners were so widely different, that it would have been quite presumptuous in me to do anything but separate from an undertaking upon which I could only have been a clog.'[581]

Watchet Harbour, 1750, probably by Robert Griffier

Coleridge worked on the poem over the following three months, adding further embellishments. He emphasised the arbitrariness of Simon Hatley's 'crime'. In shooting the albatross, Hatley, if we can believe Shelvocke, was 'hoping for a fair wind thereby' but Coleridge's Ancient Mariner has no such motive. He just goes ahead and kills the poor thing. The pointlessness of the act helps to shift the poem away from reality. It opens the gate to supernatural forces. Supernatural forces were a selling point. The previous year, Matthew Lewis had published his gothic block-buster, *The Monk*, a tale of murder, rape and black magic, with a Wandering Jew and a horrible 'Bleeding Nun' thrown in for good measure. Coleridge, despite confessing to a surfeit of 'the terrible' had written a reasonably favourable review of it in February. In the *Ancient Mariner* Coleridge gives full vent. He tweaks every paranormal string available.

Dead men stand up and sail the ship, a ghostly ship sails without any wind to propel it, the sea rots, Death plays dice with a female spectre 'The Nightmare Life-in-Death'.

But underlying everything else, the basic plot of Ancient Mariner rests on the tale of a voyage, a voyage round Cape Horn, moving from east to west against the prevailing wind, just such a voyage as the Speedwell made in 1719. The Ancient Mariner follows this route and the prevailing conditions fairly closely proceeding north to the equator, as did Simon.

The bloody sun at noon,
Right up above the mast did stand,
No bigger than the moon.

Coleridge had a wealth of material to draw on, much of it lodged in his memory. Four accounts are reckoned to have been particularly inspiring: the voyage of John Davis of the *Desire* who sailed on Cavendish's second voyage in 1591, the voyage of Captain Thomas James, who sailed from Bristol in search of a north-west passage in 1623, the voyages of Captain James Cook who mapped Australia in the 1770s and the voyage of Captain William Bligh of the *Bounty* in 1789, who sailed over four thousand miles across the Pacific in an open boat after being relieved of his command by Fletcher Christian and the other mutineers.

On 23rd March 1798 when the air was still cold, Coleridge walked the four miles from Nether Stowey to Holford, then on up the narrow lane through the deer park to Alfoxden. He carried with him the completed manuscript of the *Ancient Mariner*. That evening, by the fire in the dark, wood-panelled parlour, he read his poem aloud to the Wordsworths, no doubt with full dramatic diction, 'there is a chaunt in the recitation of both Coleridge and Wordsworth ...'[582] Later they walked back with him part of the way. 'It was,' Dorothy wrote in her journal, 'a beautiful evening. very starry, the horned moon.'[583]

Coleridge and Wordsworth decided to go for a joint publication. The idea was to raise money for a tour of Germany. It was to be a revolutionary publication by the standards of the time, tapping into alarmingly democratic modes of expression. Wordsworth wrote in the preface: 'The majority of the following poems are to be considered as experiments. They were written chiefly with a view to ascertain how far the language of conversation in the middle and lower classes of society is adapted to the purposes of poetic pleasure.'

Note the word 'majority'. *The Ancient Mariner*, as Wordsworth knew full well, was in a faux-medieval style, later somewhat sanitised. It was about as far from the language of the middle and lower classes as it is possible to imagine - in the 1790s people did not normally say 'eftsoon' or refer to 'merry minstrelsy'. In the final collection, nineteen of the poems were by Wordsworth and four were by Coleridge. Wordsworth's were of a piece with the Preface; Coleridge's were anything but. 'My compositions, instead of forming a balance appeared rather an interpolation of heterogeneous matter' he humbly confessed.

But the *Ancient Mariner* was at least a ballad. One of the radical aspects of the collection was its emphasis on the ballad form, on narrative verse, thus its title, *Lyrical Ballads*. It was published in September of that year after Coleridge and the Wordsworths were already in Germany - anonymously on Coleridge's insistence, because: 'Wordsworth's name is nothing - and to a large number of persons, mine stinks.'

Of all the poems in the simple little volume, and in spite of Wordsworth's Preface, *the Rime of the Ancyent Marinere*, is best remembered. It is the first poem in the book as well as the longest. The Ancient Mariner shoots the albatross on page 10. After that a fair south wind springs up and blows him north into the Pacific and the world of myth and the supernatural:

> *We were the first that ever burst*
> *Into that silent sea ...*

But Hatley, as we have seen, was on a different course and was not useful to Coleridge beyond the one incident, being an officer and not quite the stuff of legend. He continued to suffer bad weather and after the bad weather came the terror of capture, of wounding and a second imprisonment, 'a great variety of inexpressible troubles and hardships both by Land and Sea' as Shelvocke summed up his own voyage.[584] And when Hatley returned home there was no 'Hermit good' to forgive his sins:

> *It is the Hermit good!*
> *He singeth loud his godly hymns*
> *That he makes in the wood.*
> *He'll shrieve my soul, he'll wash away*
> *The Albatross's blood ...*

No forgiveness for Hatley and clearly there were things to forgive. He took ship for Jamaica fearing a second trial.

And then nothing. One hopes that life treated him more kindly than Coleridge's Mariner thereafter. That he got married perhaps and enjoyed some years of domestic peace.

One hopes so, but, in the end, it is perhaps reassuring that the real Ancient Mariner, having shot the world's most famous albatross, should sail off into the sunset rather than settle by the fireside with a pair of comfy slippers and a pipe. And appropriate that he should disappear from the record when on the deck of a ship - until William Wordsworth resurrects him, still on a ship, that November afternoon in 1797 and Coleridge, of generous heart and magpie memory, sees the possibilities - the ultimate act of plunder in the saga of the South-Sea men.

the End

BIBLIOGRAPHY

A de I - Archivo de Indias, Seville

AHN - Archivo Histórico Nacional, Madrid

NA - National Archives, London

OLS - Oxford Local Studies

ORO - Oxford Record Office

Adams, Henry Cadwallader (1877): *The Original Robinson Crusoe: being a narrative of the adventures of Alexander Selkirk and others.* London: Routledge and Sons.

Adams, Percy (1980): *Travellers and Travel Liars 1660-1800.* New York: Dover Publications Inc.

Adams, Percy (1983): *Travel Literature and the Evolution of the Novel.* Lexington: University of Kentucky Press.

Alsop, Thomas (1836): *Letters, Conversations, and Recollections of S. T. Coleridge.* New York: Harper and Brothers.

Arbuthnot, John (1712): *Law is a Bottomless-pit: Exemplify'd in the Case of the Lord Strutt, John Bull, Nicholas Frog, and Lewis Baboon: who Spent All They Had in a Law-suit.* London: Printed for John Morphew,

Archenholtz, Johann Wilhelm (1804): *Histoire des flibustiers, traduite de l'allemand de Mr. J.W. d'Archenholtz; avec un avant-propos et quelques notes du traducteur.* Paris: Chez Henrichs.

Arciniegas, Germán (1969): *Latin America, a Cultural History.* London: The Cresset Press.

Ashton, Rosemary(1996): *The Life of Samuel Taylor Coleridge, a critical biography.* Oxford: Blackwell.

Aughton, Peter (2000): *Bristol, a people's history* Bristol. Lancaster: Carnegie Publishing.

Ayres, Philip (1694): *The Voyages and Adventures of Captain Bartholomew Sharp and Others in the South Sea.* London: B.W.

Backscheider, Paula (1989): *Daniel Defoe, his life.* Baltimore: John Hopkins University Press.

Baer, Joel H. (1982): *The Complicated Plot of Piracy: Aspects of English Criminal Law and the Image of the Pirate in Defoe. The Eighteenth Century: Theory and interpretation vol.* 23. Lubbock: Texas Tech University Press.

Balen, Malcolm (2003): *A very English Deceit, the South Sea Bubble and the World's first great financial Scandal.* London: Fourth Estate.

Ballard, Marsh (2003): *Bristol, Sea-Port City.* London: Constable Young Books.

Barker, Juliet (2000): *Wordsworth, a life.* London: Penguin Books.

Barker, Juliet (2002): *Wordsworth, a life in letters.* London: Penguin Books.

Barker-Benfield, G. J. (1996): *The Culture of Sensibility: Sex and Society in Eighteenth-Century Britain.* Chicago: University of Chicago Press.

Barlow, Edward (1934): *Journal of a common Seaman, Barlow's journal of his life at sea in king's shipp, East & West Indiamen & other merchantmen from 1659 to 1703, transcribed by Basil Lubbock.* London: Hurst & Blackett

Beesley, Alfred (1841): *The History of Banbury: including copious historical and antiquarian notices of the neighbourhood.* London: Nichols & Son.

Bell, Ian (1992): *A Dream of Exile, Robert Louis Stevenson, a biography.* Edinburgh: Mainstream.

Bennassar, Bartolomé (1979):*The Spanish Character.* Berkeley CA: University of California Press.

Betagh, William (1728): *A Voyage around the world, being an account of a remarkable enterprise begun in the year 1719*. London: Printed for T. Combes.

Bhöm, Günter Nuevos (1963): *Antecedentes para una Historia de los Judios en Chile Colonia*. Santiago de Chile: Editorial Universitaria.

Bonner, William Hallam (1934): *Captain Dampier Buccaneer-Author*. Palo Alto: Stanford University Press.

Bourne, Ruth *Queen Anne's Navy*. Yale University Press,

Bradley, Peter T. (1939): *Narborough's Don Carlos, Mariner's Mirror 72 (1986)*, pp 465-75

Bridges, Lucas (1951): *Uttermost Part of the Earth*. Sevenoaks: Hodder & Stoughton.

Bromley, John S. (1987): *Corsairs and Navies,1660-1760*. London: Hambledon Press.

Burney, James (1816): *Chronological History of Voyages and Discoveries in the South Seas*. London: G & W Nichol.

Burns, Sir Alan (1954): *History of the British West Indies*. London: Allen and Unwin,

Byron, John (1768): *The narrative of the Honorable John Byron (commodore in a late expedition round the world) containing an account of the great distresses suffered by himself and his companions on the coast of Patagonia, from the year 1740, till their arrival in England*. London: S. Baker & G. Leigh.

Cameron, Ian (1990): *Kingdom of the Sun God*. London: Century.

Carswell, John (1961): *The South Sea Bubble*. London: The Cresset Press.

Coleridge, Henry Nelson (edit.) (1836): *Specimens of the Table Talk of Samuel Taylor Coleridge*. London: John Murray.

Coleridge, Henry Nelson and Coleridge, Sara (1911): *Biographia Epistolaris: Being the Biographical Supplement of Coleridge's Biographia Literaria vol.1*. London: G. Bell and Sons.

Collins, Jack Churton (1893): *Jonathan Swift, a biographical and critical study.* London: Chatto & Windus.

Condamine, Charles Marie de la (*1751): Journal du voyage fait par ordre du roi a l'équateur.* Paris.

Connely, William (1934): *Sir Richard Steele.* London: Jonathan Cape.

Conrad, Joseph (1928): *The Mirror of the Sea.* London: Methuen & Co..

Cooke, Edward (1712): *A Voyage to the South Sea and round the World.* London: Printed by H.M. for B. Lintot and R. Gosling.

Coombs, Douglas (1958): *The Conduct of the Dutch: British Opinion and the Dutch Alliance during the War of Spanish Succession.* The Hague: Martinus Nijhoff.

Cordingly, David (2002): *Life Among the Pirates.* London: Abacus.

Cottle, Joseph (1848): *Reminiscences of Samuel Taylor Coleridge and Robert Southey.* New York: Wiley and Putnam.

Crossley, Alan (ed.) (1990): *Victoria History of the County of Oxfordshire vol. XII*

Crow, John A. (1992): *The Epic of Latin America.* Berkeley CA: University of California Press.

Cunningham, George Godfrey (ed.) (1853):*A History of England in the Lives of Englishmen.* London: A. Fullarton & Co..

Dampier, William (1707): *Capt. Dampier's Vindication of his Voyage to the South Seas in the Ship St. George.* London: printed Mary Edwards.

Dampier, William (1999): *A new Voyage round the World.* London: Hummingbird Press.

Dampier, William (2006): *A Voyage to New Holland*, 1699. Stroud: Nonsuch Publishing.

Darlington, Philip J. Jr. (1965): *The Biogeography of the Southern End of the World.* New York: McGraw-Hill.

Darwin, Charles (1997): *The Voyage of the Beagle*. Ware: Wordsworth Editions.

Defoe, Daniel (1703): *Brief Explanation of a Late Pamphlet, Entitled The Shortest Way with the Dissenters*. London.

Defoe, Daniel (1711): *An Essay on the South-Sea Trade*. London: Printed and Sold by Morphew.

Defoe, Daniel (1713): *Reasons against the Succession of the House of Hanover*. London: J. Baker.

Defoe, Daniel (1716): *An Account of the Proceedings against the Rebels*. London: Printed for J. Baker and Tho. Warner.

Defoe, Daniel (1719): *An Historical Account of the Voyages and Adventures of Sir Walter Raleigh*. London: W. Boreham.

Defoe, Daniel (1720): *Serious Reflections during the Life and Surprising Adventures of Robinson Crusoe, with His Vision of the Angelick World*. London: Printed for A. Bell.

Defoe, Daniel (1724-7): *Tour thro' the Whole Island of Great Britain*. London.

Defoe, Daniel (1726): *The Four Years Voyages of Capt. George Roberts*. London: Printed for A. Bettesworth.

Defoe, Daniel (1974a): *Captain Singleton*. Shakespeare Head edition. Oxford: Blackwell.

Defoe, Daniel (1974b): *Colonel Jack*. Shakespeare Head edition. Oxford: Blackwell,.

Defoe, Daniel (1998): *The Life and strange surprising Adventures of Robinson Crusoe* Oxford, Oxford University Press, Oxford World's Classics.

Defoe, Daniel (1999): *General History of the pyrates*. New York: Dover Publications.

Descola, Jean (1968): *Daily Life in Colonial Peru*. London: Allen and Unwin.

Dodsley, Robert (ed.) (1771) *Fugitive Pieces on Various Subjects*, Vol. II. London:

Donoghue, Denis (1969): *Jonathan Swift, a critical introduction.* Cambridge: Cambridge University Press.

Dover, Thomas (1732): *Ancient Physician's Legacy to his Country* London: printed for the author and sold by A. Bettesworth.

Drake, Edward Cavendish (1768): *A new universal collection of authentic and entertaining voyages and travels, from the earliest accounts to the present time.* London: printed for J. Cooke.

Earle, Peter (1976): *The World of Defoe.* London: Weidenfeld & Nicolson.

Earle, Peter (1998): *Sailors, English merchantmen 1650-1775.* London: Methuen.

Edwards, Philip (1994): *The Story of the Voyage.* Cambridge: Cambridge University Press.

Elliot, George Francis Scott (1920): *Chile: its history and development.* London: T.F. Unwin.

Elliot, John Huxtable (1970): *Imperial Spain 1479-1716.* London: Penguin.

Exquemelin, Alexander O. (1969): *the Buccaneers of America with an introduction by Jack Beeching.* New York: Dover Publications.

Faber, Richard (1983): *The Brave Courtier: Sir William Temple.* London: Faber

Fausett, David (Oct., 1995): *Writing the New World. The American Historical Review, Vol. 100, No. 4,* pp. 1283-1283. Bloomington.

Fischer, Stephen (ed.) (1987): *Studies in British Privateering, Trading Enterprize and Seamen's Welfare,1775-1900.* Exeter: University of Exeter Press.

Fletcher, Francis (1628): *The World Encompassed by Sir Francis Drake.* Whitefish MT: Kessinger Publishing, 'Rare Reprints' (undated).

Fox, Christopher (ed.) (2003): *Cambridge Companion to Jonathan Swift.* Cambridge: Cambridge University Press.

Foxe, John, Blanchard Amos NS Goodrich, Charles Augustus (1844): *Book of Martyrs: Or, A History of the Lives, Sufferings, and Triumphant Deaths, of the Primitive as Well as Protestant Martyrs : from the Commencement of Christianity, to the Latest Periods of Pagan and Popish Persecution ...* Hartford: Edwin Hunt, 1844

Freile, Juan Rodriguez (1859): *Conquista i descubrimiento del nuevo reino de Granada de las Indias Occidentales del mar océano, i fundacion de la ciudad de Santa Fe de Bogotá.* Bogota.

Frey, Linda and Frey, Marsha (1995): *The Treaties of the War of the Spanish Succession.* Westport: Greenwood Publishing.

Frezier, Amadée F. (1717): *Voyage to the South Sea and along the coasts of Chile and Peru* London: printed Jonah Bowyer.

Fuentes, Carlos (1992): *The Buried Mirror, reflections on Spain and the New World.* London: Andre Deutsch.

Funnell, William (1707): *A Voyage Round the World, containing an account of Dampier's Expedition into the South Seas in the Ship St. George, in the Years 1703 and 1704.* London: printed W. Botham for James Knapton.

Galdames, Luis (1941): *A History of Chile.* Chapel Hill, NC: University of North Carolina Press.

Gill, Anton (1997): *The Devil's Mariner, a life of William Dampier, pirate and explorer 1651-1715.* London: Michael Joseph.

Glendinning, Victoria (1998): *Jonathan Swift, a portrait* Henry Holt & Co..

Green, Graham (1976): *Rochester's Monkey.* New York: Penguin Books.

Green, Toby (2008): *Inquisition, the reign of fear.* London: Pan Books.

Greenacre, Francis (1986): *The Bristol Landscape: The Watercolours of Samuel Jackso. 1794-186.* Bristol: City of Bristol Museum and Art Gallery.

Griggs, Earl Leslie (1956): *Collected Letters by Samuel Taylor Coleridge.* Oxford: Clarendon Press.

Grove, Philip Babcock (1941): *the Imaginary Voyage in Prose Fiction.* London: Holland Press.

Grove, Philip Babcock (1942): *Gildon's 'Fortunate Shipwreck' as background for Gulliver's Travels.* Oxford: Oxford University Press.

Hacke, William (1699): *A Collection of Original Voyages.* London, printed for James Knapton.

Hakluyt, Richard (1589): *The principall navigations, voiages and discoveries of the English nation, made by sea or ouer land, to the most remote and farthest distant quarters of the earth at any time within the compasse of these 1500 yeeres.* London: Bishop and R. Newberie.

Hamilton, Elizabeth (1969): *The Backstairs Dragon, a life of Robert Harley, Earl of Oxford.* London: Hamish Hamilton.

Hammond, Paul (ed.) (2002): *Restoration Literature: An Anthology* Oxford: Oxford University Press.

Harris, John DD, FRS (1705): *Navigantium atque Itinerantium Bibliotheca: or, a compleat Collection of Voyages and Travels, consisting of above four hundred of the most authentick Writers.* London: printed for Thomas Bennet.

Hatton, Ragnhild Marie (1978): *George I, elector and king.* London: Thames and Hudson.

Haws, Duncan (1976): *Ships and the Sea, a chronological review.* London: Hart-Davis MacGibbon.

Henningsen, Henning (1963): *Crossing the Equator: Sailors' Baptism and Other Initiation Rites, The Journal of American Folklore, Vol. 76, No. 299.* Champaign, IL: University of Illinois Press.

Hill, Christopher (1980): *The Century of Revolution, 1603-1714.* New York: Norton.

Holmes, Richard (1989): *Coleridge, early visions.* Sevenoaks: Hodder & Stoughton.

Holmes, Richard (ed.) (2004): *Defoe on Sheppard & Wild.* London: Harper Perrenial.

Hopkinson, Marie Ruan (1934): *Anne of England: the biography of a great queen.* London: Constable.

Howell, John (1829): *The Life and Adventures of Alexander Selkirk.* Edinburgh.

Janeway, James (1674): *Mr James Janeway's Legacy to his Friends, containing twenty seven famous instances of Gods providences in and about sea dangers and deliverances.* London: printed for Dorman Newman.

Jay, Anthony (ed.) (1996): *The Oxford Dictionary of Political Quotations.* Oxford: Oxford University Press.

Jeffries F. (pub) (1855 Jan-June): *The Gentleman's Magazine* v.198. London.

Johnson, Captain Charles (1926): *A General History of the Robberies and Murders of the Most Notorious Pirates.* London: Routledge and Kegan Paul.

Jones, Donald (1992): *Captain Woodes Rogers' Voyage round the World 1708-11.* Bristol: Bristol Branch of the Historical Association.

Jones, Louis C. (1942) *Clubs of the Georgian Rakes.* New York: Columbia University Press.

Journal of the House of Lords Vol. 13, 1675-1681 (1771), pp. 313-330: "Titus Oates's Narrative concerning the Plot".

Juan Sempere y Guarinos (1788): *Historia del lujo y de las leyes suntuarias de España.* Madrid: Impr. Real,.

Karraker, Cyrus H. (1953) *Piracy Was a Business.* Rindge N.H.: Richard R. Smith.

Katzew, Ilona (ed) (1996): *Colonial Latin America.* New York: Americas Society.

Keach, William (ed) (1997):*The Complete Poems by Samuel Taylor Coleridge*. London: Penguin Classics.

Kemp, Peter (1970): *The British Sailor: a social history of the lower deck*. London: Dent.

Kemp. Peter (ed.) (1969): *History of the Royal Navy*. London: Barker.

Kempe, Peter and Lloyd, Christopher (1960): *Brethren of the Coast, Buccaneers of the South Seas*. New York: St Martin's Press.

Knight William A. (1914): *Coleridge and Wordsworth in the West Country - Their Friendship, Work, and Surroundings*. New York: Charles Scibbner's.

Knox, John (1767): *A New Collection of Voyages, Discoveries and Travels: Containing Whatever is Worthy of Notice, in Europe, Asia, Africa and America*. London: J. Knox.

Knox, Roberts (1681): *A Historical Relation of Ceylon*. London: Richard Chiswell.

Laslett, Peter (1977): *Family Life and Illicit Love in Earlier Generations*. Cambridge: Cambridge University Press.

Lawrence, Berta (1970): *Coleridge and Wordsworth in Somerset* David & Charles.

Le Golif, Louis Adhémar Timothée (1954): *The Memoirs of a Buccaneer, Being a Wondrous and Unrepentant Account of the Prodigious Adventures and Amours of King Louis XIV's Loyal Servant ...., known for his singular wound as Borgnefesse, Captain of the Buccaneers*. New York: Simon and Schuster.

Lea H.C. (1908): *The Inquisition in the Spanish Dependencies*. New York: Macmillan Company.

Leefe, John (1978): *The Atlantic Privateers: Their Story 1749-1815*. Halifax: Petheric Press.

Little, Bryan (1960): *Crusoe's Captain, being the Life of Woodes Rogers*. London: Oldhams Press.

222

Lloyd, Christopher (1966): *William Dampier*. London: Faber & Faber.

Lloyd, Christopher (1968): *British Seamen 1200-1880 a social survey*. London: Collins.

Lodge, Thomas (1980): *a Margarite of Amerika 1596 old-spelling critical edition by James Clyde Addison, Jr*. Salzburg: Salzburg Institut fur Anglistik und Amerikanistik

Lowes, John Livingstone (1978): *The Road to Xanadu*. London: Picador.

Macintyre, Donald (1975): *The Privateers*. London: Paul Elek.

Madariaga, Salvador de (1947): *The Fall of the Spanish American Empire*. London: Hollis & Carter.

Makower, Stanley Victor (1972): *A Book of English Essays (1600-1900)*. Manchester, NH: Ayer Publishing.

Mariner's Mirror 1, 1928, pp 196-211:Rogers, BNH: "Woodes Rogers's Privateering Voyage of 1708-11".

Mariner's Mirror 15, 1924, pp 322-4: Rogers, BNH: "Dampier's Debts".

Mariner's Mirror 42, 291-301 "Bartholomew Sharp, Buccaneer", by Lloyd, Christopher

Mariners' Mirror 73, 1987, pp 385-99: Lee, CD: "Alexander Selkirk and the Last Voyage of the Cinque Ports Galley".

Markham, Clements R. A (1892): *History of Peru*. Chicago: C. H. Sergel & Co..

Marshall, Dorothy (1962): *Eighteenth Century England*. London: Longmans,

Marshall, Edward (1875): *The Early History of Woodstock Manor*. Oxford: James Parker and Co..

Mather, Increase (&&): *Remarkable Providences*. New York: Arno Press.

Mayberry, Tom (1992): *Coleridge and Wordsworth in the West Country*. Stroud: Alan Sutton.

McDermott, James (2001): *Martin Frobisher: Elizabethan Privateer.* Newhaven CT: Yale University Press.

McGrath, Patrick (1975): *The Merchant Venturers of Bristol.* Bristol: Society of Merchant Venturers of Bristol.

McMinn, Joseph (1994):*Jonathan's Travels.* Belfast: Appletree Press.

Meyerstein, E.H.W. (ed.) (1945): *The Adventures by Sea of Edward Coxere.* Oxford: Clarendon Press.

Mitchell, David (1976): *Pirates.* New York: Dial Press.

Moll, Herman (1711): *A View of the Coasts, Countries and Islands within the Limits of the South-Sea-Company.* London: J. Morphew.

Moorman, Mary (1957): *William Wordsworth, a biography - the early years, 1770-1803.* Oxford: Clarendon Press.

Murdo J Macleod (1973): *Spanish Central America, a Socioeconomic history.* Berkley CA: University of California Press.

Murphy, Dallas (2004): *Rounding the Horn. New York:* Basic Books.

Neville, Henry (1668): *The Isle of Pines or, A late discovery of a fourth island near Terra Australis, Incognita ... .* London: printed for Allen Banks and Charles Harper.

Nokes, David (1985) *Jonathan Swift, a hypocrite reversed: a critical biography.* Oxford: Oxford University Press.

Nokes, David (1995): *John Gay: A Profession of Friendship.* Oxford: Oxford Unversity Press.

Norris, Gerald (ed) (2005): *The Buccaneer Explorer, William Dampier's voyages.* Woodbridge: The Boydell Press.

Novak, Maximillian E. (2001): *Daniel Defoe: master of fictions: his life and ideas.* Oxford: Oxford University Press.

O'Neill, Michael and Sandy, Mark (2006): *Romanticism: Critical Concepts in Literary and Cultural Studies.* London: Taylor & Francis.

Palma, Ricardo (2004): *Peruvian traditions.* Oxford: Oxford University Press.

Parry Albert (1933): *Tattoo: secrets of a strange craft.* New York: Simon and Schuster.

Perry, Seamus (ed) (2000): *S.T. Coleridge, Interviews and Recollections.* Basingstoke: Palgrave.

Perry, Seamus (ed.) (2002): *Coleridge's Notebooks: A Selection.* Oxford: Oxford University Press.

Poolman, Kenneth (2000): *The Speedwell Voyage.* New York: Berkley Books.

Powell, J.W.D.(1930): *Bristol Privateers, and ships of war.* Bristol: JW Arrowsmith.

Preston, Diana and Michael (2004): *A Pirate of Exquisite Mind.* New York: Walker & Company.

Priestly, Joseph (1777): *Disquisitions Relating to Matter and Spirit.* London

Purchas, Samuel (2003): *purchas, his pilgrimage or relations of the world and the religions observed in all ages and places discovered from the creation unto this present.* 2 vols. Whitefish MT: Kessinger Publishing,

Rediker, Marcus (1987): *Between the devil and the deep blue sea: merchant seaman, pirates, and the Anglo-American maritime world (1700-1726).* Cambridge: Cambridge University Press.

Richard Holmes (ed.) (2004): *Defoe on Sheppard and Wilde.* London: Harper Perennial.

Ringrose, Basil (1893): *The dangerous Voyage and bold attempts of Captain B. Sharp and others upon the coasts of the South Sea* - contained in *The Buccaneers and Marooners of America* ... London: Sonnenschein & Co., 1893.

Ringrose, Basil (1992): *A buccaneer's atlas : Basil Ringrose's South Sea waggoner.* Berkley CA: University of California Press.

Roberts, W. Adolphe (1942): *The French in the West Indies.* Indianapolis: Bobbs-Merrill.

Robinson, Charles Napier (1911): *The British Tar in Fact and Fiction: the poetry pathos and humour of a sailor's life.* London and New York: Harper and brothers.

Rogers, N.A.M. (1997*): The Safeguard of the Sea, a naval history of Britain.* London: Harper Collins

Rogers, N.A.M.(1986): *The Wooden World.* London: Fontana Press.

Rogers, Pat (1980): *Hacks and Dunces: Pope, Swift and Grub Street.* London: Methuen.

Rogers, Woodes (1893): *a British privateer in the time of Queen Anne.* London: Diploma Press Ltd..

Rogers, Woodes (2004): *A Cruising Voyage Round the World* . Santa Barbara: The Narrative Press.

Ruiz Lopez, Hipólito (1940): *Travels of Ruiz, Pavón, and Dombey in Peru and Chile, 1777-1788.* Chicago: Field Museum of Natural History.

Sandford, Mrs Henry (1888): *Thomas Poole and his Friends.* London: Macmillan and Co..

Schouten, William Cornelis (1966): *The Relation of the Wonderful Voiage by Wm Cornelison Schouten.* Cleveland: World Publishing Co..

Schurz, William Lytle (1939): *The Manila Galleon.* New York: EP Dutton & Co..

Schwartz, Hillel (1980): *The French Prophets; The History of a Millenarian Group in Eighteenth-Century England.* Berkley CA: University of California Press.

Scott, Walter (ed.) (1814): *The Works of Jonathan Swift: Containing Additional Letters, Tracts, and Poems Not Hitherto Published; with Notes and a Life of the Author.* Edinburgh: Archibald Constable and Co..

Severin, Tim (2003): *In Search of Crusoe.* New York: Basic Books.

Shedd, William (ed.) (1854): *The Complete Works of Samuel Taylor Coleridge - notes on Robinson Crusoe*. New York: Harper and Brothers.

Shelmerdine, J.M. (1951): *Introduction to Woodstock*. Woodstock: Samppon Press.

Shelvocke, George (1726): *A Voyage round the world by way of the Great South Sea*. London: printed for J. Senex.

Smith, DN. (ed.) (1935): *Letters of Jonathan Swift to Charles Ford*. Oxford: Clarendon Press.

Smith, FN. (1990): *The Genres of Gulliver's Travels*. Newark: University of Delaware Press.

Souhami, Diana (2001): *Selkirk's Island*. New York: Harcourt Inc..

Starkey, David (1990): *British Privateering Enterprise in the Eighteenth Century*. Exeter: University of Exeter Press.

Summers, Montague (ed.) (1915): *The Works of Aphra Behn*. London: Heinemann.

Swift, Jonathan (1774): *Works of Dr Jonathan Swift Vol. VI - by Dr Arbuthnot and Mr Pope*. Edinburgh: printed John Donaldson.

Swift, Jonathan (1850): *The Works of Jonathan Swift: Containing Interesting and Valuable Papers, Not Hitherto Published; with a Memoir of the Author*. Bohn.

Swift, Jonathan (1908): *The Prose Works of Jonathan Swift v.12 (A Letter from a Member of the House of Commons in Ireland to a Member of the House of Commons in England concerning the Sacramental Test, 1709)*. London: George Bell and Sons.

Swift, Jonathan (2004): *the Journal to Stella*. Whitefish MT: Kessinger Publishing.

Swift, Jonathan (2005): *Gulliver's Travels*. Oxford: Oxford World Classics.

Taylor, George (chief mate) *Journal of the Success*. London: Ministry of Defence, Admiralty Library.

Teonge, Henry (2004): *The Diary of Henry Teonge, Chaplain on Board H.M's Shipp Assistance, Bristol and Royal Oak 1675-1679.* London: Routledge.

The Englishman, no.26, 3rd Dec. 1713: Steele, Richard

The Gentleman's Magazine v.198, 1855 Jan-June.

The William and Mary Quarterly, 3rd ser.38, 1981: Rediker, Marcus: "Under the Banner of King Death : the Social World of Anglo-American Pirates 1716-1726".

Toribio Medina, José (1887): *Historia del Santo Oficio de la Inquisición de Lima: 1569-1820.* Santiago de Chile: Imprenta Gutenberg.

Ulloa, don Antonio de and Juan, don Jorge (1760): *A Voyage to South America.* London: printed L Davis and C Reymers.

Uring, Nathaniel (1928): *Voyages and Travels of Captain Nathaniel Uring.* London: Cassel

Villena, Guillermo Lohmann (1977): *Historia Maritima des Perú, Siglos XVII y XVIII.* Lima: Instituto de Estudios Histórico-Maritimo del Perú.

Wafer, Lionel & Winship, George Parker (1903): *A new Voyage and Description of the Isthmus of America.* Whitefish MT: Kessinger Publishing.

Walter, Richard (compiler) (2001): *A Voyage round the World in the Years MDCCXL, I,II,III,IV by George Anson.* Santa Barbara Ca: Narrative Press.

Ward, Adolphus William and Waller, Alfred Rayney (1933): *The Cambridge history of English Literature.* London: Macmillan.

Ward, Ned, *Wooden World Dissected (*1707): in Lloyd, Christopher (1970): *The British Seaman 1200–1860: A Social Survey.* Madison NJ: Fairleigh Dickinson University Press.

Welbe, John (undated): *An Answer to Captain Dampier's Vindication of his Voyage to the South Seas, in the Ship St. George.* London, printed B. Bragge.

Wilkinson Clennel (1929): *Dampier, explorer and buccaneer*. Whitefish MT: Kessinger Publishing.

Williams, Glyndwr (1997): *the Great South Sea*. New Haven: Yale University Press.

Williams, Gomer (1897): *History of the Liverpool privateers and letters of Marque*. London: Heineman.

Winton, Calhoun (1964): *Captain Steele*. Baltimore: Johns Hopkins Press.

Wordsworth, Christopher (1851): *Memoirs of William Wordsworth*. Boston Ma: Ticknor, Reed, and Fields.

Wordsworth, Dorothy (2002): *The Grasmere and Alfoxden Journals*. Oxford: Oxford World's Classics.

Wycherley, George (1928): *Buccaneers of the Pacific*. Indianapolis: The Bobbs-Merrill Company.

Yapp, Peter (1983): *The Travellers' Dictionary of Quotation*. London: Routledge.

END NOTES

[1] Shelvocke (1726) 73.

Hatley

[2] Dampier (1999) 17

[3] Williams (1997) 86

[4] NA. SP 34/28/23A

[5] Betagh (1728) 108,115,244,251-3

[6] AHN seccion Inquisición, Legayo 5345, Expediente 4

[7] See pic

[8] ORO Mis DD Par Woodstock c1. His birth date being in March, he could also be described as having been born in 1684 old-style. I have used the modern style of dating throughout this book with years beginning on 1 January.

[9] NA. SP 34/28/23A

[10] Crossley (1990) 342-60, Woodstock buildings No.32

[11] Crossley (1990) 435-9

[12] Foxe (1844) 314

[13] Green, G. (1976) 87

[14] Ibid 168

[15] Hammond (2002) 253. *Love & Life, a song.*

[16] Crossley (1990) 435-39

[17] Ibid 435-39

[18] Ibid 338

[19] Shelmerdine (1951) 6. The crown retained powers to nominate new faces if it so chose. A charter of 1688 nominated a dozen new aldermen, all locals, and demoted two others.

[20] Marshall E. (1875) 425-6

[21] OLS Bladon M 1546-1976 for a transcription of the entry in the parish register.

[22] The Marquises of Powis, formerly earls of Montgomery.

[23] Green, G. (1976) 120

[24] Barker-Benfield (1996) 47

[25] ORO E215/4/D/5 This appears to be part of a collection of unused documents relating to a legal suite mounted in 1805. In total they include E215/4/D/1-6.

[26] Crossley (1990) 342-60, building no.45

[27] Crossley (1990) 342-60 building no.45

[28] ORO Blenheim Mun., box 137.

[29] OLS Woodstock C 1653-1859 for the christenings of Grace, Philedelphia, Elizabeth, Robert and William Hatley.

[30] NA. PROB 11/530, will of 'Simonis Hatley', also ORO E 215/4/D/5

[31] ORO E215/4/D/1, also Crossley (1990) 342-60, building no.49

[32] Crossley (1990) 342-60 building no.45

[33] Shelmerdine (1951) 106

[34] Little (1960) 19

[35] Rediker (1987) 13

[36] See for instance the opening pages of Barlowe (1934)

[37] NA. HCA 26/3/100

[38] Earle (1998) 22

[39] NA. C/104/36 part 1, leather-bound account book dated 1708, under 'Simon Hatley' - 'May 26 by Harbour, pay to 15 July at 35/ - £2.25s'.

[40] NA. PROB 11/530, will of Simonis Hatley

[41] Ibid

[42] William went on to be mayor nine times, thus maintaining and exceeding the family tradition - Marshall E. (1875) 425-6. He died in 1763.

[43] ORO E 215/4/D/5.

[44] ORO E 215/4/D/5

[45] The crest on the wax seal has some similarity to the crest of the Scottish Hatleys: *see* www.houseofnames.com/xq/asp.fc/Origin.EN/qx/Hatley-family-crest.htm

[46] OLS Woodstock M 1653-1836 for transcription of entry in the parish register

[47] ORO Ms Wills Oxon 213.189 (for microfilm) or 135/2/2

[48] Hentzner, Paul. *A Journey Into England*, (1598) in *Fugitive Pieces on Various Subjects*. Vol II. Dodsley, Robert (ed.) London: 1771.

[49] Beesley (1841) 150

Language of the Sea

[50] Murphy (2004) 67

[51] Macintyre (1975) 11

[52] Mitchell (1976) 52

[53] The voyage of Richard Hawkins.

[54] Williams (1997) 35. There was no other publicity in the meantime apart from a short account in Hakluyt's *Navigations* of 1589.

[55] Edwards (1994) 3

[56] *Mariner's Mirror* Vol. 42, 291-301: The 'Emperor' was an escaped slave by the name of Andreas.

[57] Ringrose (1893)

[58] Crooke and Malthus

[59] Exquemelin (1969) title page

[60] Ibid 19

[61] Williams (1997) 136

[62] All this in Shelvocke (1726) 239-266

[63] NA. SP 34/28/23A

[64] Souhami (2001) 101

[65] Lloyd (1966) 112

[66] Dampier (1999) 134

[67] Rogers W. (2004) 122

[68] Arciniegas (1969) 84/5

[69] Lodge (1980) 42 (originally published 1596). Lodge conceived the plot while billeted in the Jesuit College in Santos, in Brazil, during Thomas Cavendish's last

voyage, and wrote it shortly after during nearly two months of appalling weather in the Straights of Magellan. His 'introduction to gentleman readers' makes clear his dislike of Cavendish: 'som foure yeres since being at sea with M. Cavendish (whose memorie if I repent not, I lament not) it was my chance in the librarie of the Jesuits in Sanctum to find this historie in the Spanish tong ...'.

[70] Lodge (1980) 40

[71] Rogers W. (2004) 63

[72] Frezier (1717) 84-5

[73] Shelvocke (1726) 107

[74] Arbuthnot (1712)

[75] Rogers W. (2004) 108

[76] Frezier (1717) 250

[77] Ibid 298

Gentlemen Venturers

[78] Swift (2005) 7 'a Letter from Capt. Gulliver to his Cousin Sympson'.

[79] Grove (1942)

[80] Novak (2001) 639 re Daniel Defoe: *Compleat English Gentleman.*

[81] Rediker (1987)158

[82] Rogers W. (2004) 98

[83] Wafer (1903) 37

[84] Williams (1997) 92

[85] Cordingly (2002) 30

[86] Novak (2001) 260

[87] Swift (1908)

[88] Frey (1995) 639

[89] Swift (2005) 7

[90] Edwards (1994) 39 cit. Williamson, J.A.: introduction to *A Voyage to New Holland*, 1939.

[91] The voyage of the *Roebuck* was a government sponsored expedition to explore the coast of New Holland (Australia) 1699-1701. On the way out, Dampier quarrelled with his first lieutenant, George Fisher, and left him in prison in irons in Bahia, Brazil. Fisher got back to England before Dampier and worked to get his revenge. Dampier had joined the Navy for this expedition and was therefore subject to naval discipline. The end result was a court martial on 8 June 1702 when Dampier was found guilty of 'very hard cruel usage towards Lt. Fisher'.

[92] Swift (2005) 275

[93] Wafer (1903) for all this.

[94] Ibid 64

[95] Ibid 101. *Utopia* had been recently published in a French translation.

[96] *L'Histoire d'un Voyage Fait en Terre du Bresil autrement de l'Amerique* by Jean de Lery, a Calvinist, first published 1578. Villegaignon's settlement was also intended to be a place of refuge for French Protestants.

[97] Hatley had already been captured and was spending his second period in prison in Lima.

[98] Shelvocke (1726) 405-6

[99] Dampier (1999) 79

[100] Edwards (1994) 40 *re* Funnell (1707) 23

[101] Dampier's portrait in the National Portrait Gallery

the Hand of the most High

[102] Rediker (1987)179,184

[103] *Journal of Edward Coxere* cit. Earle (1998) 104

[104] Dampier (1999) 237

[105] Ibid

[106] Mather chap.1

[107] Rogers W. (2004) 178

[108] Mitchell (1976) 16. A commission in this sense being a Letter of Marque.

[109] Crow (1992) 189

[110] Ibid

[111] Fletcher (1628) 58

[112] Wycherley (1928) 71

[113] Dampier (1999)26

[114] Archenholtz (1804) 269

[115] Williams (1997) 77

[116] Wycherley (1928) 176

[117] Williams (1997) 77

[118] Exquemeling (1969) 12 (in the intro. by Jack Beeching)

[119] Exquemeling (1969) 187

[120] Marshall D. (1962) 105

[121] Fuentes (1992) 168

[122] Madriaga (1947) 186

[123] *Journal of the House of Lords Vol. 13, 1675-1681 (1771)*, pp. 313-330: "Titus Oates's Narrative concerning the Plot".

[124] *Catholic Encyclopedia*: Oates, Titus

[125] Shelmerdine (1951) 106

[126] Novak (2001) 83

[127] Shelmerdine (1951) 106

[128] Schwartz (1980) 108

[129] Ibid 79

[130] Novak (2001) 559

[131] Betagh (1728) 117

[132] Novak (2001) 276

[133] Hamilton (1969) 47

[134] Ibid

[135] Ibid 81

[136] Backscheider (1989) 10

[137] Part of a short verse fixed to the door of St. Patrick's Cathedral, Dublin on the day of Swift's installment as Dean in 1713 cit.Cunningham (1853) 195.

the Voyage of the *Cinque Ports*
[138] Lloyd (1966) 33 This was following Coxon's capture of Santa Marta in 1677.

[139] Ibid 34

[140] Ibid 35

[141] Elliot GFS. (1920)104

[142] Archenholtz (1804) 319

[143] Dampier (1999) 110

[144] Portugal and Savoy left their alliance shortly after the war started.

[145] Souhami (2001) 29

[146] Lloyd (1966) 99

[147] Ibid 97

[148] Macintyre (1975) 1

[149] Earle (1998) 120

[150] Lloyd (1966) 98

[151] Wilkinson (1929) 185-6

[152] Lloyd (1966) 98

[153] Souhami (2001) 48

[154] see *Mariners' Mirror 73*,385- 399: "Alexander Selkirk and the Last Voyage of the Cinque Ports Galley" by Lee, C.D. Selkirk is often referred to as the 'master' of the Cinque Ports but I have preferred to follow the arguments put forward by C.D. Lee in this article for details concerning Selkirk's status and his relationships with Stradling and Dampier.

[155] Welbe (undated) 2

[156] Ibid

[157] Name once used for the Falkland Islands

[158] Rogers W. (2004) 73

[159] NA. C 24/1321

[160] Ibid

[161] Funnell (1707) 18

[162] Defoe (1998) 64

[163] Crow (1992) 182. England, Holland and France had similar systems, but unlike Spain they had strong industries and could supply their colonies at relatively reasonable prices. In 1651, Cromwell passed the Navigation Act, making the use of English ships a requirement for all British trade.

[164] Ibid

[165] Ibid 341

[166] Rogers W. (2004) 2

[167] Betagh (1728) 314.

[168] Ibid

[169] NA. C 24/1321 Sheltram's deposition cit. Souhami (2001) 71

[170] Funnell (1707) 49

[171] Dampier (1999) 85

[172] Funnell (1707) 44-5

[173] Ibid

[174] Dampier (1707) 3

[175] Funnell (1707) 26

[176] NA. C 24/1321

[177] Rogers W. (2004) 72

[178] Ibid 71

[179] Funnell (1707) 55- for this and the following account.

[180] Williams (1997) 5

[181] Walter (2001) 227

[182] Dampier (1999) 88

[183] Ibid

[184] Lloyd (1966) 115

[185] Funnell (1707) 68- for this and much of the following narrative

[186] Ibid 84

[187] Ibid 221

the Voyage of the *Duke* and *Duchess*

[188] Aughton (2000) 8

[189] Yapp (1983) 265: Letter from Alexander Pope to Martha Blount, 19 November 1739.

[190] Ballard (2003) 40

[191] McDermott, James p.176

[192] Adams's *Chronicle of Bristol* cit. Aughton (2000) 60

[193] Magna Brittania, early 1700s, cit. Aughton (2000) 7

[194] Celia Fiennes 1680 cit. Greenacre, Francis, foreword

[195] Rediker (1987) 162

[196] Barlow, Edward p.34

[197] Jones D. (1992) 4. Dampier had made clear his interest in such a voyage in a postscript to his *Vindication* of 1707: '... I am ready to satisfy any committee of Merchants how Practical and Expedient it is to put it into Execution forthwith.' However, Wilkinson (1929) 205 asserts that the voyage had been decided upon in principle before Dampier's return.

[198] Ballard (2003) 67

[199] McGrath (1975) 1

[200] Jones D. (1992) 5

[201] Knox J. (1767) 122

[202] Jones D. (1992) for this and other details of fitting out.

[203] Lloyd (1966) 128

[204] Cooke (1712) introduction

[205] Lloyd (1966) 129

[206] Rogers W. (2004) 12 states that Simon was taken on as Third Mate. However, Captain Edward Cooke in his introduction lists shares due to each rank and,

according to this list, second mates were due 5 shares. Account books of the *Duchess*, in NA. C/104/37 part 2, show that Hatley was due 5 shares in total so it seems that although Simon was described as Third Mate by Woodes Rogers, he had the substantive rank of second mate.

[207] Jones D. (1992) 5

[208] Rediker (1987) 89

[209] Ibid 90

[210] Ibid 11

[211] Earle (1998) 48

[212] Rediker (1987) 281

[213] Ibid 238

[214] Backscheider (1989) 101

[215] Rediker (1987) 238

[216] Earle (1998) 202

[217] Williams (1997) 144, re NA. C 104/160

[218] NA. C 104/36 part 1

[219] Ibid

[220] NA. C 104/36 part 1

[221] I have followed both Edward Cook's and Woodes Rogers's accounts for most of the voyage of the *Duke* and *Duchess*. They supplement rather than contradict each other.

[222] Wordsworth D. (2002) 141

[223] Rogers W. (2004) 9

[224] Glendinning (1998) 161

[225] NA. C 104/36 part 1

[226] Macintyre (1975) 5

[227] Rogers W. (2004) 11

[228] Painting in the National Maritime Museum

[229] Rogers W. (2004) 13

[230] Teonge (2004)

[231] Rediker (1987) 165

[232] Cordingly (2002) 113

[233] Backscheider (1989) 237

[234] Ibid

[235] Wycherley (1928) 303

[236] Rogers W. (2004) 15

[237] Ibid 19

[238] Fletcher (1628)

[239] Funnel (1707) 5

[240] Rogers W. (2004) 24

[241] Fletcher (1628) 12

[242] Earle (1998) 85

[243] Rogers W. (2004) 25

[244] Hacke (1699) 5

[245] Funnell (1707) 12

[246] Rogers W. (2004) 34

[247] Funnell (1707) 11

[248] Rogers W. (2004) 28

[249] Funnell (1707) 11

[250] Rogers W. (2004) 29. (Angra dos Reis is now a town of well over 100,000 people.)

[251] Cooke (1712) 26

[252] Rogers W. (2004) 29

[253] Ibid 30

[254] Ibid 59

[255] Cooke (1712) 31

[256] Rogers W. (2004) 61

[257] Murphy (2004) for this and other facts concerning the southern seas.

[258] Cooke (1712) 33

[259] Ibid

[260] Walter (2001) 123

[261] Cooke (1712) 35

[262] Rogers W. (2004) 71-3 for Selkirk's rescue.

[263] Ibid 83, also Cooke (1712) 120

[264] Cooke (1712) 104

[265] Ibid 79

[266] Cooke (1712) 121

[267] Rogers W. (2004) 83 for Lobos Islands

[268] Ibid 84

[269] Ibid 86

[270] Archenholtz (1804) 289

[271] NA. C 104/37 part 1: 'a list of what men of the Duk's wass att taking the Marquiss & in the Duchess' boat …'

[272] Rogers W. (2004) 89

[273] Ibid 103

[274] Cooke (1712) 138 &145

[275] A de I V, Quito 167 cit. Little (1960) 87

[276] Rogers W. (2004) 96

[277] A de I V, Quito 167 cit. Little (1960) 95

[278] Rogers W. (2004) 98

[279] Little (1960) 97

[280] Rogers W. (2004) 101

[281] Ibid 105

[282] Ibid 113 states that there three black and three white. However a large vellum-bound account book in NA. C 104/37 part 2 mentions, 'Negroes lost with Mr Hatley 06'.

[283] Cooke (1712) 153

[284] Little (1960) 101

[285] Rogers W. (2004) 112

[286] NA. SP 34/28/23A

[287] Rogers W. (2004) 113

good dogs were Tories

[288] Ibid p.143

[289] Ibid p.204

[290] Cooke (1712).353

[291] Ibid

[292] Rogers W. (2004) 162

[293]Captain Pincherty had banking connections in Paris and offered bills of exchange payable in London for a ransom.

[294] Rogers W. (2004) 166

[295] NA. C 104/37 part 1 'a list of men of the Duk's ... Simon Hatley - lost'.

[296] NA. C 104/60 Thomas Dover to the owners, 11 Feb. 1711, cit. Williams (1997) 155

[297] NA. C 104/60. Vanbrugh to Coldney, 27 Aug. 1710, cit. Williams (1997) 158

[298] Hamilton (1969) 35

[299] Ibid 104

[300] Hamilton (1969) 180

[301] Nokes (1995) 130

[302] Backscheider (1989) 288

[303] Carswell (1961) 40-59

[304] *A South Sea Whim*, cit. Carswell (1961) 58

[305] Backscheider (1989) 447

[306] British Library: East India Company, Minutes of the Court of Directors, 1710-12, 450: cit. Little (1960) 142: also Souhami (2001) 165, quoting D/19 & E/11, Oriental and India Office Collection.

[307] Cooke (1712) 456

[308] Little (1960) 145

[309] *Mariners' Mirror 29*, 196-211: cit. Little (1960) 145 and Lloyd (1966) 153

[310] Souhami (2001) 166 re Burney Collection of Early Newspapers, British Library

[311] Williams (1997) 43

[312] Jones D. (1992) 19

[313] Ibid

[314] Ibid 13

[315] Connely (1934) 245&328 and Little (1960) 159

[316] Steele, David *Autocrats at a Coffee House* cit. Makower (1972) 58

[317] Adams (1983) 127

[318] *The Englishman* no.26, 3rd Dec. 1713

[319] Jones D. (1992) 19-20

[320] *Mariners' Mirror* 73, 1987, pp 385-99

[321] Williams (1997) 172

[322] NA. C 35/317, f. 451v. cit. Williams (1997) 173

[323] Williams (1997) 169, also Little (1960) 157

[324] *Mariners' Mirror* 73, 1987, pp 385-99

[325] NA. C 35/317, f. 451v. cit. Williams (1997) 173

[326] NA. C 24/1321 pt.1

[327] Macintyre (1975) 131 & Williams (1997) 171

Lima and the Ancient Mariner

[328] NA. SP 34/28/23A

[329] Rogers W. (2004) 177

[330] See chapter 3 page …

[331] Betagh (1728) 244

[332] Ibid

[333] Frezier (1717) 218

[334] Ibid

[335] Ibid 209

[336] Descola (1968) 299

[337] Ibid 78

[338] Rogers W. (2004) 110

[339] Ibid

[340] Galdames (1941) 136

[341] Frezier (1717) 219

[342] Ibid

[343] Ibid 209 describes the location of the central prison in 1711.

[344] NA. SP 34/28/23A

[345] Ibid

[346] Descola (1968) 82

[347] Ibid 109

[348] Crow (1992) 217

[349] Bennassar (1979) 98

[350] Ibid 203

[351] Rogers W. (2004) 177

[352] The graffiti is obscure. This is my reading.

[353] Galdames (1941) 67

[354] Descola (1968) 191-3

[355] Crow (1992) 209

[356] Markham (1892) 171

[357] Toribio (1887) vol.2, chap.25

[358] Little (1960) 77

[359] Lloyd (1966) 112

[360] Descola (1968) 154

[361] AHN, seccion Inquisición, Legayo 5345, Expediente 4

[362] Ibid

[363] Ibid

[364] Bennassar (1979) 85

[365] Ibid

[366] Rogers W. (2004) 178

[367] Ibid

[368] Frezier (1717) 185

[369] Jones D. (1992) 20

[370] NA. C 104/37 part 1 cit. Williams (1997) 158

[371] Jones D. (1992) 20

[372] NA. C 104/160 'Smart Money for wounds and disablement' cit. Jones D. (1992) 21

[373] Little (1960) 169

[374] NA. C 104/36 part 2: Account book 1712-12 p.31. 25 Apr. 1714 cit. Williams (1997) 159

[375] Williams (1997) 159

[376] NA. C 104/37 part 1 'a list of men of the Duk's ... Simon Hatley - lost'.

[377] NA. C/104/36 part 1 & C/104/37 part 1. The £180 10s 2d is made up of £76 12s of wages in lieu of shares for 38 months and 14 days (after stoppages) and of £103 18s as the dividend on 2.5 shares.

[378] Rediker (1987) & Earle (1998)

[379] Hopkinson (1934) 351

[380] Cordingly (2002) 224

[381] Jones D. (1992) 21

[382] NA. C 104/37 part 2: *Account book for the Duke* gives Selkirk's shares as identical to Simon Hatley's. However, Lloyd (1966) 155 states that Selkirk was rated as a master by this time and received £800. I have stayed with the smaller figure.

[383] Little (1960) 157

[384] Hart, W.H. *Notes and Queries*, 30 March 1861, cit Souhami (2001) 186

[385] Ibid 191

[386] Williams (1997) 160

[387] NA. C 104/37 part 2

[388] Defoe (1711)

[389] Carswell (1961) 66

[390] Ibid p.67

[391] Hatton (1978) 226

[392] Ibid 233

[393] Backscheider (1989) 376

[394] Hatton (1978) 226

[395] Poolman (2000) 1

[396] Betagh (1728) 8

[397] See page ...

[398] Admiralty Library (Portsmouth) MS 18, f. 2v.: *Shelvocke's manuscript journal* cit. Williams (1997) 198. Also Betagh (1728) 11

[399] NA. PROB 11/530, Quire nos. 223-262: will of Simonis Hatley

[400] ORO E 215/4/D/5.

[401] Crossley (1990) Buildings Woodstock: The house remained in the possession members of the Hatley family until 1812 and the bankruptcy of one Thomas Hatley, hatter.

[402] Shelvocke (1726) xviii.

[403] Campbell *Navigantium atque Itineratum Bibliothece*, I, cit. Williams (1997) 198

[404] Shelvocke (1726) xxiv

[405] Ibid

[406] Ibid xxiii

[407] Ibid xxii

[408] Lloyd (1968) 88

[409] Shelvocke (1726) xxiii

[410] Betagh (1728) 16

the Albatross

[411] Williams (1897) 5

[412] Betagh (1728) 14

[413] Shelvocke (1726) 6

[414] Ibid 7

[415] Betagh (1728) 23

[416] Shelvocke (1726) 12

[417] Betagh (1728) 25.

[418] Ibid 26

[419] Ibid 30

[420] Barlow (1934) 86

[421] Crow (1992) 249

[422] Frezier (1717) 24

[423] Ibid

[424] Ibid

[425] Arciniegas (1969) 91

[426] Ibid 111

[427] Shelvocke (1726) 23

[428] Betagh (1728) 43

[429] Shelvocke, (1726) 32

[430] Ibid 38

[431] NA. HCA 15/37 'S': Instance papers 1718-30: affidavits of James Morville, William Burrow, George Gill and Jacob Robins.

[432] Betagh (1728) 34

[433] Ibid 39,40

[434] Shelvocke (1726) 47

[435] Ibid

[436] Ibid 49

[437] The following quotations from Shelvocke (1726).

[438] Dampier (1999) 50

[439] Murphy (2004) 225

[440] Shelvocke (1726) 72

[441] Edwards (1994) 47

[442] Murphy (2004) 303

[443] *The Observations of Sir Richard Hawkins* cit. Williams (1997) 26

[444] Translation from Spanish

[445] Betagh (1728) 53-5

[446] Shelvocke (1726) 80

[447] Ibid 81

[448] Elliot GFS. (1920) 60, also Frezier (1717) 63-4

[449] Frezier (1717) 83

[450] Shelvocke (1726) 100.

[451] Frezier (1717) 53

[452] Shelvocke (1726) 138

[453] Betagh (1728) 72

[454] Shelvocke (1726) 151

[455] Journal of George Taylor, Chief Mate of the *Success*, cit. Betagh (1728) 127

[456] Wycherley (1928) 306-7

[457] Frezier (1717) 151

[458] Betagh (1728) 103

[459] Wilkinson (1929) 83

[460] Shelvocke (1726) 175

[461] Betagh (1728) 105

[462] Ibid 243

[463] Dampier (1999) 74

[464] Nicholas Laming, the boatswain, died 'of fatigue' on the journey – Betagh (1728) 105.

[465] Betagh (1728) 252

[466] Betagh received better treatment than his fellow captives for a number of reasons: 1. His friendship with a French Captain, Fitzgerald, a native of St. Malo then in Lima. 2. Betagh had an association with Admiral Sir Charles Wager who destroyed the Spanish treasure fleet off Cartagena in 1708. Don Pedro Midranda, the Spanish Admiral on the *Brilliant*, had been Wager's captive and had been well-treated by him and wanted to repay the courtesy. 3. Betagh was Irish and had been brought up a Catholic and perhaps played on this even though he had joined the Church of England many years previously.

[467] Betagh (1728) 279

Crusoe and Gulliver

[468] Holmes (2004) xi

[469] Backscheider (1989) 414

[470] Defoe (1998) 131

[471] Defoe (1998) 139

[472] Shedd (1854) 316

[473] Souhami (2001) 191-3

[474] NA. C II/52/31 and C II/297/61 (1714-58) for the petitions of Frances Candis and Sophia Bruce regarding Selkirk's will, cit. Souhami (2001) 201

[475] Ibid

[476] Rediker (1987) 47

[477] Souhami (2001) 204

[478] Williams (1997) 201

[479] Wycherley (1928) 316 & Betagh (1728) 237

[480] Betagh (1728) 204 & Shelvocke (1726) 467

[481] See page …

[482] Betagh (1728) 180

[483] Williams (1997) 200

[484] Shelvocke (1726) 368-70.

[485] Ibid 448

[486] Williams (1997) 201

[487] Backscheider (1989) 452

[488] *The Commentator,* 1 July 1720, cit. Backscheider (1989) 453

[489] Carswell (1961) 131

[490] Balen, Malcolm p.137

[491] Carswell (1961) 154-5

[492] Ibid 146

[493] Ibid 175

[494] Balen (2003) 147. (The total rental income from all lands and properties in Britain did not at this time exceed £14,000,000 per year - Backscheider (1989) 456.)

[495] Carswell (1961) 201

[496] Betagh (1728) 203

[497] Ibid 204

[498] Ibid 228

[499] NA. HCA 15/37 'S': Instance papers 1718-30: affidavits of James Morville, William Burrow, George Gill and Jacob Robins.

[500] Betagh (1728) 204

[501] Shelvocke (1726) 371

[502] Betagh (1728) 203

[503] Ibid 205-6

[504] NA. HCA 15/37 'S': Instance papers 1718-30: affidavits of James Morville, William Burrow, George Gill and Jacob Robins, also John Theobald, James Moulville etc.

[505] Wycherley (1928) 359 & Poolman (2000) 153

[506] Betagh (1728) 230

[507] NA. HCA 15/37 'S': Instance papers 1718-30: affidavit of John Burloigh, turnkey at the Marshalsea Prison, 7 November 1722.

[508] Betagh (1728) 253

[509] Collins (1893) 194

[510] Swift (2004) 221

[511] Swift (1774) vol VI, 62

[512] Ibid

[513] Ibid

[514] Swift (1725): Letter to Alexander Pope, 29 September 1725.

[515] Scott (1814) 445: a remark by Swift to the poet Edward Young.

[516] Coleridge (1836) 93

[517] Smith (1990) 26: Swift, letter to Charles Ford, 1723: cit. Novak (2001).

[518] Smith (1935) xl

[519] See page ..

[520] Swift (2005) 271

[521] Little (1960) 199

[522] Swift (1850) vol.2, 572: Letter from Edward, Earl of Oxford, 2 November 1724

[523] Ibid 146

[524] *The Gentleman's Magazine* v.198, 146

[525] Shelvocke (1726) x.

[526] Ibid 'Dedication'

[527] Ibid ix

[528] Betagh (1728) 'Dedication'

[529] Walter (2001) 56

[530] Little (1960) chap.13

[531] Backscheider (1989) 527

[532] Poolman (2000) 154

[533] Ibid

[534] National Maritime Museum - database of Maritime Memorials

[535] Betagh (1728) 33

[536] Ibid

Coleridge

[537] Rediker (1987)

[538] Mayberry (1992) 21

[539] Jay (1996) 384: Philip Henry Stanhope: Notes on Conversations with the Duke of Wellington, 4 November 1831

[540] Perry S. (2002) 55

[541] Perry S. (2000) 8

[542] Lawrence, (1970) 67: re *Journal of Charlotte Poole*

[543] Holmes (2004) 60.

[544] Ibid 60

[545] Perry S. (2000) 45

[546] Sandford (1888) 96-7: letter to Mr Haskins, 22 September 1794

[547] Holmes (2004) 79

[548] Ibid

[549] Alsop (1836) 199

[550] Lowes (1978) 123

[551] Holmes (2004) 100

[552] Sandford (1888) 142-3

[553] Coleridge (1911) 106: Letter to Charles Lloyd senior, 15 Oct. 1796.

[554] Mayberry (1992) 66

[555] Barker (2000) 128

[556] Sandford (1888) 125

[557] Knight (1914) 231

[558] Keach (1997) 66

[559] Holmes (2004) 82

[560] Griggs (1956) vol.1, 322: cit. Holmes (2004) 138

[561] Ibid 598

[562] Priestly (1777)

[563] O'Neill & Sandy (2006) 32: Letter to William Sotheby, Sept. 1802.

[564] Holmes (2004) 152

[565] Mayberry (1992) 88

[566] Griggs (1956) vol.1, 334 cit. Mayberry (1992) 92

[567] Lawrence (1970) 163

[568] Holmes (2004) 156: Report of Home Office Agent

[569] Barker (2000) 133

[570] Mayberry (1992) 98

[571] Ibid

[572] Griggs (1956) vol.1, 71

[573] Holmes (2004) 167: the most probable date is 14 October 1797.

[574] Ibid 162

[575] Ward (1933) vol.4, 106

[576] Purchas (2003) vol.1 intro.

[577] Holmes (2004) 163 re Purchas, Bk.4 chap.13

[578] Holmes (2004) 196

[579] Barker (2000) 138

[580] Wordsworth C. (1851) 107

[581] Keach (1997) 499: a memoir dictated to Elizabeth Fenwick, 1857.

[582] Barker (2000) 151

[583] Wordsworth D. (2002) 150

[584] Shelvocke (1726) 468

Index

254

Defoe, Daniel 2,23,24,25,28,38,39,
  67,75,86,108,137,182,192,197;
  writing *Robinson Crusoe* 138,
  175-8
Doughty, Simon 83
Dover, Dr Thomas 78,86,92,96,99,
  101,107,108
Drake, Sir Francis 16,33,34,157
Duchess of Marlborough *see*
  Churchill, Sarah
Duck, Henry 96,99
Duke of Marlborough *see*
  Churchill, John
Duke of Wellington *see*
  Wellesley, Arthur

Edward II of England 59
Edward VI of England 63
Elizabeth I of England 5-6,16,63
Estcourt, Thomas 44,46
Esterlin, Thomas 128
Eugène, Prince of Savoy 63
Ezquemelin, Alexander 17-18,

Farnese, Isabella 137
Finch, John 65
Fleming, Simon 88
Fletcher, Francis 16,33
Foe, James 176
French, Humphry 69
Frezier, Amadée 22,120,148
Fricker, Edith 198
Fricker, Mary 195
Fricker, Sarah 195,196,198,
  199,200,201
Frobisher, Martin 60
Fry, Robert 93
Funnel, William 29,30,46,53

Gay, John 189
George I of Britain 135
Gill, George 185
Gils, Jacob 128
Girard, Captain 151
Godfrey, Agent 151
Golden Caps 41

Goldney. Thomas 44
Gopson, Richard 24,27
Gregory, Blagrove 11,140
Griffiths, David 181
Guiscard. Marquis de 109-10
Guy, John 60

Hackluyt, Richard 205
Harley, Robert, Earl of Oxford 67,
  108-10,112,115,117,133,135,138,
  189
Hatley, Mary (Simon's mother) 4,7,
  8,10,11,140
Hatley, Mary (Simon's sister) 8,11,
  140
Hatley, Ralph 10,
Hatley, Robert (Simon's
  grandfather) 7
Hatley, Robert (Simon's uncle) 8
Hatley, Simon, childhood and
  general background 4,7-9,10,
  11,17,39,40,44,140,176,178,188;
  apprentice 4,9-10,59-61,196; third
  mate 2,10,31,65,67-8,71,74,76-7,
  78,82-4,88-9,93-6,99,150; lost at
  sea 102-3,104,107,118,134;
  prisoner in Lima 2,3,4,10,19,119-
  22,124,126-30,168-70; between
  voyages 133,134,135; Second
  Captain 2,3,11,15,30,139-143,
  145-7,149-50,152-4,156-7,159,
  160-1,,165-8,182.187,190;
  after second imprisonment
  180,184,185,191,192,207,
  211,212
Hatley, Symon 4,7,8,10,37,140
Hatley, William 8,10,140
Hawkins, Sir John 63
Hendrie, Agent 152,158
Henry I of England5
Henry III of England45
Herbert, Philip Seventh Earl of
  Pembroke 7
Hollidge, John 63,67,112
Hoxford, Samuel 47
Hucks, Joseph 194

255

Hudson, (boatswain of the *Speedwell*) 151
Hughes, Edward 139,141,152,184

James, Captain Thomas 60
Jay, John 59
Johnson, Esther (Stella) 189
Joseph Ferdinand, Prince of Bavaria 44

Keimer, Samuel 138

La Jonquière Mns 150-1,
Lacanta, Chief 27
Lamb, Charles 201,203
Larraín, Don Fransisco 162
Law, John 181
Lewis, Mathew 209
Lodge, Thomas 21
Louis XIV of France 22,36,37,38, 44,138
Lovell, Robert 195

Macanaz, Melchor Rafael 36
Magee, W. 163
Magellan, Ferdinand 83,85
Mansa, Emmanuel 153-4
Mather, Increase 32
Mendoza, Louis de 83
Mesnager, Monsr. 138
Mitchel, Robert 139,141
Montague, Basil 204
Montague, Lady Mary Wortley 183
Montaigne, Michel de 28
More, Thomas 28
Morgan, Edward 46,47
Morgan, Henry 16,35,36,41
Morsilio, Don Diego 169

Narborough, Sir John 16,35
Neruda, Pablo 157
Newton, Isaac 181

Oates, Titus 37
Oms y de Santa Pau, Don Manuel de 126

Oxenham, Sir John 15,16,
Oxley, Henry 126

Page, William 79
Parker, John 65
Peixoro, Floriano 149
Pepys, Samuel 65,142
Philip II of Spain 21
Philip V of Spain 44,126,137
Philip, duc d'Anjou *see* Philip V of Spain
Pickering, Captain Charles 46,47,80
Pigafetta, Antoniao 21
Pincherty, Monsieur 105,106
Pinney, Azariah 197
Pinney, John 197,199
Pinney, John Praetor 197
Poole, Henry 195
Poole, Thomas 195,196,198-204, 206
Pope, Alexander 58,183,189
Priestley, Joseph 201
Purchas, Samuel 205
Pyper, George 45

Quesada, Gaspar de 83
Quesada, Jiménez de 20-1

Randall, Second Lieutenant 159,162
Ray, James 61
Ringrose, Basil 2,17,18,24
Robenolt, Adam 45
Roger, Noblett 71
Rogers, Captain Woodes
Rogers, Captain Woodes 2,20,22, 23,24,25,50,64,67, 124,129,130, 145,150,188,194; voyage of the *Duke* 64,72,74-86,89,101,105-8; capture of Guayaquil 92,94,96-9; after the return of the *Duke* 111, 114,115,116, 134,135,136,191
Rogers, John 94
Rousseau, Jean Jacques 28

Salado, Mathew 126
Sawkins, Captain Richard 2

256

Schouten, William 155
Selkirk, Alexander 2,19,24,31,39,
   40,44,46,48,53,54,176,178,188;
   voyage of the *Duke* 80,86,88,
   89,91,98,99; after the return of the
   Duke 112,114,115,116,135-6,179-
   80,187
Sharp, Captain Bartholomew 2,23,
Shelvocke, George, 3,18-19,22,23,
   28,30,39; preparation for voyage
   of the *Speedwell* 139-143; voyage
   of the *Speedwell* 145-56,158-60,
   163-4,180-1; after the voyage of
   the *Speedwell* 180,183-5,190,191,
   192
Shepherd, James 61
Shutter, Christopher 63
Sidney, Sir Philip 7,8
Southey, Robert 195,196,197
Sproke, John 167,169
St. Albyn, Langley 202,204
St. Albyn, Mrs Lancelot 202
Steele, Richard 114,136
Steven, Turner 146
Stevenson, Robert Louis 125
Stewart, Mathew 152,184
St-John, Henry 109,135,187
Stradling, Thomas 19,24,40,
   46-54,62,80,86,119,123,169
Swan, Captain Charles 20
Swift, Jonathan 23,25,26,28,29,40,
   108,186-90

Thelwall, John 203
Tiller, Edward 126
Tiller, Walter 126
Underhill, George 65

Vanbrugh, Carlton 76,82,91,108
Vespucci, Amerigo 80,149
Vial, Sara 157
Villegaignon, Nicholas Durand de
   28

Wafer, Lionel 2,27,
Walpole, Robert 181,183

Walsh, James 204
Watling, Captain John 2,165
Wellesley, Arthur 193

Lightning Source UK Ltd.
Milton Keynes UK
16 February 2010

150163UK00001B/52/P